**Anita Prażmowska** is Professor o
London School of Economics and Polit
include *Civil War in Poland 1942–194*
*Britain and Poland 1939–1943: The Betra*

*I dedicate this book to my daughter Miriam who has been my companion and a constant source of happiness.*

# Poland

## A MODERN HISTORY

ANITA PRAŻMOWSKA

I.B. TAURIS

LONDON · NEW YORK

New paperback edition published in 2013 by I.B.Tauris & Co Ltd
6 Salem Road, London W2 4BU
175 Fifth Avenue, New York NY 10010
www.ibtauris.com

Distributed in the United States and Canada Exclusively by Palgrave Macmillan
175 Fifth Avenue, New York NY 10010

First published in hardback in 2010 by I.B. Tauris & Co Ltd

ISBN: 978 1 78076 288 3

A full CIP record for this book is available from the British Library
A full CIP record is available from the Library of Congress

Library of Congress Catalog Card Number: available

Printed and bound by CPI Group (UK) Ltd, Croydon, CR0 4YY

# CONTENTS

# ABBREVIATIONS

| | |
|---|---|
| AK | Armia Krajowa – Home Army |
| AL | Armia Ludowa – People's Army |
| AWS | Akcja Wyborcza Solidarność – Solidarity Electoral Platform |
| BBWR | Bezpartyjny Blok Współpracy z Rządem – Non-Party Block for Co-operation with the Government |
| BCh | Bataliony Chłopskie – Peasant Battalions |
| COP | Centralny Okręg Przemysłowy – Central Industrial Zone |
| GG | *Generalgouvernement* |
| GL | Gwardia Ludowa – People's Guard |
| KNP | Komitet Narodowy Polski – Polish National Committee |
| KOR | Komitet Obrony Robotników – Workers' Defence Committee |
| KPN | Konfederacja Polski Niepodległej – Confederation of Independent Poland |
| KPP | Komunistyczna Partia Polski – Communist Party of Poland |
| KPRP | Komunistyczna Partia Robotnicza Polski – Communist Workers' Party of Poland |
| KRN | Krajowa Rada Narodowa – Homeland National Council |
| LRP | Liga Rodzin Polskich – The League of Polish Families |
| MW | Młodzież Wszechpolska – All Poland Youth |
| ND | Narodowa Demokracja – National Democrats (also known as Endecja) |
| NKN | Naczelny Komitet Narodowy – Supreme National Council |
| NSZ | Narodowe Siły Zbrojne – National Armed Units |
| PKWN | Polski Komitet Wyzwolenia Narodowego – Polish Committee of National Liberation |
| PO | Platforma Obywatelska – Citizens' Platform |
| PiS | Prawo i Sprawiedliwość – Law and Justice |
| PSL | Polskie Stronnictwo Ludowe – Polish Peasant Alliance |

| | |
|---|---|
| PPR | Polska Partia Robotnicza – Polish Workers' Party |
| PPS | Polska Partia Socjalistyczna – Polish Socialist Party |
| PPS | Frakcja Rewolucyjna |
| PPS | Revolutionary Fraction |
| PPS | Lewica |
| PPS | Left Wing. |
| PZL | Polski Związek Ludowy – Polish Peasant Association |
| PZPR | Zjednoczona Polska Partia Robotnicza – United Polish Workers' Party |
| RPPS | Robotnicza Partia Polskich Socialistów – Workers' Party of Polish Socialists |
| SD | Stronnictwo Demokratyczne – Democratic Alliance |
| SDKP | Socjaldemokracja Królewstwa Polskiego – Social Democracy of the Polish Kingdom |
| SDKPiL | Socialdemokracja Królestwa Polskiego i Litwy – Social Democracy of the Polish Kingdom and Lithuania |
| SdRP | Socjaldemokracja Rzeczpospolitej Polskiej – Social Democracy of the Polish Republic |
| SL | Stronnictwo Ludowe – Peasant Alliance |
| SLD | Sojusz Lewicy Demokratycznej – Democratic Left Alliance |
| SN | Stronnictwo Narodowe – National Front |
| TRJN | Tymczasowy Rząd Jedności Narodowej – Provisional Government of National Unity |
| UB | Urząd Bezpieczeństwa – Security Bureau |
| UD | Unia Demokratyczna – Democratic Union |
| UPA | Ukraińska Armia Powstańcza – Ukrainian Insurrectionist Army |
| WRiN | Wolność, Równość i Niepodległość – Freedom, Equality and Independence |
| ZPP | Związek Patriotów Polskich – Union of Polish Patriots |
| ZSL | Zjednoczone Stronnictwo Ludowe – United Peasant Alliance |
| ZWC | Związek Walki Czynnej – Union of Active Struggle |

# PREFACE

The nationalist revolutions of the twentieth century have been driven by peoples' conviction of the uniqueness of their history and destiny and the contribution of that history and destiny to the international commonwealth. This is followed by a journey to a common destination of weak states and squalid dictatorships. This journey is unique only in language, geography, and the personnel administering them. The people have been largely unable to face the challenge of building a modern state, let alone contributing positively to international affairs.

The Polish–Lithuanian Commonwealth ceased to exist in January 1795. Poland re-emerged onto the European map in November 1918. The two dates span a time of great economic and political changes in Europe, which affected the Polish areas as much as they did the rest of the continent. In Western Europe, by the beginning of the twentieth century, the political power of the landed classes was destroyed. Representative governments were the norm. Economic progress was linked to industrialisation and the growth of the middle class. While areas east of Germany lagged behind, the West European model of governance and economic development was the paradigm according to which Poles would find their way out of poverty and foreign domination.

Poland presents an interesting historic case of progression from a republic of the gentry and nobility to a liberal polity. The self-proclaimed leaders of the Polish nation first fought for independence. When this failed, they were forced to address the question of whether the nationalist agenda and modernisation could be pursued simultaneously. The trauma caused by the two successive failed national uprisings in 1830 and 1863 forced Polish nationalists to look beyond the restoration of the Polish Kingdom. During both, the gentry had played a prominent role in the planning and fighting which ensued. As a class, the gentry carried the consequences of

the collective punishments wreaked upon the nation after Russia re-
established control over its Polish territories. The reappraisal which
followed each failure and the exodus of the insurrectionists into exile in Western Europe, stimulated the debate on what exactly they
had sought to achieve. The inevitable conclusion was that, in order
to succeed, the uprising needed broader support among the Polish
people. Confronting the partitioning powers, the insurrectionists
needed the support of the urban dwellers and of the peasants. The
gentry had failed, in spite of seeing themselves as the carriers of the
national identity and the epitome of everything they considered
to be Polish. The debate progressed from addressing the iniquities
of serfdom, to considering the wider impact of industrialisation on
poverty, backwardness and economic dependence. Thus, the quest
for national self-determination became inextricably linked with the
vision of modernity and economic progress.

By the outbreak of the First World War, it was agreed that independence would result in the establishment of some form of representative government. From the French Revolution onwards, the
concept of citizenship was debated within the progressive liberal
communities. While the brief period of Napoleonic administration
of parts of Poland had meant that reformed state and legal systems
were introduced into Polish areas, the partitioning powers also determined the pace of political changes in Poland. In areas under
Austrian and Prussian control, the Poles had gained the right to
representation and learned to use properly functioning legal systems to challenge state decisions. Through contacts with West European progressive thinkers, Polish exiles had addressed the issue of
Polish independence through the prism of radical and revolutionary ideas. Contacts with Russian revolutionary thinkers, likewise
injected into the debate the conviction that full participation in
governance should be the aim of those fighting for Polish independence. Polish leaders in exile and those in areas under Austrian,
German and Russian control had realised that independence could
only be achieved if the international consensus between the three
partitioning empires was broken. They were therefore aware of the
need to understand the European balance of power. Thus, at the beginning of the twentieth century, Polish nationalism was progressive and forward thinking, incorporating most modern concepts

on the nature of liberal institutions and on citizen participation. If Poland was to emerge from the collapse of the European political consensus, it would be governed in accordance with the most up to date political models.

The quest for independence dominated and ultimately defined the debate on Poland's restoration. National self-determination was the single most important objective. The nationalist revolution in Eastern and Southeastern Europe led to the subordination of debates on the political and economic models to this objective. This raised questions about modernisation in accordance with the liberal model of elected representation and free market principles. In 1918, Poland gained independence because of the collapse of the three partitioning powers. Nevertheless, its borders, in particular the eastern, northern and southern, were defined through a series of conflicts with neighbouring states. The narrowing down of the debate to the defence of Polish territorial gains had an impact on discussions concerning governance and economic progress. Polish nationalism, from being associated with progressive thinking, became exclusive, inward-looking and, ultimately, provincial. During the interwar period, the debate on Polish right to independence was narrowly perceived as merely the right of Poles to make this decision, while rejecting claims made by other national groups to the same right. Thus the policies of the newly emerged Polish state towards Ukrainian and Byelorussian desire for statehood were aggressively dismissive. Those hopes were seen as a challenge to Polish interests. Polish nationalism shed its earlier association with revolutionary ideals and modernist visions. Although independent, Poland ostensibly continued to be ruled in accordance with democratic principles. In reality, by the end of the 1930s, it was ruled by a regime which was no more than a military coterie. Ostensibly democratic in form, the government showed little inclination to protect the rights of all citizens equally. Instead it focused on a narrow nationalist agenda. In the economic sphere, state intervention and military expenditure remained high. The restriction of citizens' rights and democratic representation was repeatedly justified by the need to defend national interests.

After the Second World War, the communist regime offered a different model of modernisation. Industrialisation was to be implemented at a rapid pace. This was paralleled by attempts to increase agricultural production through land consolidation and introduction of technology. Communist social policies likewise intended to transform backward, rural communities into a part of modern, urban society. Communism provided access to education and employment. But the development of any form of civil associations was held back. The national assembly's authority was nominal, as the real authority rested entirely with the Communist Party. The paradox of communist rule was its program of rapid modernisation without citizens' participation in governance. The communists were not averse to using nationalist slogans to extend their popular appeal. The Communist party was unflinching in its determination to maintain its grip on all state functions. However it also maintained that national interest was of paramount importance.

The fall of communism in Poland and the economic and political transformation which followed, once more opened the debate on the importance of the national interests in the process of democratisation. Post-communist parties all wanted to see Poland establish closer trading and political links with West European states. However, they were quick to learn that their own appeal to the electorate would be strengthened if they could present themselves as staunch defenders of Polish interests. This explains the need to demonise international finance and to exaggerate the impact of communism and foreign ideas on Polish life. Their commitment to democracy has never been in doubt. However, the parties which emerged after the fall of communism have faced the dilemma of creating their own identity. Whereas nationalism proved to be a winning slogan, modernisation and progress towards closer integration into Europe have not been easy to present as synonymous with furthering Polish objectives. The contradictions between nationalism and modernity in Poland remain unresolved.

# INTRODUCTION

When the First World War came to an end, the map of Eastern and South-eastern Europe was transformed. New states emerged, where they had not existed before the war. Some were new entities. Others had historic links with kingdoms that had been earlier absorbed into what had been the Austro-Hungarian, German and Russian Empires. The common feature about all the new states was their national leaders' claim to represent the will of a given national group and with that the right of that group to govern itself. Peace treaties were negotiated and signed during the two years after the cessation of hostilities. These confirmed the victorious powers' approval to the break-up of the three European and Ottoman empires. There is an assertion that the redrawing of the map of Eastern and South-eastern Europe was the result of these peace treaties. This is historically incorrect. The emergence of new states was the result of various factors. One was the military collapse of the empires. Another was the loosening of their administrative and political control over areas inhabited by national groups with a strong sense of identity. A final factor was the growth of national self-awareness. The peace treaties, most notably the Versailles Treaty of 28 June 1919, reflected in most cases pragmatic acceptance by the British, French and US governments of what had already happened. This was namely the collapse of the European empires and the emergence of states based on the claims of vocal national groups to independence and the right to self-determination.[1]

Of the Successor States, as they came to be collectively referred to, Poland was the best known. The Polish question had been the subject of international agreements and disagreements in equal measure. It had also attracted the attention of prominent thinkers and campaigners. The destruction of the Polish–Lithuanian Commonwealth at the end of the eighteenth century came to be perceived as an international injustice.[2] The Poles fought hard to regain independence through national uprisings and by extensive lobbying in European capitals. During the course of the nineteenth century, the growth of nationalist ideologies made it increasingly difficult for European powers to deny that the Poles had a right to independence. Nevertheless, it was only the military defeat of the powers, which had earlier occupied Polish territories, that made it possible for an independent Polish state to emerge after the war.

Successive generations of the Polish elite had fought for independence through the nineteenth century. When that had proved impossible they sought not only to maintain, but also to develop Polish language, culture and a distinct identity while under foreign control. To them, the emergence of an independent Polish state was more than a culmination of their hopes and aspirations. Critically, that emergence was perceived as a reversal of a great historic injustice. During the second half of the nineteenth century and the opening years of the twentieth, progressive thinkers in Europe viewed the Polish question as no less than a touchstone of European morality. The Poles' were unwilling to accept foreign tutelage. The brutality and arbitrariness of the partitioning powers' policies, in particular after the 1863 insurrection, attracted widespread international support and admiration. This made it possible for the Polish question to become not merely an internal matter between the three partitioning powers, but an international cause.

Thus, the restoration of the Polish state onto the map of Europe appeared to be a just act ending the war. That single act stands out from among the many decisions made at the end of the war. For the Poles it marked a new era. An era in which they had not only to assume responsibility for their own fate but build the foundations of a new state.

The Polish–Lithuanian Commonwealth had been a multinational and multireligious state in which the concept of citizenship was confined to those of noble rank. Wealthy burghers and traders had no such status. The peasants and the urban poor had at best only an awareness of their belonging to a region, or religious group. They rarely, if at all, perceived themselves to share a common heritage or political objectives with the nobility. The main power struggle within the early modern period was between the nobility and the crown. It was then that the nobility developed a sense of Polish national awareness defined by language and culture, though not by religion.[3] After the partitions, attempts to re-establish the power of the Polish–Lithuanian Commonwealth and then to shake off foreign tutelage were led by the nobility, with little reference to other social groups or their needs. This situation changed when successive uprisings failed. During the latter part of the nineteenth and the opening years of the twentieth centuries, wider sections of the community were affected by and involved in the debate on independence. The Polish–Lithuanian Commonwealth ceased to be a model for a future state. New concepts of statehood and of citizen participation were being debated. The insurrectionist tradition was gradually being replaced with a willingness of the wider sections of the community, to shoulder the responsibility for making pragmatic and difficult decisions to respect and work within the political framework of a state. This particularly applied to the male community. This, in turn, called for agreements on patterns of economic development and on foreign relations. During the century of foreign tutelage, opposition to the occupation powers had been elevated to being the sole most important indicator of commitment to Polish nationalism. Nevertheless, debates on independence called for an economic vision and political models for the future and, more importantly, for realism. The clash between the strength of nationalist sentiments and the desire to build solid foundations for the evolution of a modern state was inevitable. For Polish thinkers the real test would be that of whether it would be possible to move on from a stance characterised by a negative attitude towards state institutions to that of modern citizenship. This modern citizenship was one in which democracy bestowed on all the right to participate in decision making. Conversely, it also demanded allegiances to the state.[4]

The political institutions of the restored Polish state were modelled on democratic principles, which assumed the full participation of citizens of the state in the process of governance. The Poles had to adapt to the new situation. In the first place, they did this by accepting that they were no longer subjects of foreign states but citizens within their own state. In the second place, the now citizens of a Polish Republic had to find a common political language. The state, which emerged from the military conflagration of the First World War, was independent. But, more importantly, it was modern. It was administered on the basis of up to date political ideas and encapsulating contemporary concepts of a relationship between the state and its citizens. The issue of the resurrected Polish state had been the subject of extensive soul-searching which went back to the failed uprisings. Each unsuccessful attempt to throw off foreign occupation invariably led to debates on the way forward. Debates were also conducted on what had been the causes of disunity and military failure. In identifying what had been the reasons for these disasters, questions were raised about the relationship between the fight for independence and social reforms. Thus, even before independent Poland appeared on the map of Europe, generations of Poles had debated, discussed and mulled over the question of just what type of Polish state this would be.[5]

On 3 January 1795, the Polish–Lithuanian Commonwealth ceased to exist. 11 November 1918 is the accepted Independence Day. The period between these two dates was a time when Polish national awareness developed and was tested in adversity. The complexities of that period moulded the character of Polish nationalism.

The destruction of the Commonwealth was in the first place made possible because of Russian, Austrian and Prussian cooperation throughout the eighteenth century. Henceforth, the fate of areas inhabited by Poles was determined by the extent of unity between the three. Thus, the European balance of power had, from the outset, an impact on the Polish question and was therefore a critical issue in Poland's restoration. Successive leaders of Polish insurrections fully grasped this issue and tried to exploit it. Austrian, German and Russian rulers always weighted carefully the impact of disunity between them on the Polish question. Conversely, the Poles tried to exploit differences between the three and between each of the empires and the other European powers to gain support for an independent Poland. Thus, the fate of the Commonwealth and the issue of its restoration were always very closely connected to the European balance of power. This balance of power could raise hopes for independence or dash them. This dashing of hopes occurred when disunity between the partitioning powers proved short-lived. French, British and Turkish wishes to weaken the three partitioning powers were never strong enough to undermine the empires' hold on their Polish lands. Nonetheless, the other European powers' interest in constraining the partitioning empires always held out the prospect of some support for the Poles. Polish political exiles were a widely observed phenomenon in nineteenth-century Europe, either fleeing persecution in their own lands, or seeking to participate in wars against Poland's enemies. Thus the Polish question remained in the public eye, attracting compassion, anxiety or support, depending on the circumstances. The Poles, likewise, came to appreciate the relevance of the European balance of power to their own cause. At the same time, the exile communities of Poles were exposed to new political ideas. They were frequently accidental and sometimes intentional participants in revolutionary outbreaks during the turbulent years of the first half of the nineteenth century. Thus, all debates on the restoration of Poland were invariably linked to several factors. The first was an understanding of how the new political ideas generated by the European revolutions would undermine the ruling elites. Another was how to destroy the reactionary consensus and through that initiate wars against the three powers which had partitioned Poland. Poland's independence could not be secured without destroying the European balance of power. Leaders of the successive insurrections came to understand that full Polish participation was necessary to achieve independence. The debate moved from advocating national insurrections led by the gentry and national elites, to the realisation that social, political and economic reforms were necessary to build national unity. Thus radical reforms came to be seen as an integral element of the debate of independence.

## THE PARTITION OF THE POLISH–LITHUANIAN COMMONWEALTH

Stanisław August Poniatowski, the last king of the Polish–Lithuanian Commonwealth, was forced to relinquish the throne in 1795. In 1572 Zygmunt II August (1548–1572) of the Jagiellonian line died. From this point onwards, the nobility of the Commonwealth appropriated the right to choose the new king. Henceforth, each successive king was elected at a gathering of the nobility. At these gatherings international princes, neighbouring monarchs and what would nowadays be described as lobby groups bid for support of the nobility, the wealthy magnates and the lesser gentry. Inevitably, with each successive election the power of the nobility was increased. Whereas the role of the crown, and therefore also that of the state, was diminished. This in itself did not have an adverse impact on the internal life of the Commonwealth as the gentry, through provincial assemblies, took a direct part in local affairs. Furthermore, elected monarchs were constrained in their desire to employ the resources and the armies of the Polish-Commonwealth in order to pursue dynastic ambitions elsewhere. This is what happened during the rule of the Vasas, Sigismund III (1587–1632) and Władysław IV (1632–1648). Both, though elected kings, refused to relinquish their claims to the throne of Sweden and involved the Commonwealth in extensive military conflicts in pursuit of objectives in Scandinavia. Subsequently, the Saxon August II (1697–1733) and his successor August III (1733–1763) embroiled the Polish–Lithuanian-Commonwealth in extended wars against Sweden. This led to political dependence on Russia. During these years, the gentry fought against the exchequer being depleted in pursuit of foreign ambitions and the deployment of the army in wars that had little to do with the Commonwealth's interests. In the process, powerful magnates pursued their own interests. Internal conflicts thus divided the magnates from the gentry and the nobility, as a social group, from the Crown.

During the seventeenth century and beginning of the eighteenth century, the Commonwealth was involved in a number of economically and militarily disastrous wars. In 1654, Russia invaded the Ukraine and Lithuania. This emboldened the Swedish king to march on Poland and to destroy the Polish elected Vasa king's claim to the Swedish throne. The main battles between Russia and Sweden were fought on Poland's territories. The Commonwealth survived that crisis. Nevertheless, the regional balance of power was shifting. In the meantime, a Cossack uprising in the Ukraine ravaged whole swathes of South-eastern parts of the Commonwealth. In 1683 the Turkish threat to Western Europe was forestalled by Jan III Sobieski's (1673–1696) defeat of the Turks outside Vienna. The Poles' role had been of crucial importance in this campaign. However, they ultimately secured little benefit from it. The Commonwealth was increasingly becoming dependent on Russia. In 1698 August II, the Saxon king of Poland, resumed war with Sweden, this time in alliance with Russia and Denmark. Swedish military victories led to the pillaging of large parts of the Commonwealth. It was never to recover its status and political power, while the neighbouring states did. Russia, in particular, benefited during the Northern Wars, increasingly interfering in the Commonwealth's internal affairs.[6] During the War of Austrian Succession and the Seven Years' War, the two western neighbours, Austria and Prussia, grew in power.[7] The culmination of that process was the dismemberment of the Commonwealth by the three neighbouring powers, Prussia, Austria and Russia.[8] The final chapter of the history of the Commonwealth was one in which the interests of the Russian empress came in conflict with the reforming zeal of Stanisław August Poniatowski (1764–1795), the newly elected king, hitherto her protégé.

The election of what turned out to be the last Polish king marked a final attempt by the enlightened section of the Polish nobility to reverse the Commonwealth's decline and to strengthen the state through a series of reforms.[9] Poniatowski had, though, become the king of the Polish–Lithuanian Commonwealth because the Russian Empress Catherine needed to have in Warsaw a monarch who would not disrupt her plans for war against the Turkish Empire. What the empress would not allow her protégé to do was to reaffirm the Commonwealth's independence. She achieved this by blocking reforms and encouraging the anarchic behaviour of sections of the nobility. This was especially applied to those distrustful of attempts to limit their liberties. In her desire to keep Poland weak and dependent, she had allies in Prussia and Austria. The Prussian king, Frederick II, accepted that the Commonwealth was in the Russian sphere of influence. The Austrians had a different motive for agreeing with Russian policies in relation to Poland. They remained anxious about Turkey, and therefore supported Catherine's plans for war with the Ottomans.[10]

The Polish and Lithuanian magnates and the gentry were in any case not united. Some supported Poniatowski's reforms. Others saw in his efforts a threat to their rights. As a result, they were willing to support Russian policies, which ostensibly aimed at supporting their freedoms. However in reality these policies were aimed at reducing

the impact of the reforms. In August 1772, Prussia, Austria and Russia signed the the three-power agreement. This marked the first stage
of the destruction of the Polish–Lithuanian Commonwealth. Over
30 per cent of the territories were taken over and incorporated into
the boundaries of the neighbouring states. Poniatowski was allowed
to retain the title of the King of the Polish–Lithuanian Commonwealth. Although he pushed on with reforms, increasingly gaining
the support of the enlightened nobility, the Commonwealth was
not able to assert itself against its neighbours. In January 1793,
Prussia and Russia agreed to the Second Partition of the Polish–
Lithuanian Commonwealth. Earlier attempts to implement rapid
and wide-ranging political changes were of no avail. On 3 May
1791, taking advantage of Empress Catherine's preoccupation with
the war against Turkey, reformists gathered around the king. He
convened the Sejm, the assembly of nobles, to approve a new constitution. The 3 May reforms reflected the substance of the debates,
which had been taking place within the intellectual community
since the First Partition. Both the ideas of the Enlightenment and
events taking place in France, encouraged a questioning approach
to the problems of the Polish–Lithuanian Commonwealth. Hugo
Kołłątaj and Stanisław Staszic were two prominent thinkers of the
period. They advocated limiting the political power of the impoverished gentry. They wanted the concept of citizenship to be defined
along with the rights of these citizens. At the background of their
recommendations lay the realisation that the power of the state
needed to be balanced by the responsible actions of citizens, who
would be politically active. Manufacture and trade flourished in the
major towns of the Commonwealth. This led to the growth of a
wealthy strata of townspeople, whose economic influence needed
to be recognised. The authors of the 3 May Constitution did not go
so far. They hoped to limit the rights of the impoverished gentry
and grant the wealthy town dwellers citizens' rights, though as yet
no political power. Although the reformers were successful in gaining the Sejm's approval for the constitution, they were ultimately
defeated when Russian troops attacked in May 1792. A number
of leading magnates and their clients from within the lesser gentry were unwilling to approve reforms which would have reduced
their much cherished privileges. They sided with the Russians and

condoned Russia's interference in the internal affairs of the Commonwealth. The 3 May Constitution was henceforth seen as a missed opportunity, nevertheless, one marking a stage in the great debates on the role of the state and the concept of citizenship.[11]

Modern European history has been moulded by the ideas of the Enlightenment, the French Revolution and the Industrial Revolution. Events in France had an immediate and major impact on political developments of the time. The year 1789 marked the end of the old order in France and the beginning of a new one. In this new order the concept of a citizen replaced that of a subject. Philosophers and political thinkers put forward a new concept of authority. This concept was the expression of the will of the people and challenged political rights and privileges, which, until then, had depended on birth and inheritance. The French Constitution defined citizens' right to participate in state decision making. It also suggested that there was a political entity defined as the nation. As old institutions were abolished, so the declaration of the rights of individuals suggested that men had not only a say in state matters, but that they had civil rights which were inalienable. In the case of Eastern Europe, and in particular in the Polish case, the impact of ideas emanating from France was distinct. This was due to the fact that the Commonwealth was experiencing the trauma caused by the first two partitions. The concept of the republic of the nobles was being challenged. In addition to this, constitutional and nationalist ideas were being generated in equal measure by the French Revolution. The growing power of the middle classes and townspeople, came to be seen as integral elements of the debate on the subject of reforms which would save Poland. The nobility could no longer claim, without fear of contradiction, to be the real representatives of the Polish nation.[12]

Polish political leaders in exile anticipated that the Russians would complete the destruction of the Commonwealth with a final partition. They therefore planned an uprising.

On 25 May 1794, Tadeusz Kościuszko led the insurrection. It started in Kraków but quickly spread to other parts of the Commonwealth. The insurrectionists faced a critical dilemma. On the one hand, they needed the support of the gentry. However, for the uprising to be successful, it had to involve wider sections of the community, notably the serfs and townspeople. Many people were affected by the egalitarian ideals of the French Revolution. They believed that the military campaign against the combined Russian and Prussian forces had to be a national one. From the outset the serfs were active in supporting Kościuszko's insurrection. This, in turn, led him to call for the abolishment of serfdom. During fighting in Warsaw, poor sections of the town population were fully active in defending the city. The leadership of the uprising mobilised and came to depend on the support of the serfs and the townspeople. This was inevitably followed by demands for the abolishment of serfdom and for the granting of political rights to the townspeople. Nevertheless, it was the quest for freedom and the rapid growth of nationalism that became the signal feature of political developments in Polish areas. The partitioning powers recognised that Polish nationalism had the capacity to become a revolutionary force, which could impact on the whole region. They were brought together not merely by the desire to suppress Polish attempts to regain independence. Moreover, by a realisation that Polish nationalism had to be suppressed in principle. Polish nationalism was becoming increasingly tainted by romantic and revolutionary ideals. There were concerns that it would generate similar sentiments among the subjects. The insurrection failed and on 3 January 1795 the Third Partition spelled the end of the Polish–Lithuanian Commonwealth. Henceforth, all debates concerning the return of Poland to the map of Europe would inevitably raise the question of the form in which Poland was to be restored. It was doubtful that the borders of the pre-1772 Commonwealth could be secured. Critically, at a time when the political and economic life of Europe was rapidly changing, all debates on the future of Poland raised inevitable questions as to its future political institutions.[13]

The Revolutionary and Napoleonic Wars affected Europe as a whole. They led to the dissemination of the ideals of the French Revolution. France was until 1815 waging wars against the three partitioning powers. This led many Poles to hope that, with France's military victory, an independent Poland would be restored. Reformers were critics of the political chaos which made the partitions possible. Nationalists' emotions found an echo in the principles carried forth by the French armies. These two groups looked to France for deliverance and for political models. To the Poles the Napoleonic Wars appeared to be a time of hope and revolutionary zeal. Polish exiles in France and those in the Polish lands viewed Napoleon as a potential liberator and a friend of the Polish cause.[14] During the French campaign in Italy, nearly 20,000 Polish exiles formed into legions and fought with the French army. This unconditional support for Napoleon wavered slightly when he signed peace treaties with Austria and Russia in 1801. However, when hostilities were resumed, the Poles in Western Europe and in Polish territories once more rallied to the French side. The Poles took up arms to participate in the forthcoming military confrontation with Russia. Napoleon turned out to be a fickle friend. When he had an upper hand against Poland's enemies, he focused on France's long-term military objectives, rather than supporting the Polish cause. The Treaty of Tilsit was signed by Napoleon and Prussia on 8 July 1807. As a result of this, the Duchy of Warsaw was created. It comprised most territories earlier incorporated into Prussia during the Second and Third Partitions. These were the Warsaw, Płock, Bydgoszcz, Kalisz and Poznań areas. The port city of Gdańsk was not included within the borders of the Duchy, instead becoming a Free City. The previously Prussian town of Białystok was successfully claimed by Russia. After a brief war with Austria, France was victorious. Austrian Galicia, including the towns of Lublin, Zamość and Kraków were added to the Duchy's territory. Napoleon's opportunistic solution of the Polish question fell short of what the Poles hoped for. Nevertheless, although a French puppet state, the Duchy was to be governed along the most up to date political and philosophical lines generated by the French Revolution. A professional and trained administration, backed by a secular educational system, represented a challenge to the power of the old nobility and the church. A legislative system based on the Napoleonic Code aimed to guarantee civil liberties and equality between the sexes. Serfdom was abolished in law. However, so long as the issue of land ownership was not fully resolved, it is doubtful that the peasants felt the benefit of the change in their legal status. Only 30 per cent of the territories previously comprising the Polish and Lithuanian Commonwealth made up the Duchy. These were nevertheless ethnically Polish regions, notably including the two old capitals, Kraków and Warsaw. Impressively, the Duchy was to be governed in accordance with the constitution, which introduced uniformity and consistency throughout the territories.

In 1812 the Franco-Russian War was resumed with disastrous consequences for Napoleon. His army was defeated and retreated from Moscow and suffered heavy casualties. In April 1814 Napoleon abdicated and, by the Treaty of Vienna, Prussia, Austria, Russia and Britain decided the fate of post-Napoleonic Europe. For the Poles this marked the end of their hopes for the restoration of the Commonwealth. The fate of the Duchy was determined as a result of conflicts and compromises between the four main protagonists. Britain, Prussia and Austria were intent on blocking Russian ambitions in Europe. Therefore Russian attempts to claim the Duchy were opposed. Prussia re-established control over Poznań, now renamed as the Duchy of Posen. Austria regained areas in Galicia, but agreed to the creation of the City Republic of Kraków. The remaining parts of what had been the Duchy came under Russian control, though they were not incorporated directly into the empire. The Kingdom of Poland, or Congress Poland, as it was better known, was an autonomous state. It was united with the Russian Empire by the fact that the Tsar of Russia became the King of Poland. Although it had its own assembly, in reality it was entirely dependent on Russia. Many of the reforms introduced during the Napoleonic period remained in place, most notably the Napoleonic Code. Thus Congress Poland retained its distinct national composition and, although within the Russian Empire, it was governed by progressive and modern laws.[15]

Having defeated Napoleon, the European powers were committed to preventing any further challenges to the established order. At the same time, there was no denying the fact that Polish nationalism was a force to be reckoned with. Therefore Prussia, Austria and Russia had more in common than the desire to counteract the spread of revolutionary ideas. The Russian tsar claimed control over Congress Poland. He was nevertheless willing to grant the Poles autonomy within the empire, as well as more extensive political rights than those enjoyed by his other subjects. Prussia and Austria likewise accepted that the Poles had a claim to their own language and culture. Nevertheless, the common perception was that any attempts by the Poles to gain independence would be a challenge to the authoritarian regimes of the three powers. Moreover, they would most likely be motivated by revolutionary nationalism. If not defeated, this could spread to other parts of Europe. The three partitioning powers did not pursue any agreed policies towards territories inhabited by Polish communities. In each case, politicians in Vienna, Berlin or St Petersberg made decisions as to whether to maintain the political institutions introduced during the Napoleonic period without reference to each other. Henceforth, Polish areas incorporated into the three empires developed at a different pace. This was a result of distinct policies determined by the interests of each regime. In spite of this, the Poles increasingly saw themselves as sharing a common destiny.

Polish national leaders in the Polish areas and political exiles abroad varied in their attitudes towards the partitioning powers. Some saw advantages in cooperating with the authorities in the hope that this would lead to increased autonomy. Others viewed Poland's destiny in terms of outright independence and disagreed with efforts to reach any accommodation with the three empires. The latter refused to abandon plans for national uprisings. To succeed, the leadership of military insurrections would have to gain the support of Poles from all three empires and not just from one. National uprising occurred because of issues specific to one area. However, every insurrection had affected other areas and was always planned to inspire and mobilise Polish-inhabited territories. Military plans were initially considered more important than the preparation of political programmes. It was assumed that an uprising could be sustained by an appeal to Polish national sentiments. However, more specific plans for the future Polish state faced the insurrectionists with more complex dilemmas. Polish nationalism was a militant, angry and, at times, desperate quest for the right to national self-expression. It focused on fighting for independence, but rarely addressed with equal force the issue of a political programme within the nation state. Only successive failures of national uprisings forced Polish communities and their leaders to assess the degree to which they were able to rally Poles to the call for independence and thus to question those leaders' claim to represent the will of the Polish people. From those reassessments came the realisation that, for any national insurrection to be successful, its planners and leaders would have to address issues such as serfdom and the political rights of the townspeople and ultimately the working classes.

During the course of the nineteenth century several uprisings occurred in Polish territories. As each failed, the policies of the partitioning powers towards the Polish question became more repressive. The uprisings failed to overthrow foreign tutelage and to appeal to all sections of the Polish community. This, in turn, led to reflection and debates. Within the growing Polish exile communities in European capitals and in the Polish-inhabited areas, the failed national uprisings and the severity of retribution resulted in a process of national soul-searching. This touched upon political, economic and social issues.

## THE NOVEMBER UPRISING

The November Uprising broke out on 29 November 1830. It started in Warsaw, when a group of conspirators tried, but failed, to assassinate Grand Duke Constantine, the tsar's brother. They had hoped that events in Warsaw would lead to a national uprising. What they lacked was a clear programme as to what would happen next, once the fighting started. Many of the young conspirators had been army officers and had consciously modelled themselves on the revolutionary progressive Italian Carbonari. The Polish generals and the Sejm deputies did not agree with the insurrectionists and would have nothing to do with the young men's plans. Failure to link the call for a national uprising to reforms in the village, most notably abolition of serfdom, meant that the peasants remained distrustful. Although in Warsaw young apprentices joined in street fights with the Russian troops, tradesmen and shopkeepers were cautious. The reality was that the Polish economy had benefited from trade with the Russian Empire and economic stability tempered their willingness to support the call for independence. The Sejm's decision to declare Poland independent led to a full-scale Russian military intervention. In the confrontation with Russian troops, Polish units secured notable victories. Nevertheless, internal conflicts between the leaders of the uprising and Russian determination meant that by May the uprising was doomed. In September, Russian troops occupied Warsaw. Tsar Nicholas I abolished the constitution and the Sejm. In principle, Congress Poland continued to be administered as an independent state. However repression was increased. Polish remained the official language. Nevertheless, the University of Warsaw was shut and censorship was imposed.

In their plans for an uprising, the young leaders had been inspired by revolutionary upsurges in Western Europe. The July Revolution in Paris and events in Belgium led them to believe that an uprising in Congress Poland would be followed by similar ones in France. They believed that this would embolden Prussia to take military action against Russia. This did not happen. Nor did the Poles in Austrian- and Prussian-controlled areas rise in support of their co-nationals in Russian areas. Their, plans built on the assumption that all that was needed was an event which would act as a spark, igniting the fight for Polish independence and possibly even a Europe-wide solidarity campaign. These had to be reviewed. Once in exile, the revolutionaries debated and revisited the failures and successes of the uprising. The mood of despair was accentuated by the presence of eminent poets and writers. Adam Mickiewicz and Juliusz Słowacki are outstanding examples of the Polish Romantic literary tradition. They gave expression to the sense of yearning for the lost fatherland. Frederyk Chopin's piano composition was based on Polish folk music and struck a chord with the émigré community. Patriotic and romantic ideas were enhanced by contacts with mystical and Theosophical groups, so fashionable in those days. The notion took root among the exiles that suffering and separation from the homeland were a necessary purgatory before Poland could re-emerge.

At the same time, leaders of the uprising considered why it had failed. One group, led by Prince Adam Czartoryski, gathered at the Hotel Lambert in Paris. They laid stress on the need for international support for any future uprising. The radicals formed a party known as the Democratic Society and declared themselves to be the Young Poland movement. References were made to Italian revolutionary thinkers while stating that Poland would be reconstructed only when a popular uprising took place in all the partitioning states.

It quickly became apparent that the failure of the November Uprising and the consequences of its defeat could not be easily reversed. Plans for a new uprising were hatched and agents travelled from exile communities to Polish areas. However, Poles in the homeland had become more cautious and refused to heed the romantic notion of the call of the nationalist bugle. In areas under Prussian, Austrian and Russian control, the authorities had learned to exploit class hostilities between the Polish gentry and the peasants. Plans hatched in the relative safety of exile had decreasing relevance to events evolving in Polish-inhabited regions, thus reducing the authority of the émigré organisations. In 1846, in the relatively free Republic of Kraków, a revolutionary government was established. The response of the Austrian authorities was to encourage the peasants to attack the Polish landlords. This they did in Western Galicia, an area of poverty and backwardness. When the last remnants of the insurrection were destroyed, Kraków was incorporated into Austria. Many Polish exile leaders and populist thinkers had been convinced that a national uprising should start with a peasant revolt. They had to rethink their tactics.

The Europe-wide revolutionary activities of the 1848–49 period are generally referred to as the Spring of Nations. These led the émigré leaders and Poles to hope that German and Austrian revolutionaries would support their national aspirations. As it turned out, neither considered the Polish cause so important as to include a commitment to the restoration of an independent Poland in their programme. A Polish uprising in the Poznań region was quelled with the agreement of the German liberals. In the meantime, the Austrian authorities undermined attempts by the Polish landlords to base an uprising on a radical programme. They did this by issuing a decree abolishing serfdom. The Poles were active in many of the revolutions that swept through Europe during those two years. Their hopes were cruelly disappointed though. Continuing attempts were made to exploit all international conflicts and put the Polish question on the international agenda. However, accommodation with the authorities became the norm in Poland. Thus, while a sense of national unity prevailed, the Poles increasingly focused on cultural expression rather than on plans for a national uprising. Poles in each of the partitioning states became part of the economic, political and social life of those empires. Henceforth, their responses and ideas were moulded by what they experienced on a daily basis.

# THE JANUARY UPRISING

On the night of 14/15 January 1863, a new uprising broke out in Congress Poland. It had been preceded by two years of conflict between the Poles and the Russian tsarist authorities. The Russians offered compromises. At the same time, the police and Russian troops in Warsaw acted with extreme brutality against the civilian population. Sections of the Polish nobility still believed that an accommodation could be reached with the Russian authorities. However, students, young officers and Warsaw artisans, calling themselves 'The Reds', assumed the initiative. The link between national liberation and political reforms was made explicit from the outset. A political programme was quickly issued in which the abolition of serfdom and emancipation of Jews, two highly contentious issues, were mentioned. At the same time, fraternal support from abroad was sought. For a year, the Poles fought a guerrilla war against Russian troops. Militarily, they had not been successful and, even though the peasant issue had been addressed, in the villages, support was patchy. In European capitals, liberals proclaimed their support for the Poles. The British, French and Austrian governments protested at the Russians' mistreatment of the Poles, but little was done to aid them. Prussia and Russia had, in the meantime, signed an agreement to cooperate on the Polish issue. When the uprising collapsed, Russian retaliation was brutal. The remaining signs of Polish autonomy were destroyed. Congress Poland was now integrated into the Russian Empire and renamed Vistula Land. In due course, the use of Polish language was forbidden and the process of Russification was instigated throughout areas under Russian control. Russian became the official language and the language of instruction in schools. The Catholic Church, which was considered to be inextricably linked with the Polish national identity, was repressed. Contacts between Polish bishops and the Vatican were made difficult and church activities in society were monitored. Landowners who had either participated in, or assisted the insurgents, lost their estates and thousands were sent into punitive exile in the Russian interior. Thousands of Poles fled to the West, once more forming exile communities. Here the trauma of the uprising, as on previous occasions, became the subject of endless debates and conflicts.

The January Uprising was the most dramatic of all Polish attempts to regain independence. Its failure led to reflection and with that a further degree of acceptance of the inevitable. If Polish identity was to be retained, then other means of defending it had to be found. The political and cultural importance of the nobility had been reduced. The gentry in all insurrections had been the most active section of Polish society. In the January uprising it had been made to suffer the consequences of its actions. Through repression, the Russians sought to politically destroy that group of the Polish community. The gentry was losing its pre-eminence in the political life of areas under Russian control. At the same time, changes in patterns of production and developments in agriculture were undermining the landed gentry's financial position.

The last quarter of the nineteenth century was a time of great economic and political transformations in Europe. These, in turn, led to the emergence of new political parties. In Polish-inhabited territories, similar changes took place. In Poland, West European ideas and new ideologies fell on fertile ground. At the same time, contacts between Polish nationalists and conspiratorial organisations in the Russian Empire, extended the range of debates. Due to the oppressive nature of the tsarist empire all political organisations were banned. This, in turn, led to the development of secret Anarchist and terrorist organisations with which Poles had some contact. Nevertheless, in Polish territories political debates were inextricably linked to the main issue of the fight for independence.

After 1863, Russian policies towards territories of the previous Polish and Lithuanian Commonwealth, became more determined. Polish presence in Lithuanian areas was reduced by displacing landowners and forbidding them to purchase land. In their place, Russians were allowed to buy land. The tsarist authorities encouraged non-Polish communities – Lithuanian, Byelorussian and Ukrainian – to separate from Poland and integrate into Russian culture. At the same time a growing sense of national awareness within those communities meant that they no longer saw their future through the prism of the Polish quest for independence. In the same way that Poles debated the issue of national self-expression, Byelorussian and Ukrainian national leaders also came to consider the possibility of establishing their own national state. Polish claims to represent the interests of those who, in the past, had been part of the Commonwealth, became irrelevant and were, in fact, resented. The tsarist authorities viewed the Uniate Church, loyal to the Church of Rome, as a betrayal of the Orthodox Eastern faith. As a result, it was singled out for persecution and was targeted as part of a policy of reducing the Western orientation of the Ukrainian ethnic groups.

In Vistula Land the consequences of Russian policies were very complex. By a *ukase* of 2 March 1864 serfdom was abolished, freeing peasants from personal servitude and obligation to till the land of the landowner. This destroyed the authority of the gentry and created a free peasantry with an entitlement to land. Thus the last vestiges of feudalism ended. At the same time, encouraged by fiscal policies and the abolishment of tariff barriers between the Russian Empire and the Vistula Land, Polish areas experienced an industrial revolution. During a brief period, a rapid pace of economic change affected whole districts. Warsaw, Łódź, Piotrków, Białystok, and areas of the Dąbrowa Basin became industrial centres. Economically, Polish territories enjoyed the full benefit of having access to the protected markets of the Russian Empire. Industrialisation, in turn, led to the emergence of a working class and, with that, clandestine socialist organisations. These were critical of the iniquities of the capitalist system.[16]

It was inevitable that trauma was caused by the January Uprising, its failure, the repressions that followed and, finally, the economic developments. This generated a new mood of despondence. The previously cherished Romantic and messianic ideas glorified suffering, death and sacrifice as part of the great national struggle and resurrection. These were replaced by ideas in which economic progress and stability were signs of progressive thought. Economic development was considered to be a precondition for national liberation and with that came discussions of the benefits and applicability of the democratic institutional model to the Polish question. New thinkers were critical of the ideas which had been part of the past republic of the nobility and sceptical of the likelihood of the next uprising being successful where the previous had failed. They advocated social and economic progress. This current in Polish political thinking came to be known as Positivism. Several eminent writers wrote in that vein, focusing on the usefulness of education, scientific development, engineering and medicine. Bolesław Prus and Aleksander Świętochowski are good examples of authors who saw themselves as part of the Positivist trend.

Russian repressions hit the landed gentry particularly severely. Many were either stripped of their estates, sent into exile or went into voluntary exile. This, in turn, increased the importance of the home environment in maintaining knowledge of the Polish language and culture. Polish language, literature and culture were no longer taught at schools and could not be used in public. The duty to teach children Polish therefore fell to the mothers. In many educated families, usually belonging to the gentry, men were absent. They had either perished during the uprisings, or had been punished for having been directly involved in them or in supporting them. When insurrectionists left for exile in Western Europe, they were rarely accompanied by their families. This left the women to manage the estates and bring up the next generation. The role of Polish mothers thus became critical in fostering national self-consciousness. The myth of a Polish mother became particularly important during this period. She had a sacred responsibility to maintain Polishness and to transmit the knowledge of the language, history and culture to the next generation. This became no less than a woman's national duty. Two of the prominent authors of the period were women who closely associated with the Positivist trend in literature. Maria Konopnicka and Eliza Orzeszkowa were both critical of the gentry's preoccupation with fomenting uprisings while ignoring the social consequences of industrialisation. The social consequences of the failed uprisings, in particular on women, were discussed in literature.

At the same time, the extensive tsarist bureaucracy and army offered employment opportunities for educated Poles. Entry into the ranks of both was regulated by state examinations and progression was defined by clear rules. In daily life many Poles faced intimidation and discrimination. However, once they had passed state examinations, they were assured of state employment and were able to enjoy the same benefits as did the other subjects of the Russian Empire. A strong sense of injustice and anger united the

Polish community. However, in Russian areas there were those who accepted the inevitable and made careers for themselves.

In Polish areas under Russian domination, political issues could only be addressed with extreme caution, if at all. In schools, authorities strove to root out any indications of national awareness and political opposition to Russian domination. Thus, all debates on issues relating to Poland's past independence and hopes for future sovereignty and of reforms could only be conducted in conspiratorial groups. The tsarist system was the most repressive of the European regimes. In 1905 Tsar Nicolas II was persuaded by his advisors to agree to a number of reforms. The most important of these was the decision to allow for the elections to a State Duma. The limited concessions had been preceded by a war with Japan during which the Russian Empire faced military defeat. In 1905, strikes and street fighting engulfed the industrial towns and centres of European Russia. Initially, reforms promised by the tsar, suggested a willingness to build democratic institutions. Russian subjects were allowed to form parties and trade unions. In spite of initial high expectations for change, disappointment set in quickly as the tsarist regime made extensive use of emergency laws to suppress genuine freedom. This, naturally, had an impact on the nature of debates taking place in Polish areas, radicalising both liberal and socialist groups. The inevitable conclusion was that the tsarist system could not be reformed and would thus have to be destroyed in a forthcoming revolution.

In Polish areas incorporated into Prussia and Austria, political developments took a different course. In both, the establishment of constitutional political systems decreased the Poles' preoccupation with insurrections as the only way of redressing grievances. In both cases, Polish citizens came to enjoy the same rights as did all other citizens, as state organisations worked relatively efficiently and so did the courts. The result was that Poles became fully active in the political life of both empires. This in turn, meant that the Poles in both became members of legally defined parties and trade unions and gained experience of parliamentary politics.

The fate of Polish territories under Prussian control was determined by two major events: the German unification and Bismarck's policies of extending and consolidating German presence in areas inhabited by Poles. These policies were applied to Pomerania, Silesia and Eastern Prussia, all areas with a high proportion of ethnic Poles. After 1815, Prussia was awarded control of the Grand Duchy of Posen, which in due course was incorporated into Germany. Prussia had supported Russia during the January Uprising. It took punitive measures against attempts by Poles from areas under Prussian control, who wanted to support or join the uprising in Congress Poland. When Germany was united in 1871, the Prussian Landtag, the state assembly, made decisions relating to the Polish question. The Prussian attitude towards the Poles was clearly negative and, as a result, a policy of Germanisation was implemented. This was aimed at either destroying the Polish communities or integrating them fully into German life. Nevertheless the Poles, as citizens of the German state, had the right to participate in the political life of united Germany. Poles had the right to vote to the Landtag and the Reichstag, which made decisions relating to matters of state. Poles sent their own representatives to both assemblies. Cooperation with German parties proved to be minimal and the nationality issue proved an obstacle to unity, even in the case of the socialist parties and trade unions.

In 1873 Chancellor Otto von Bismarck embarked on a confrontation with the Catholic Church. His aim was to break down the independence of the German states and to fuse them more closely. He perceived the Catholic Church to be an obstacle in that process. In Prussia, the Catholic Church was seen as having a particularly strong bond with the Polish community. Bismarck's *Kulturkampf*, as it came to be known, had the dual role of reorganisation and of destroying the Catholic Church. From 1872 onwards, Polish language teaching was finally restricted, resulting in the closing of all Polish schools. German became the language of instruction in all elementary schools. By 1876 the same policies were implemented in secondary schools. In 1886, Bismarck established a very generously funded Colonisation Commission. The aim was to buy up land from Polish landlords and to enable German colonists to settle in the eastern regions. This was done through the use of existing laws and by granting subsidies to enable colonists to buy land. While the Polish communities were affected by the closure of schools and discrimination, the well-functioning legal system allowed them to fight back. This they did by raising funds to prevent land buyouts and even establishing a Land Bank and the Bank of the Association of Workers' Co-operatives, both highly respected financial institutions. The formation of peasant cooperatives and associations of Polish landowners reduced the impact of the Prussian attempts to economically undermine the Polish community.[17]

Thus, Polish areas incorporated into the German state developed a distinctly different community response to attempts at destroying Polish national self-awareness from that in the Russian Empire. The Poles fought back by making full use of the Landtag and the Reichstag to voice grievances. Recourse to courts was frequently a successful way of opposing discriminatory policies. However much the Poles felt themselves to be persecuted, they, nevertheless, came to trust democratic institutions and to work within the legal framework.

Austrian responses to the Polish question were determined by the empire's weakening position in Europe, military defeats and, finally, by rivalry with Prussia, which resulted in the creation of a Prussian-dominated united German state. In 1866, after military defeat in a war with Prussia the Austrian emperor decided to primarily seek an accommodation with the Hungarians. The Poles benefited from this policy. While Hungary's status within the empire was guaranteed, other national groups were given further rights as autonomous regions. In the Russian and Prussian parts of Poland repression was increased after 1863. However, in Austria, direct intervention in Polish-inhabited regions was relaxed. In 1868, Polish Galicia was granted autonomy within the Hapsburg Empire and in due course was allowed to have its own assembly. Austrian rule in Galicia was based on cooperation with the nobility. They, in turn, appreciated that they had a lot to gain from supporting Austrian policies. Local administration was made responsible for local matters and there was support for schools in which Polish remained the language of instruction. These things maintained the close relationship between the Polish nobility and the Austrian state. The Jagiellonian University in Kraków and the University in Lwów were reopened. Galicia and Kraków became oases of Polish national self-awareness.

Nevertheless, Polish areas under Austrian control remained economically the most backward regions of the Austrian Empire. In Congress Poland and in Poznań in Prussia, both powers destroyed the power of the nobility. Under Russian rule, the middle classes and those connected with industry and trade benefited. In Prussia, the need to counteract colonisation policies and the fact that agricultural produce commanded high prices led to the introduction of efficient farming methods. Both the landowners and peasants had an incentive to modernise. In areas under Austrian control, the situation was entirely different. These were areas little affected by industrialisation. In villages, a patchwork of dwarf holdings prevailed, in most cases insufficient to support a family. For the peasants, emigration to the USA was the only escape from poverty. For the nobility, there were few incentives to modernise their estates. The Austrian authorities allowed the nobility to retain their old privileges and monopolies. This ensured continuing stagnation in agriculture and the absence of incentives to industrialise. Politically, the Polish community was closely integrated into the life of the empire. Poles had the right to send representatives to the Austrian Reichsrat, where they were very active. Many of the Polish aristocrats associated so closely with Austria that they did not feel obliged to support specifically Polish issues in the assembly.

There were repressive policies by the Russian authorities towards areas of the previous Polish–Lithuanian Commonwealth. There was also a general growth of national self-awareness among all the ethnic groups in East Europe. These two factors inevitably stimulated extensive debates on exactly how Polishness was defined. The initial fight was for restoration of the Commonwealth. However, by the middle of the nineteenth century, the debate had progressed beyond that aim. In the Polish case, unlike West Europe, there was no Polish state and thus the definition of Poland and of a Pole was more difficult to pin down. Still, there was no doubt that Poles shared a strong sense of national awareness, defined by language, culture and a historic past. In the case of the nobility, the educated, and among the growing ranks of the middle class, this awareness of a common identity transcended the boundaries imposed by the partitioning powers and, although never evenly, continued to develop in all Polish-inhabited areas.

After the failed January Uprising, each of the partitioning powers became more closely involved in drawing up long-term plans
for areas under their control. This, accompanied by the sense of de-
spondency which overcame Poles, led to the emergence of trends,
which have been described as 'loyalism'. Loyalists were thinkers
who pointed to the high human cost of the uprising and cautioned
against further military action, which, if it failed, could result in
the physical destruction of the Polish nation. They were fearful that
any further evidence of insubordination could lead to repressive
measures. Loyalism was also based on a careful assessment of the
international situation. Until the January Uprising, Poles generally
assumed that the partition of Poland was viewed in most European
states as an injustice. Their hopes that revolutionaries and liberals
would be always sympathetic to the Polish cause were dashed after 1848/49. At this time it emerged that liberals could be every bit
as nationalist as their conservative opponents. Still hopes lingered,
that with the change of power balance, there would be an opportunity to reconstruct the Commonwealth. These hopes were finally
destroyed in the 1870s. Prussian victory in the war with France and
the unification of Germany was followed by a relatively long period
of international stability. France was a state that Poles had always
believed to be sympathetic to their cause. But it was defeated. Austria was the least oppressive of the partitioning powers. But it lost
out to united Germany. Polish leaders were only too well aware that
Germany and Russia were united on the Polish question. Peripheral
powers, such as Britain and the Ottoman Empire, no longer mat-
tered. Britain had no interest in the Polish question. The Ottoman
Empire had condemned the partition of Poland and had previously
welcomed Polish refugees. However it was now no longer a player
in European politics. The conclusion was that the defence of Polish
national identity had to be achieved by accepting the inevitable and
by trying to find areas of compromise with the authorities in the
hope of decreasing restrictive policies.

Loyalism was thus not always a sign of weakness, but more a
reflection of pragmatism. Writers and intellectuals defined themselves as Positivists and were connected with trends which rejected
insurrections. These were men and women who chose to focus
on cultural and economic developments as a means of defending

Polish identity. A strong element in their programme was a focus on establishing schools, cooperatives, self-help circles and model farming. Positivist thinking was dominated by ideas of organic work and support for work and projects that would lay down the foundations for future national development. Prominent exponents of Positivist ideas were Aleksander Świętochowski, Piotr Chmielewski and Bolesław Chlebowski. Authors such as Henryk Sienkiewicz, Bolesław Prus and Eliza Orzeszkowa identified themselves as Positivists. They maintained the teaching and use of the Polish language. They believed that by empahasising the distinctiveness culture and religion, that Polish identity would survive and be fostered until such a moment when a Polish nation state would emerge.

Loyalists were more strident in their criticism of the nationalist culture based on the gentry and its preoccupation with insurrections. They effectively accepted that the rapid economic transformation of Polish-inhabited territories meant that the middle classes were becoming politically and economically more important. To them, economic stability and economic reforms became a priority. During the 1880s and 1890s Congress areas were being economically transformed due to Russian policies. The main exponents of loyalism in these areas were industrialists, bankers, financiers and members of the wealthy middle class community. Of those, Antoni Wrotnowski, Kazimierz Krzywicki, Włodzimierz Spasowski and Erazm Piltz were the best known. Advocates of the Loyalist theory, in particular the wealthy nobility with strong links with the tsarist administration, and new financial magnates and industrialists were more open about their conviction that Poles should accept their place in the Russian Empire. They suggested that the propertied classes should set an example to other Poles by being loyal to the governments of the partitioning powers.

In Polish areas under Prussian control, Loyalists were able to make full use of the existing democratic organisations to defend Polish interests. Thus Polish deputies to the Prussian Landtag and the Reichstag used both institutions to oppose laws limiting the rights of Poles to buy land and voted against subsidies for the Colonisisation Commission. Acceptance of the state of affairs led to the development of ideas. The battle to maintain Polish ownership of land and the development of cooperatives and enterprises became a priority. The fight to retain and maintain a sense of Polish national identity was thus conducted through opposing German economic encroachment. The great debates on the survival of the nation without a state were conducted in areas of Congress Poland. But they did not have their equivalent in Prussian-controlled territories.

In Austrian Galicia, Loyalist tendencies were widespread. This was due to the fact that Austria had granted Galicia autonomy and the right to a local assembly. The main debates were, therefore, not focused on the issue of opposition but on the question of how to obtain and secure freedoms, which Vienna was clearly willing to grant the Poles. The dilemma was whether to support the federalist or the centralised model of the empire and which of the two would be most advantageous to the Poles. One example of Galician Loyalism occurred in 1866, when the Galician assembly forwarded to the emperor a letter promising loyalty in return for further freedoms. Far from seeing the Austrian Empire as a 'Prison of Nations', the Galician Conservatists felt that within Austria, Polish national consciousness could be cultivated and developed. After 1869 a group of young conservatives started publishing a series of pamphlets called *Stańczyk's Portfolio (Teka Stańczyka)*, in which they debated the role of the recent uprisings. This led to further debates and, most notably, to the definition of the concept of nation. Stanisław Koźmian developed the concept of a nation being not a political entity but a community of people who are bound by shared customs, language and traditions. Both groups, without condemning the January Uprising, laid less stress on the concept of a state representing the interest of a nation and accepted that several nations could coexist in one state. They effectively suggested that Polish interests would be best served if Polish territories remained within the Austrian Empire. This conclusion was no doubt caused by a growing anxiety about the process of Russification in Congress Poland and an anxiety that if Austria were to be further weakened, she might lose Galicia to Russia. The main focus of the conservatives' activities was to develop Polish schools and sponsor cultural activities and Polish language publications. These were then easily smuggled into the Russian territories.

The passage of time also took its toll on the debates concerning Poland's fate. At the end of the century, the young generation
felt that the events after the January Uprising were history, as were
the Positivist solutions. Once more, a willingness to seek inspira-
tion from the great days of the past manifested itself. It was then
that Henryk Sienkiewicz wrote his Trilogy, which harked back to
past days of glory, even if not always giving a historically accurate
picture of that past. Jan Matejko's paintings, likewise, were deeply
inspirational to generations which had no personal experience of
either the struggle for independence or of the immediate consequences of its failure. Arthur Grottger and Maksymilian Gierymski
painted in the same nationalist vein. By the end of the nineteenth
century, new ideas emerged challenging earlier attitudes and, in fact,
developing more precise political objectives. These changes were a
reaction to the increasing sterility of the debates conducted after the
January Uprising. They also reflected the changing social structure
of the Polish population, where the working class and peasants now
increasingly sought to speak with their own voices.

The policies of the partitioning powers towards Polish territories
had, at times, unexpected results. The destruction of Polish language teaching in areas under Prussian control and the establishment of high-quality compulsory schooling in German in no way
prevented Polish children from learning Polish. Once illiteracy was
abolished, learning to read in Polish was the next logical step. In
Austrian Galicia, backwardness in the villages was endemic, but the
Poles were able to publish Polish language books and newspapers.
Censorship in Galicia was least oppressive. The borders between
the three sections of Polish-inhabited areas were porous and therefore allowed for a great degree of interchange of ideas. The end of
the nineteenth and the beginning of the twentieth centuries were
times which could be described as those of increasing mass participation in social and political life. Moreover, Polish areas were not
cut off from the rest of Europe. The development of efficient railways
meant that from within Congress Poland it was possible to travel
to St. Petersburg and Odessa. From Kraków Poles went to Vienna
and from Poznań, Berlin was within easy reach. Polish territories
were not just the crossroads between the West and East, they were

the territories whose inhabitants were as much part of the Russian Empire as being citizens of powerful and economically advanced West European states. They were more so than ever before part of the intellectual and political debates which flourished in East and West Europe.

# 1 Poland on the Eve of the First World War

At the end of the nineteenth century and the beginning of the twentieth century, nationalism as a political ideology came to play an increasingly important role in Europe. In the Polish case, the growth of Polish nationalism was not constrained by the boundaries of the three partitioning empires. Poles who had been incorporated into the Russian Empire, believed themselves to be a spiritual and cultural community with Poles in the Austrian and German Empires. More importantly, Polish leaders did not feel they were merely addressing the Polish question with reference to specific problems faced by Poles in one of the three empires. They felt they were addressing the Polish question in its entirety, even though they lived in areas ruled by governments of differing political character. Nevertheless, while it is possible to see how the Polish-inhabited regions developed distinct characteristics, a sense of national unity persisted and increased over time.

Polish political thinkers faced two dilemmas. The first was the dilemma of how Poland was to regain independence. At the same time, closely linked to that debate, was the question of the form in which Poland was to be restored. These two issues led to the question of modernisation. The Poles' efforts to modernise the Commonwealth had failed. Henceforth, all political, social and economic decisions would be made by the three partition powers. While implementing their own modernisation programmes, they aimed at integrating the Polish areas into their own territories and separating

## *The Dismemberment of the Polish–Lithuanian Kingdom during the Second and Third Partitions*

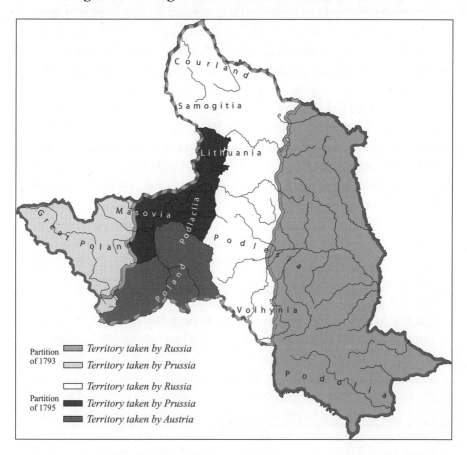

them from other Polish lands. Thus the process of economic and political modernisation took place and was paralleled by the attempt to
destroy the Polish nation. This led to profound dilemmas within the
Polish communities. They came to view state activities with distrust,
even if they were economically beneficial to the Poles. Critically, it
led to the emergence of the perception that the nationalist question
was more important than progress towards modernisation.[1]

If economic and social developments are considered in separation from cultural self-expression, the picture was complex at the
beginning of the twentieth century. Like other East and Southeast
European areas, Polish-inhabited regions continued to be generally
economically underdeveloped, with a heavy dependence on agriculture. In most cases, agriculture was desperately backward and
villages were overpopulated. The most obvious way out was through
emigration, mainly to North America, where the Polish communities formed a sizeable diaspora. At the beginning of the twentieth
century, the USA restricted the number of immigrants from backward parts of Eastern Europe. This and the growing birth rate increased pressure in the countryside. At the end of the nineteenth
century, village life was still dominated by the landowners, who
controlled the local economy. In most cases the economic power of
the landlords was mirrored by them retaining political control over
the villages. When universal franchise was introduced, the landlord
had means of ensuring that the peasants would cast their votes as
instructed. This was the case in the Austrian and German areas.
But the situation was far from uniform or static. An eminent historian has pointed out that at that time Poland was not an 'economic
reality'.[2] At the turn of the century, discrepancies between the backward, neglected countryside, and areas affected by industrialisation,
became more pronounced. The process of industrialisation was always patchy and coexisted side by side with the traditional village
community economy. At the same time, extensive state involvement encouraged and facilitated industrial development. Therefore
primitive manufacturing methods continued while modern, up to
date, usually foreign-owned industrial plants were introduced into
the region. Industrialisation and the development of extensive railway systems had a big impact on Polish areas. In addition, the trade
policies of the partitioning powers were of critical importance in

determining the speed and pattern of development. The Russian
and German Empires formed extensive markets protected by tariff barriers. Polish areas benefited from being part of those closed
economic regions.

In Pomerania and the Poznań regions, which were under Prussian control, agriculture was more advanced than in the Russian or
Austrian Empires. In Berlin there was a natural desire to support this
region for its high-quality agricultural production, which economically complemented the industrially advanced areas of Germany.
Labour mobility was made possible by the development of a railway system and peasants were able to move from the agricultural
Poznań region and seek employment in Germany or Silesia. Chancellor Otto von Bismarck formulated policies in relation to Polish
inhabitied areas. In doing this, he followed his predecessors who
had aimed at integrating the Polish areas into the Reich. In the
first place, he sought to destroy the Polish gentry and the Catholic
Church – both of which he saw as carriers of dangerous liberal
ideas.[3] The first move was to destroy the Catholic Church's control over education. Thus the process of Germanisation had two
purposes.[4] In this policy of denationalisation and integration of the
Polish community into the Reich, Bismarck sought to reduce the
amount of land held by the Poles. This was done through the state
which acted as an agent in the process of buying land from Polish landowners and encouraging German colonisation.[5] The result
was conflict with the Polish community which only marginally reduced the amount of land held by the Poles. An unexpected result
was the development of Polish peasant cooperatives, self-help associations and local banks. Polish peasants had the incentive and
means of fighting back, as their property rights were protected by
the well-functioning German legal system to which they had recourse. At the same time, they were encouraged to improve production and to modernise. Savings and credit companies and agricultural circles were the by-product of the Poles' attempts to counter
German policies.[6] In Polish parts of Prussia, agriculture became advanced and productive, with villages becoming prosperous and economically stable. At the same time, Poles in the German Empire
were well educated and easily assimilated into industry as a skilled
workforce.

In Silesia, textile and coal mining formed the basis of the industrial takeoff. At the end of the nineteenth century, coal mining and steel production came to dominate Upper Silesia, which became one of the most industrially advanced regions in Europe. In Silesia, colonisation and industrialisation led to changes in the population structure. The Polish presence was visible in agricultural areas and in the Katowice coal-mining region. Most industrial production was financed by either German or foreign capital. Most managerial and skilled posts were held by Germans, which from the outset caused ethnic tensions.[7]

The situation in the Polish areas which had been incorporated into the Austrian Empire was very different. In 1868, Polish Galicia was granted autonomy. Although an assembly was constituted to administer the region, it was not until 1865 that the Austrians allowed the Poles to assume full responsibility for local issues. After years of neglect, Agendor Gołuchowski, the imperial governor, implemented policies aimed at, in the first place reforming the educational system and improving the infrastructure. At the turn of the century, the provision of elementary education was considerably better than in areas under Russian control. However shortage of funds and conflicts among Polish conservatives, who dominated the Galician Sejm and administration, meant that the region continued to be backward. The issue of education had exercised the minds of the conservative landowners. They were unhappy at the prospect of the peasants having access to education, which would provide them with knowledge beyond the basic literacy levels. Conflicts between the landowners and the peasants continued into the twentieth century. At the same time, the economic situation was difficult. Agriculture suffered from years of neglect. In villages, poverty was endemic, as was illiteracy. In some areas industry made its mark, but in most cases the local population benefited little from new economic activities in the region.[8] Oil exploration, dominated by foreign capital, was a good example of the way industrial activities bypassed the region. In Austrian Polish areas, small-scale and light industries usually meant food processing. Sugar beet production constituted some agricultural progress. As a direct result, sugar refining developed in the Ukrainian regions.

Even on the eve of the outbreak of the First World War, politics in the Galician Sejm were dominated by particular groups. These groups firmly believed that the Poles had a lot to benefit from loyally supporting the empire. The main issue of debate was whether to seek a larger degree of autonomy within the Austrian Empire, or full independence. By then, they were united in supporting educational reforms. Most of the politicians came from landed backgrounds. They therefore did not feel comfortable supporting industrial developments. They also distrusted those calling for investment as this would encourage the transformation of the local economy.[9]

In Austrian Poland, the ethnic composition of the community was very diverse. This was particularly the case in Eastern Galicia, where the Ukrainian population increasingly resented the Poles' domination of local political life and the economy. In addition, 11.5 per cent of the inhabitants of the regions were Jewish. Some members of the Jewish communities were unconstrained by discriminatory laws. These members tended to be fully active in all areas of the economic life of Polish Austria. This varied from small-scale retail activities, to banking and industrial entrepreneurship. Before the outbreak of the First World War, up to 75 per cent of local trade was in Jewish hands. The Jewish community, outside the cultural centre of Kraków, remained unassimilated.[10]

Within areas under Russian control the economic situation was entirely different. The abolishment of serfdom in 1864 reduced the economic and political role of the landed gentry but stimulated the growth of village communities. In Congress Poland, the process of transforming village life was delayed in comparison with other parts of Europe, in particular Western Europe. Economic development was nevertheless of great interest to successive Tsarist governments. The first stages of economic modernisation occurred during the first thirty years of the nineteenth century while serfdom was still in place. In the Polish areas, manufacture and trade were advanced in relation to the Russian areas. Customs barriers between Congress Poland and the Russian Empire had been abolished in 1856. This meant that the Polish areas were then able to take full advantage of the vast markets offered by the empire. This led to the emergence of several important industrial zones in Congress Poland, notably the

Dąbrowa Basin, the town and district of Łódź and, finally, the towns of Białystok and Warsaw. The industrial revolution in the Polish areas was made possible by the opening up of the Russian markets to goods produced in Congress Poland. Congress Poland was protected by the establishment of tariffs between the Russian Empire and the neighbouring states. The Polish regions benefited economically from the economic changes taking place in the empire. Nevertheless, Russian policy had always ensured that the emergence of an industrial and middle class did not pose a challenge to the autocratic Tsarist system. Thus, in addition to maintaining a strong control over economic activities, the Tsarist administration encouraged foreign investment. That way, although Congress Poland was the centre of industrial production and sent over 70 per cent of its goods to the Russian Empire, the Poles did not reap the full financial benefits of trade between the Congress areas and the Russian Empire. Politically, the system remained impervious to change until 1905. Following defeat at Japan's hands and strikes and riots, which rocked the foundations of the regime, Tsar Nicholas II relented and agreed to political reforms.[11]

The Jewish community in Congress Poland was swelled by an influx of Jews from the empire. This was due to the policy of confining Jews to the Western European parts of Russia, the so-called Pale of Settlement. The Jewish population made up 14 per cent of those living in Congress Poland. In some cases, particularly in the eastern districts, over 50 per cent of the population of a given town was Jewish. The issue of assimilation was extensively debated by Jews and non-Jews alike. Jewish life in the Russian Empire was constrained by laws which applied only to that community. Despite this, Jews played an important role not merely in the economic life of the small towns, but also in trade with the Russian regions.

In spite of the different pace and character of economic changes affecting Polish territories, there were similarities. The rapid and extensive development of railway networks had a dramatic impact on all communities. In all three cases, the partitioning powers had an interest in financing and supporting the process. Military considerations still played an important role in their plans. Nevertheless, it was only natural that trade, movement of goods and migration of workers to places of employment was rapidly accelerated. As the three empires financed the expansion of the railway system, they hoped to integrate the Polish areas into the empires. At the time of the outbreak of the First World War, railway lines connected Polish regions with Vienna, Berlin and St. Petersburg, though few cut across the frontiers of the three empires. The Russian railway gauge was different from that used by the Austrians and Germans, making it impossible to run trains directly and without interruption from the East to the West. This situation created problems once an independent Polish state emerged after the First World War. Due to this, Polish economists had to grapple with the fact that Poland did not have a railway system which would serve Poland and its capital. Before the war it was easier for Poles to travel from Warsaw to Odessa than to Berlin.[12]

At the end of the nineteenth century and the beginning of the twentieth, the nature of the political debates had gone beyond the debate of the role of the nobility and ways of combating village backwardness. Industrialisation and the emergence of new social groups connected with industry, created new political dilemmas. Industrialisation had led to greater disparities in wealth. The political demands of those involved in manufacture and industry were increasingly different from those of the gentry and peasants. Conflicts between the workers and the industrialists led to new forms of political activism, to debates and with that to the formation of different priorities. Polish community leaders and intellectuals were only too well aware of the way industrialisation destroyed traditional societies and led to exploitation of workers and their families. In the Polish case, political debates could not address the workers' question without, at the same time, referring to the fact that there was no Polish state. Thus, the two emerging political trends – the nationalist and the socialist – were initially linked and had in effect the same roots. In each of the partition areas, the political debate and the nature of political organisations, which emerged at the end of the nineteenth century, continued to be defined by the character of the regime. In the German and Austrian cases, trade unions and political parties were accepted as legal organisations. The introduction of manhood suffrage meant that most working men had an awareness of how the liberal democratic system worked and how it could be used to their advantage. In the Russian Empire, all forms of dissent were illegal, and there was no right of free association. Only in 1906 did the Tsar allow for the formation of an elected assembly and accepted that political organisations could be formed. These factors determined the character of political movements and had an impact on the programme they put forward.

From the outset, political thinkers and Polish nationalists realised that to be successful they had to appeal to Poles living in all three partition areas. At the end of the nineteenth century, political organisations and parties emerged. These became the accepted way to pursue political objectives either within the parliamentary system or in conspiracy. They not merely sought to build links between the three, but they also claimed to represent the aspirations of all Polish communities. Links within the Polish territories were consolidated by the fact that activists frequently had to move from one partition area to another in order to evade arrest. This particularly affected politically active Poles in Congress Poland, who moved to Kraków, from where they were able to maintain contact with conspirators in the Russian Empire. Polish language publications were, likewise, disseminated from the Austrian areas where they could be published legally. They were then conveyed to regions under Russian control, where censorship was very restrictive.

The Polish communities in exile were a factor in the building of links between activists and organisations. They frequently experienced economic hardship and were often the object of surveillance by the local police forces in various West European capitals where they had sought sanctuary. In spite of this, these men and women continued campaigning for the restoration of a free Poland. By necessity they associated with political exiles from other regimes. This frequently led to a very vibrant exchange of ideas. Thus, exile Poles were exposed to the most up to date political ideas and discussions. From these, they derived intellectual stimulation to address Poland's problems. When looked at from that background of discussions of political ideas, Poland's problems were no longer so unique. Nevertheless, relations between exile political leaders and those in the Polish territories were never easy. In principle, they shared the same objectives, namely the restoration of an independent Poland. To that aim they supported each other and facilitated the dissemination of new ideas and publications. But in reality, relations between the exile communities and Poles were uneven. Some exiles tended to dwell on the past, rehearsing past failures and, on the basis of a limited understanding of what was happening in Polish areas, hoped to spark off another great national insurrection. Socialist, and even anarchist ideologies, advocated a revolutionary transformation of the political life of Europe. Some tried to apply these ideas to the still industrially backward Polish territories. In Polish territories, social inequalities and the political and economic consequences of industrialisation tended to increasingly dominate the debate on the restoration of Poland.

A number of organisations emerged in exile and in the Polish territories during the second half of the nineteenth century. The national democratic movement emerged from the coming together of these organisations. What these organisations had in common was the rejection of the positivist acceptance of the foreign tutelage and their desire to involve all people in the fight for independence. In Warsaw, a weekly publication *Głos* (The Voice), the first copy of which was published in 1886, led the debate on the subject of an independent Polish state. Its readership was confined to intellectuals and students. They came to disagree with what they thought was a preoccupation with economic advancement at the expense of the national agenda. Jan Ludwik Popławski established the weekly with Józef Potocki. He drew a link between the rural community and the survival of Polish national identity. The peasants (in Polish 'lud', which can also mean 'the people') were extolled for their supposed organic relationship with the land and for having maintained ancient traditions and ways. In his preoccupation with the peasant community, Popławski was also criticising the emerging industrial and middle class strata for having, supposedly, abandoned a commitment to Polish nationalism. According to the intellectuals connected with the *Głos*, the way forward was not only to work towards increasing people's national awareness but also to bring the peasants directly into the fight for independence.[13]

In Lwów, *Przegląd Społeczny* (The Social Review) voiced similar dilemmas. Its editor Bolesław Wysłouch also focused on the peasants as the true soul of the Polish nation. The Lwów thinkers shared with their counterparts in Warsaw the conviction that the community as a whole should be politically active in independent Poland.

Wysłouch went further in stating that Poland should emerge as a
state governed in accordance with modern democratic principles.
Both groups made reference to socialist and democratic principles
with which they were acquainted.[14]

During his exile, Zygmunt Miłkowski published a brochure in
1887, which was widely disseminated in Poland. The author suggested in it that the aim of the partitioning powers was the destruction of the Polish nation. In the circumstances, the Poles had no
option but to fight back. But that battle would require careful and
consistent planning. Miłkowski drew attention to the loosening of
ties between the three partitioning powers, which he believed would
in due course result in conflict. He therefore advocated that young
people should prepare themselves for that moment when a national
insurrection would result in the defeat of Poland's enemies. These
ideas found a ready echo with the university and high school students in Congress areas, who bore the brunt of Russian repressive
measures and Russification policies.[15]

Zygmunt Balicki was a student activist who had fled Congress
territories and, in exile had met Miłkowski. In 1887 he established
a youth organisation which set out as its programme the fight for
an independent Poland. An interesting feature of this initiative was
a desire to bring together youth activists from the three partition
areas. The Związek Młodzieży Polskiej (Association of Polish Youth,
also known as 'Zet' ), which was thus established, was committed
to social and political justice. Its members were to prepare to fight
for independence. But they were also to be committed to combat
social and economic injustices in society.[16]

In 1887 a number of Polish exiles in Switzerland established the
Liga Polska (Polish League). This was an organisation whose aim was
to coordinate the exiles' activities with those in Polish territories. By
1888 Popławski, Balicki and the leadership of the Zet had combined
forces with the Liga Polska. Henceforth, they worked closely together, focusing on developing a network of organisations, both in
Polish territories and in exile. The organisation structure was aimed
at training and preparing young people, mainly students, to assume
a leadership role not only in the fight for independence but also
in linking with the peasants. Great stress was put on educating the

masses, developing a sense of national solidarity and encouraging self-help and cooperative organisations.[17]

With time, the movement became clearer in its identity, distancing itself from socialist and Marxist egalitarian principles with which it had initially agreed. In 1893, the Polish League assumed the name of the National League. The debate on how individual Poles could further the national cause continued and in due course the main ideological tenets of what came to be known as national democracy were defined. By then, the leading light of the movement was Roman Dmowski, a one-time Warsaw student activist.

In May 1897 Dmowski announced the formation of the National Democratic Party, which would encompass all three partition areas. It would be some time before this plan became a reality. Nevertheless, this announcement recognised the growing popularity of the movement.[18] In 1903 Dmowski published his first major work, *The Thinking of the Modern Pole*, in which he outlined what were to later become the main themes of his ideology. His analysis of the failed uprisings led him to assert that the nobility, who had organised the national uprisings, were not the true representatives of the Polish nation. Instead, he asserted that it was the common people, the peasants and workers who had a claim to being the nation.[19] The key assertion made by Dmowski was that Poles constituted a nation, defined by a commonality of language, culture and heritage. Dmowski believed that nations were in conflict with each other. The specific problem faced by the Poles was that they did not have a state and that left the Polish nation particularly vulnerable. This was both because of conflict with Russia and Germany, and also because there was a threat that the Poles would lose their own national self-awareness. The aim of the new movement was to defend the interests of the nation, which stood above those of individuals. This was to be done through involvement in youth circles, sport groups, paramilitary organisations and self-education and cooperative circles. During the following years, Dmowski developed his ideas further. He advocated cooperation with the Russian Empire, believing that the Poles and the Russians faced, in Germany, a common enemy. At the same time, Dmowski disagreed with pan-Slavic theories. These theories suggested that the Russian nation would, given an opportunity, overwhelm the Poles. Dmowski's theories were deeply anti-Semitic, suggesting that the Jewish people were a parasite within the Polish nation, likely to destroy its vitality.[20]

In 1897, the national democratic programme was published first in Congress areas but was accepted by the Poles in other partition areas. In the meantime, national democrat activists concentrated on educational programmes, especially among the peasants, whom they identified as the true carriers of the national spirit. Dmowski was not opposed to capitalism, industrialisation or modern economic developments. On the contrary, his theories addressed the need for a future Poland to be both industrialised and economically and militarily strong. He nevertheless put the well-being of the nation above the profit motives, seeing industrial conflict as a possible source of the nation's weakness. This is where Dmowski and his followers disagreed with socialists. National democrats hoped for a society in which economic conflicts would be overcome and all the nation's resources and potential would be harnessed for the common good. Interestingly, though Dmowski and his followers glorified the alleged national purity of the Polish peasant, they were adamant about the need to defend the dignity of those working in industry, particularly in order to limit exploitation.

At the beginning of the twentieth century, the national democratic movement made headway only in Congress Poland, while Poles in Austria and Prussia were less inclined to support a movement that was critical of any accommodation with the partitioning powers.[21] In Prussia, this changed in 1902 when Kaiser Wilhelm II initiated an aggressive anti-Polish policy. Further restrictions on the teaching of religion in Polish raised fears about Germanisation policies. The national democrats were referred to as the Endecja. They benefited from these developments, as those who had earlier advocated a conciliatory policy towards the German authorities, lost ground.[22] In the 1903 and 1905 elections when three Polish national democrats were elected to the Prussian assembly, the party felt that it had secured modest but significant victories. During that time, the Endecja made few inroads within the Austrian areas where the activities of the conservative, socialist and peasant parties offered the national democrats few openings.

Unlike the gradual emergence and definition of the principles of the national democratic movement, socialism was a creed with which Poles in exile and those in Polish territories were familiar. Throughout the nineteenth century, relations between West European revolutionaries and exile Poles had been in most cases very good.[23] West European activists had condemned their own governments for being passive during the January Insurrection and gave material and organisational support to the exiles who fled from Polish territories.[24] Polish exiles had been active in the formation of the First International. They were also conspicuously present in most revolutionary upsurges during the nineteenth century, from the Hungarian Revolution to the Paris Commune. Polish thinkers in exile were familiar with the teaching of Marx and Engels. Marx condemned the West European governments' indifference to the fate of Poland. This conveyed an impression that socialists were generally in support of Polish independence. Nevertheless, Polish political émigrés, even those who were involved with the First International, considered the need to fight for an independent Poland to be a priority, more important than the quest for a socialist society. It is known that emissaries from the International travelled to Polish territories trying to build up a Polish section. This leads to suggestions that revolutionary agents introduced Marxist ideas into Polish territories from the West and students enrolled in German universities. The alternative hypothesis is that Polish students at Russian universities were drawn into underground activities, mainly the Russian conspiratorial organisation Zemlya i Volya. Through these contacts they participated in the debates on the applicability of the Marxist doctrine to Russia. This was a society which still had not experienced industrialisation and was still a monarchist dictatorship. It can be accepted that Poles travelling to the West and those studying in Warsaw, Vilna, Moscow, St. Petersburg and Odessa would have been aware of the significance of the Marxist doctrine as a theory which sought to explain the rapid economic and political changes taking place in the Russian Empire.[25]

In 1878 a group of young Polish socialists based in Warsaw prepared a *Programme of Polish Socialists*. These were Ludwik Waryński, Kazimierz Hind, Szymon Diksztajn and Stanisław Mendelson. They were all one-time students and socialist activists. This was sent for

comment to a group of Polish socialists in Geneva and finally published in Brussels. The *Programme* was based on the Communist
Manifesto. It assumed the inevitability of class conflict, which would
ultimately lead to a revolution, and the establishment of a socialist
order. This was a first attempt at coordinating the activities of various disparate socialist organisations. An interesting point about it is
that it refused to address the issue of independence for Poland. By
1880 Waryński and a number of young revolutionaries, fleeing the
threat of arrest, found themselves in Geneva. Socialist refugees from
various countries were thus brought together and debated further
the aims of the Polish socialist programme. By then it had come to
be known as the Brussels Programme.[26] An issue that divided socialists in Geneva was that of Poland's independence. Waryński's group
believed that the socialist revolution and international solidarity
should be the main objective of the Polish socialist movement. His
protagonists were led by Bolesław Limanowski. His political experience had been that of organising workers' organisations in Lwów.
He believed that in the first place, young Polish socialists should
fight for the establishment of an independent Poland with democratic institutions. This, in due course, would be replaced by a socialist system.[27] Thus, the two main strands which persisted within
the Polish socialist movement, manifested themselves from the
outset.

In 1881, Waryński returned to Warsaw, where he sought to
build up a centralised socialist movement. In 1882, a programme
of the International Social-Revolutionary Party – The Proletariat –
was announced.[28] The organisation lasted only until 1884, when
its leaders were arrested and were either executed or sent into penal
exile to Siberia. During its brief period of existence the leadership
maintained contact with comrades in Geneva. The Proletariat was
a section of the International, but at the same time, fraternal links
were established with the Russian revolutionary organisation *Naro-
dnaya Volya*. The unresolved debate on the primacy of the national
agenda in relation to the socialist programme, came to divide Polish
revolutionaries, along with new issues. Waryński believed that immediate action should be taken to challenge the authorities. Strikes
were organised and links were forged with workers. The leadership
of the Proletariat considered the use of terror to be a legitimate tactic

in fighting the state and individuals associated with it. Some revolutionaries disagreed with this line. They claimed that the Proletariat should focus on long-term plans and on building solid links with the working class.[29] Thus the main lines of debate which would divide socialists in the future were already outlined at the end of the nineteenth century.

When the Tsarist authorities destroyed the Proletariat, various smaller, revolutionary socialist organisations continued to function in Congress Poland. However, the issue of a centralised Polish socialist organisation continued to preoccupy socialist thinkers. A factor which added urgency to their considerations were the consequences of the economic crisis of 1890–91. This had resulted in strikes and mobilisation of workers. Workers' activists and socialists in each partition felt that they had to respond to the situation. At the same time, it was considered important that Poles should speak with one voice in the Second International. In January 1892, Polish socialists in the Austrian partition, came together to form a Galician Social-Democratic Party. In Prussia, with the encouragement of the German social democrats, Poles moved in the same direction. In November 1892, responding to news of these developments, a group of émigré socialists met in Paris to discuss the future programme of a socialist party. They then consulted with comrades in Polish territories and jointly tried to address issues which emerged specifically in relation to questions of cooperation between Polish and Russian socialists. The result was the formation of Polska Partia Socjalistyczna (Polish Socialist Party – PPS) in February 1893. From the outset, Polish socialists abroad and those in the areas under Russian control, failed to agree on a number of contentious issues. One of the most extensively discussed issues was that of whether the fight for Polish independence should take precedence over the need to secure political concessions. Although that key question was left unresolved, it marked a stage where Polish socialists moved away from the previous internationalist line towards a tacit acceptance that national independence was a priority.[30] During a meeting of the PPS in Vilna, which subsequently came to be known as the party's 1st Congress, a young activist, Józef Piłsudski, was given the task of clarifying the party's relations with Russian revolutionary organisations. His conclusion, accepted by the PPS, was that the Poles should collaborate with the Russians only if support would be given to Polish claims for independence.[31]

The publication of what came to be known as the Paris Programme, and attempts to unite the socialist movement had the opposite effect to that intended. In addition, it brought to the fore divisions. Of those, the most vocal and theoretically most rigorous was the Social Democracy of the Polish Kingdom (Socialdemokracja Królewstwa Polskiego – SDKP), which emerged in 1894. Its key spokesmen and ideologues were Róża Luxemburg, Julian Marchlewski, Leon Jogiches and Adolf Warski. PPS and SDKP differed on a number of key issues, most notably the importance of the struggle for national independence, cooperation with Russian revolutionaries and on working class solidarity. The PPS was cautious in its response to the Russian revolutionaries' desire for collaboration, putting the fight for an independent Poland at the top of the list of its objectives. SDKP, on the other hand, expressed anxiety about workers being distracted from the fight for political concessions by patriotic slogans. In its closing resolution, the 1st Congress of the SDKP, declared the party's main aim would be the fight for the destruction of the Tsarist system and the establishment of constitutional democracy. Polish and Russian workers were to jointly strive to those ends. Polish independence was described as 'an utopia' and was therefore a distraction from the proletariat's main objective, namely, class war. The SDKP remained a minority party within Congress Poland and when the Tsarist police destroyed the party's underground organisation, the remaining members moved towards the PPS. In 1899, an attempt was made to rebuild the social democratic movement. Feliks Dzierżyński led the initiative in Warsaw. In Vilna, Mieczysław Kozłowski established a workers' organisation. In December 1899, the Warsaw and Vilna social democrats made contact with social democrats Edward Sokołoski and Piotr Suknalewicz in Lithuania. They then contacted the leadership of the SDKP, who were in exile, with a proposal to form a new organisation. In 1900, these efforts resulted in the formation of the social democracy of the Polish Kingdom and Lithuania (Socialdemokracja Królewstwa Polskiego i Litwy – SDKPiL). This party claimed direct links to the Proletariat. It was opposed to placing the Polish national issue in the forefront of its political objectives. Instead, it emphasised the

importance of building a constitutional democratic system and, ultimately, a socialist regime. The Polish question, according to the
party's programme, would depend on the achievement of the first
objective. This would, in fact, be of lesser consequence than the
fight for socialism. This was the line earlier put forward by Luxemburg in 1895, when she declared that the destruction of capitalism
had to come first, before the Polish aspirations of the nation could
be satisfied. The so-called Luxemburgist line was adopted by the SD-
KPiL. However, its leaders were only too well aware that by putting
the issue of Poland's independence in such terms, they risked losing
the working class vote.[32]

The PPS was the best organised socialist party in Congress
Poland. However, its influence did not extend to the German and
Austrian areas. Earlier relations with the nationalist movement
were ended as the socialist movement became more clearly defined,
both, ideologically and organisationally. The main publication of
the PPS was the *Robotnik* (The Worker). Periodically, the party's
structure and network were depleted by arrests. Nor was it a party
which was ideologically united. Within the PPS, a vocal left wing
group emerged. They were critical of a number of issues, most
notably of the party's stress on the nationality issue. But also of
its uneasy relationship with the Russian revolutionaries and of
its continuing references to the reconstruction of Poland on its
pre-partition borders. The issue of terrorism did not go away. The
Second International had expelled from its ranks the anarchist
movement. This had favoured terror and assassinations as legitimate
means of furthering the workers cause. However Polish socialists,
in particular those active in Congress Poland, maintained links
with revolutionary and terrorist groups within the Russian Empire.
The great debates on the role of the peasants and the place of
industrialisation in a backward agrarian society formed the crux of
the debates in the emerging social democratic movement in Russia.
These had a relevance to the dilemmas faced by Polish socialists.

The primacy of the national question affected relations between
Polish and Jewish socialists. Initially, Jews had joined the PPS and
the SDKPiL. PPS, in particular, was keen to attract Jews to its ranks.
These were Jews who saw themselves as Poles and associated with
the Polish quest for independence. In 1897, a Jewish Socialist Party,

usually referred to as the Bund, was formed. This was the culmination of a process of separation of the Jewish community from the
mainstream socialist movement. Initially this had led to the building of the Jewish workers' organisation within Congress Poland.
Piłsudski had already noted, in 1893, that Russian and Lithuanian
Jews were dominating the Jewish movement. This drove a wedge between Polish and Jewish socialists.[33] Thus, at the turn of the century,
the socialist movement faced a number of doctrinaire and organisational problems. All of this combined to weaken the movement,
in spite of its apparent numerical strength.

One of the most interesting developments at the end of the nineteenth and the beginning of the twentieth centuries was the emergence of the peasant movement. This section of society was usually
associated with backwardness and political ignorance. They came
to form distinct parties, which fully participated in the political life
of the empires. More interestingly, they formulated programmes of
their own. In each of the partition areas, the peasant movement
developed differently. This depended on the economic situation,
relations with the Polish nobility and, finally, the administrative
and legislative structures. In this process, two trends can be dis-
cerned. On the one hand philanthropists, churchmen and enlightened members of the nobility sought to educate and economically
support the poor peasants through encouraging self-help organisations. On the other hand, there is evidence that, at the end of the
nineteenth century, peasants became adept at using courts and appeal procedures as means of redress against the landowners' greed
and arbitrariness. A further factor which had an impact on the political maturing of the peasant community was the state of relations
between the landed gentry and the village. There were attempts to
drive a wedge between Polish landowners and the peasants or to
support them. These attempts, along with the policies of the partitioning powers towards Polish landowners, had an impact on the
character of the developing peasant movement.[34]

Within Austrian Galicia, conflict between the landowners and
the peasants was particularly strongly defined. When Galicia was
granted autonomy, the power of the nobility was increased. Instances of abuse and exploitation of the poor and backward peasants also increased. Since peasants had the right to vote for

representatives to the *Reichsrat*, they came to appreciate the relevance to involvement in the political life of Galicia and Austria. During the period 1861–67, peasant deputies sat in the local assembly. At the same time, enlightened landowners and Catholic clerics independently undertook to try and raise the economic and educational standards in the Galician village. Bolesław Wysłouch and a Jesuit, Stanisław Stojałowski, were the first. They initially focused on improving levels of agriculture and combating backwardness. But they were not solely concerned with the economic situation in the village. Their actions were motivated by the conviction that the peasants represented the spirit of the nation. They rejected the increasingly obsolete idea that the gentry were the custodians of Polish identity.[35] The first peasant party, the Stronnictwo Ludowe (Peasant Alliance – SL), was established in July 1895 in the town of Rzeszów. Its main aim was to prepare for the forthcoming elections to the local assembly. In its programme the SL went beyond campaigning for land reform. The peasant electoral committees had clearly understood the relevance of the local and central political institutions to not merely their daily life, but in resolving many of their problems in the long term. They therefore made reference to the need to reform the educational and judiciary systems and to the importance of electoral reforms.[36]

The year 1903 marked the next stage in the development of the peasant movement. During that year, the SL changed its name to the Polskie Stronnictwo Ludowe (Polish Peasant Alliance – PSL) and announced a wider political programme.[37] The new programme staked the party's claim to representing the interests of the poor and middle peasants. It also appealed to all working people. It therefore transcended narrow community interests. It demanded that aristocratic privileges should be abolished and that all people should enjoy the same opportunities. The PSL reasoning was that, through their labour, whether physical or intellectual, men gained political rights and acquired duties and obligations. The PSL programme called for the Polish territories to be accorded the same rights as were enjoyed by the Hungarians. It clearly claimed to speak on behalf of the Polish nation. The programme was more precise in what it considered to be the nation. The true representatives of the nation were not the nobility but the 'people', in effect, the toilers. The party

programme addressed a number of difficult issues, such as the place
of the Jewish community in the Polish state. The PSL saw assimilation or the right to emigration as the only two solutions. The rights
of other national groups were recognised as being on par with those
demanded by the Poles. The PSL was determined to secure electoral
victories in Galicia. However, the 1903 programme appealed to all
those who considered themselves to be Polish nationals.[38]

During the period before the outbreak of the war, the PSL came
to enjoy electoral successes both in the Galicia and in elections to
Vienna. In 1907 the PSL had secured 16 seats in the Vienna assembly, while in 1911 it held 22 seats. After these victories the PSL's
development as a political force stalled. In many ways, this was inevitable, as parliamentary successes required the party to decide on
political tactics and willingness to forge alliances. The key issue was
the need for the peasant deputies to vote with other Polish deputies
in the Vienna assembly. There, they faced the choice of either allying themselves with the conservatives, or the much more radical
national democrats. It was believed that divisions within the peasant community had led to the emergence of party factions and, with
that, to the weakening of the party's distinct contribution in the Vienna and Galician assemblies. However, it would now appear that
conflicts on the party's way forward were responsible for this. There
is no denying the fact that the emergence of a peasant party marked
a very important stage in the political maturing of that section of
the community. Moreover, it laid the foundation of a programme
in which the peasants addressed the national issue. Henceforth, the
peasant party spoke boldly of being the party of the Polish people.[39]

Within the Prussian and Russian areas, the development of a
distinct peasant movement lagged behind or was subordinated to
the emergence of other political parties. In Prussian Poland, this
was due to Bismarck's attack on the Catholic Church and on all
signs of Polish national self-expression. This drew the gentry and
the peasants together. The landowners and the peasants were, in
equal measure, affected by the Prussian colonisation drives and the
policies of buying up land from Polish nationals. The response of
the community leaders was to focus on economic development and
mutual help which brought the two together. This reduced the gulf
between the landowners and the peasants and focused attention on

ways of reducing and fighting the state's attempts to strip Poles of their land.

No peasant party emerged in the Poznań district, Mazovia and the coastal areas including Gdańsk. Instead, peasant circles, cooperatives, self-help organisations and banks acted as focal points of rural activism. These advised peasants on improved agricultural methods, advantageous trade opportunities and ways of reducing debt. Through that, they fought the state's attempts to force the peasants to sell their land. They were usually associated with specialist journals and self-help publications. Bismarck's policies amounted to a wholesale attack on Polish nationals. Therefore the response of the community was to fight back not merely to retain the right to land, but also to remain Polish and to resist the process of Germanisation.

In Congress Poland, the peasant movement was late in developing. This was because serfdom had been abolished only in 1864. Even then, the Tsarist authorities had little interest in encouraging the development of an economically stable village economy. The Tsarist regime had always distrusted the Polish gentry, in particular after the two national uprisings, and tried to drive a wedge between it and the peasant community. The Act of Emancipation had awarded the peasants the land which they had earlier cultivated. However, the unresolved issue of communal rights remained a bone of contention between the peasants and the landowners. Emancipation led to the emergence of vast stretches of poor peasants' farmsteads. These were characterised by low production, overpopulation and land hunger. At the same time, landowners had to adjust to the new reality of not being able to use serf labour. In many cases they failed to adjust, became bankrupt and had to sell their land. The peasants rarely understood the complexities of the Tsarist Emancipation Act. They distrusted the landowners, believing that they had been cheated out of their land and denied the use of common lands. The landowners were still convinced of their leadership role in the fight against the Tsarist regime. They paid little heed to the problems faced by the peasants and indeed contributed to the poverty in the village by retaining disputed lands and rights.

The only bridge between these two communities was education. Progressive sections of the landed gentry sympathised with the peasants' plight and were anxious about the lack of educational opportunities. They made efforts to remedy the lack of schooling in Polish and, to that purpose, they set up secret literacy groups. In the 1880s these efforts mirrored the activities of Russian revolutionaries. They believed in the need to foment revolutions from within the peasant community. The *Narodnik* or Populist movement was relatively weak in Congress Poland. But it did provide one of the few ways those national leaders made contact with the peasants. In the 1890s the newly emerging socialist conspiratorial groups, analysed the consequences of the growth of a working class in Tsarist Russia. In addition to this, they still considered the likely role of the peasants in any future revolution. The peasant movement was late in developing in Congress Poland. However, from the outset, it aimed at redressing the national divisions caused by the Russian authorities and sought to raise educational levels and national awareness.[40]

In March 1905, in Congress Poland, a group of agronomists and educated people espousing progressive ideas publicised a declaration. This declaration announced the formation of a peasant party, which took the name Polski Związek Ludowy (Polish Peasant Association – PZL). Its programme was prepared by a committee and, as a result, was far from coherent. Nevertheless, it outlined the basic principles of the new party. In spite of assertions to the contrary, this was not a programme which had been drawn by the peasants themselves. It had more of an appearance of a call to the peasants to take action along lines sketched out by the progressive thinkers. The authors had had strong links with the PPS and had been exposed to the great revolutionary debates on the relevance of the Marxist doctrine to a predominantly agrarian community. Therefore, the programme's foundations were socialist. The peasants were to speak with their own voice and to reject the patronage of the national democrats. They were to fight for an independent Poland in which all privileges would be abolished and all would enjoy equal citizens' rights. It was assumed that the PZL's aim was the establishment of an elected assembly to which peasants would send their representatives. However, just what would be the role of the state was left unclear. Perhaps influenced by anarchist ideas, the authors of the declaration referred to self-rule and the formation of producers' cooperatives. But little was said about the relationship between citizens and the state. In 1906, the Tsarist regime allowed for the formation of parties and free associations. Until this time, the PZL could only function as a conspiratorial organisation. They were always threatened by the police and limited in their ability to link up with those on whose behalf it purported to speak, namely the peasants. The peasants continued to be a central, nevertheless elusive, element in the party's activities. The PZL's success never matched that of the PSL, which had a sound organisational structure and appeared to present a coherent programme.

A crisis was experienced by the Russian regime during the years 1904–1906. This marked a watershed in the stages which led to Poland becoming an independent state. Many Polish leaders, seeing the Russian Empire in trouble, believed this to be an opportunity to either forward the Polish cause or to at least weaken the staunchest enemy of Polish nationalism. The international crisis and the ensuing social and political conflicts raised hopes that Poland could become an autonomous region within the Russian Empire. The possibility of Poland securing independence was also considered. These hopes, invariably, led to heated debates and, with that, to conflicts on just what form that state would take. The closer Poles came to realising their much cherished hope for independence, the more intense were the debates between various factions and groups. Until then, these factions and groups had focused on methods of achieving independence. They had only generally discussed theoretical aspects of the future state and had not considered its future structure and its ideological objectives.

The Russo–Japanese war broke out on the night of 8/9 February 1904. The Japanese Navy attacked the Russian-held Port Arthur. By May 1905, Russia was not merely militarily defeated, she was humiliated and on the brink of internal collapse. Tsar Nicholas II was under pressure from his advisors who cautioned that the empire would succumb to revolutions. Due to this, he signed the Portsmouth Peace Treaty with Japan. In Polish areas of the Russian Empire, the war was seen as an opportunity to ally with Russia's enemy. The Japanese legation in Warsaw encouraged this view. Two political leaders made the perilous journey to Tokyo to discuss the implications of the war on Polish hopes. Piłsudski represented the major faction of the PPS. He was convinced that the Russo-Japanese conflict was merely an opening salvo of a conflict between the imperial powers. Piłsudski hoped that the USA and Britain would, in due course, ally themselves with Japan. He therefore assumed that the Japanese would financially support a national uprising. In the summer of 1904 Piłsudski arrived in Tokyo. He did not find the Japanese helpful or supportive of his plans. The Japanese authorities were unwilling to allow the Polish leader access to Polish prisoners of war. In addition to this, it turned out, another Pole had prevailed on the Japanese not to aid Piłsudski. Roman Dmowski, the leader of the national democrats, had also made his way to Tokyo. There he discouraged the Japanese from supporting Piłsudski. As Roman Dmowski himself admitted, the main purpose of his journey to Tokyo was to prevent the Japanese from supporting PPS' plans for an uprising. Piłsudski believed that Russia stood on the brink of defeat, as the regime was facing not merely the threat of a military collapse but also of an internal revolution. Dmowski, on the other hand, was convinced that Russia was far from defeated and that an uprising in Poland would be put down with the usual ruthlessness. Thus, he concluded that the Poles should work on the assumption that the fall of the Tsarist Empire was not imminent and that only with time would it succumb to internal problems and become weak. Only then would it be possible for the Poles to negotiate an autonomous status. To the Japanese High Command, Dmowski put an argument that Poland was of use to them. The Russians were obliged to constantly maintain troops in Congress Poland, thus constraining Russia's ability to take action against Japan. As it turned out, Dmowski's stark realism appealed to the Japanese military leader, who decided not to support Piłsudski, and instead gave Dmowski financial support throughout the Russo-Japanese war.[41] Neither political leader fully took into account the extent of disaffection which the war and its consequences engendered within the Polish community. In fact, like other community and political leaders, they underestimated the extent of anger caused by economic dislocation and conscription to the Tsarist army. The extent of working class political maturity and the determination of the urban dwellers to confront the Russian troops was as much a surprise to the Russians as it was to the Polish political leadership.

The first signs of resistance to the Russians emerged when the Poles refused to comply with mobilisation notices. Violent clashes with the police and Cossack units, which were usually deployed against demonstrators, continued throughout the summer of 1904. PPS was the first of the political parties to see in these an opportunity to spark a national uprising. The question was whether this small conspiratorial party could inspire the Polish community to take the critical step of moving from merely spontaneous attacks on Russian troops, to a mass insurrection.[42] This seemed dubious, as in 1904 demonstrations were mainly caused by anti-war sentiments. On 13 November, a melee between demonstrators and the police took place on Grzybowski Square, in Warsaw. This resulted in fatalities. PPS had, in fact, intentionally caused the conflict at a time when Catholics were leaving the nearby church. Their hope was clearly to cause a major confrontation and, possibly through that, trigger an uprising. This did not happen, even though anti-war demonstrations became more violent.

In 1905, the situation changed. On Sunday 22 January, in Petrograd, army and Cossack units attacked innocent people who, led by priests, intended to put to the Tsar a letter of supplication. The regime's overreaction resulted in over a thousand casualties. This became the spark which ignited first riots, and then, more carefully planned fighting against the army. The Tsar's authority was irreparably destroyed. More dangerously for the regime, major town and industrial areas were engulfed in fighting. During this, armed workers combined to form strike committees, the soviets, and fought the army. Russian revolutionaries were caught unprepared by the magnitude of the strikes and fighting. What was noticeable was the degree of organisation and political maturity shown by the workers. The bloody events of 1905 brought together the revolutionary groups and the workers. Had it not been for the loyalty of the army and the Tsar's grudging willingness to make political concessions, the regime's survival would have been doubtful.

News of the Petrograd massacre travelled to Polish towns swiftly. SDKPiL opposed the PPS preoccupation with the nationalist question and declared its support for the Russian revolutionaries.[43] PPS hesitated, not sure whether to call for a national uprising. In the circumstances, neither party determined the course of events. Strikes broke out in Warsaw factories and soon spread to other major industrial towns, most notably Łódź and Lublin. On 28 January, a successful general strike paralysed Warsaw. Unemployment and the economic depression, which had hit the urban population most heavily, was a factor in the events which unfolded in the Polish areas. This, in turn, increased instances of strikes and conflict with the police. By the spring of 1905, tension rose in the industrial town of Łódź. where, the workers responded to employers' attempts to bring in new labour by staging occupation strikes. The breakthrough in the political parties' attempts to assume a leadership role in the strikes, took place in spring. It has been suggested that this was not so much due to the success of their tactics, but because the factory management tried to open negotiations with the workers and agreed to the appointment of factory committees.[44] These, in turn, attracted the attention of both the PPS and the SDKPiL, who saw them as embryonic revolutionary groups. Not only the socialist parties noted the workers' organisational successes. Dmowski initially condemned the PPS for fomenting strikes, accusing it of encouraging mass action while having no means of controlling it. The nationalist movement was fearful that the socialists were acting out of loyalty to the Russian socialist movement. They tried to counter calls for strikes and demonstrations. Both movements stood to gain from the mobilisation of the disaffected workers.[45]

In Russian territories, the regime struggled to regain control. Lack of policies and economic problems meant that the waves of strikes spread. They culminated in a General Strike in October 1905. The initial spontaneous character of these events was visibly transformed by the growing structure of the soviets. The soviets grew bolder in their demands and clearer in their objectives. On 13 October, the Petrograd Soviet of Workers' Deputies came into being. This signalled a determination to coordinate strikes and fighting in the streets. Tsar Nicholas II reluctantly and grudgingly bowed to his advisors' suggestions. On 17 October, he published a manifesto promising to introduce civil liberties and establish an elected Duma. A promise of increased autonomy was made to national groups, which had been active in the strikes and street fighting throughout 1905. These concessions were followed up by brutal repression. The result was that strikes and street manifestations continued and culminated in an uprising in Moscow in November.

Despite this, workers increasingly returned to work. By the beginning of 1906, the regime was able to re-establish its authority.

In the Congress areas, the workers rather than political parties and organisations, took the lead in organising strikes. Dmowski publicly condemned plans for a national uprising, arguing that it would be unlikely to succeed and would only result in bloodshed. At the same time, the PPS and its activists met in March and debated whether the striking workers should focus on the fight for independence or on toppling the Tsarist regime, which would in due course lead to Poland gaining independence. It would seem that the workers, unswayed by these dilemmas, continued to mobilise the fight against the regime and against factory owners alike. During May 1905, a wave of strikes engulfed industrialised parts of Congress Poland. In June, mass demonstrations against police and army brutality led to street fighting. This has since been defined as an uprising in Łódź. On 10 November, martial law was imposed in Polish areas of the Russian Empire. This finally led to the decrease of strikes. Political parties looked back on the recent events, considering what had been signs of unexpected working class political maturity. Reflections on their own role in the future fight for an independent Poland were equally important.

The Russo-Japanese war and the turbulent events of 1905 led the national democrats to conclude that it was time to form a party. The aim of this party would be to prepare for independence. Thus, in the spring of 1905, the Stronnictwo Demokratyczno-Narodowe (National-Democratic Party – ND) was constituted in Warsaw. From the outset, Dmowski insisted that the party's initial aim should be autonomy within the Tsarist Empire. Having observed the strikes of that year, Dmowski concluded that the socialists had a bad influence on the working class and needed to be stopped. His view was that the two movements – nationalist and socialist – represented two moral stances, one a positive and engaged, while the second he equated with a lack of moral values. While not all national democrats agreed with his analysis, the party ultimately moved towards a head-on confrontation with the socialists. In order to prevent the workers from being ostensibly exploited by socialists, the party sought to build bridges with the workers, to educate

them and persuade them of the primacy of the national agenda. At
the same time, nationalist workers organisations were formed and
encouraged to confront socialist organisations on the streets. This
led to street battles between armed sections of the nationalist and
socialist organisations. Elections to the first Duma took place in the
April of 1906. Russian and Polish socialists decided to boycott the
elections and this gave the national democrats an opportunity to
secure 25 seats. Dmowski was disqualified from standing because
of a technicality. But he joined the second Duma, when it was
convened in February 1907. In spite of their numerical strength,
the national democrats made no impact on decisions concerning
Polish issues. Dmowski was unwilling to seek alliances with Russian
deputies and merely addressed issues relating directly to the Polish
question. He therefore failed to forge potentially helpful alliances.
Hopes that Poland would, in due course, be granted autonomy
were not realised. Dmowski had, in particular, pinned his plans on
the Duma being the starting point of a dialogue between the loyal
Polish deputies and the Tsarist regime. As the likelihood of an international conflict increased, so Dmowski defined his and his party's
programme. He took the view that, were Germany and Russia to go
to war, the Polish question would naturally divide them. The winner
of that military conflict would nevertheless still have to address the
Polish problem. Dmowski believed that Germany was Poland's prin-
cipal enemy. He hoped that Russia would win and that would, in
turn, lead to Poland benefiting from its earlier support for Russia.[46]

Divisions within the PPS had manifested themselves even before
the outbreak of the Russo-Japanese war. The workers mobilisation
took place in the industrial centres of Congress Poland. The events
of 1904–5 merely accentuated internal conflicts. These conflicts primarily focused on the issue of whether the fight for independence
should precede or take place parallel with the struggle to establish
socialism. A group, which came to be known as the 'Elders', maintained that Polish socialists had little to gain from cooperation with
Russian socialists, whom they dismissed as weak. They furthermore
believed that only once an independent Poland was established,
would the struggle for socialism have a realistic chance of survival.
Younger activists rejected this piecemeal approach and advocated
a revolutionary struggle, both for independence and for socialism.

They believed that fraternal cooperation with Russian comrades was advisable. Referring to the Second International's call for socialist unity, they advocated cooperation with the SDKPiL.[47]

The extent of strikes and workers' mobilisation caught both sections of the PPS by surprise. They joined and fully participated in strikes and fighting which engulfed the industrial areas. However, it was clear that the workers had not depended on the leadership of the Socialist Party and had instead organised themselves spontaneously. In the spring of 1905, the 'Young' section of the party, took over the leadership, confidently anticipating that the strikes would lead to an empire-wide revolution which would overthrow the Tsarist regime. At the same meeting, a decision was made to form a Combat Organisation within the party. During the coming year this Combat Organisation embarked on high-profile terrorist acts, blowing up railway bridges, attacking military objects. On 19 May 1905, they also attempted to assassinate the newly appointed governor of Warsaw.

By the end of 1905, socialist leaders had to accept that a revolution would not take place. Repression and economic problems reduced the workers' desire to take to the streets. This did not decrease the virulence of ideological conflicts within the party and indeed the 'Elders' and the 'Young' sections continued to vie for the leadership. The former put Piłsudski in charge of the Combat Organisation. They insisted that individual acts of terror still had the potential of sparking an uprising which would lead to national liberation. Leaders of the 'Young' section insisted that the party should instead build links with the masses. The IX Party Congress was convened in Vienna in November 1906. It formalised the split between the two groups. The 'Elders' still believed in the primacy of the fight for independence. They were expelled from the PPS. Refusing to accept that decision, they formed a party which took the name of PPS-Frakcja Rewolucyjna (PPS-Revolutionary Fraction). The 'Young' section defined itself as PPS-Lewica (PPS-Left Wing).[48]

Piłsudski became the unquestioned leader of PPS-Frakcja Rewolucyjna. Initially, he and other leaders still maintained that acts of terror, instigated by the Combat Organisation, would lead to a national uprising. But, by 1907, they had to admit that this was not going to happen. In the circumstances, Piłsudski started to think of a way of preparing for military action against Russia. In these plans, he took into account the international situation, which would allow the Poles to ally themselves with Russia's enemy. In their calculations, the Hapsburg Empire was likely to go to war against Russia. The logical next step was to prepare plans for military action by training riflemen who would be capable of confronting Russian units. Piłsudski increasingly removed himself from the PPS political activists and focused on military issues, in particular after the Combat Organisation collapsed due to arrests. He finally moved to Kraków, where, in 1908, the Związek Walki Czynnej (Union of Active Struggle – ZWC) was formed. From 1910 the Austrian authorities allowed the ZWC and associated paramilitary organisations, the so-called riflemen clubs, to register as legal organisations. During the following years, all parties made plans along those lines. However Piłsudski's group was most successful in bringing together disparate paramilitary organisations. The main focus of the ZWC increasingly became military action to the neglect of more precise debates on the character of the future independent state.[49]

In October 1908, Austria-Hungary occupied Bosnia-Hercegovina. The scene looked to be set for a conflict from which the Poles could benefit. Piłsudski's vision was that the Poles would make a direct military contribution. This would, in turn, lead to their establishing a civilian administration. Though still only in the embryonic stages of planning, this vision looked likely to be realised.

# 2   The First World War
and the Emergence of
Independent Poland

When the First World War broke out, Polish leaders realised that the European crisis offered them an opportunity to present the Polish question as a matter of international significance. This was an eventuality which had been discussed extensively within the Polish communities in exile and in Polish territories, long before the crisis of 1914 broke out. Initially, it was hoped that the Poles in the three partition areas would be able to press for an increase in the rights to national self-expression. For the first time since the Polish and Lithuanian Commonwealth Kingdom had ceased to exist, the three partitioning powers were at war with each other. This generated a sense of optimism in Poland. The partitioning powers broke the consensus on the Polish question. This opened the possibility of the Poles either pledging their loyalty to, or conditionally supporting, the war effort of the power which would be most receptive to Polish demands. The duration of the war, the course of military developments and, ultimately, the collapse of the Russian Empire, and then the defeat of the German and Austro-Hungarian Empires, left a political vacuum in Central Europe. By the end of the war, the Poles were able to establish first a civilian authority in Warsaw and then consolidate the borders of the new state.

The war began with the assassination of the heir to the Austro-Hungarian throne by a Serbian terrorist. In response, Austria-Hungary attacked Serbia on 28 July 1914. Within the next few days, in accordance with existing international agreements, Russia,

France and Britain lined up against Germany and Austro-Hungary. Hostilities between Russian troops and Austro-Hungarian and German units raged over Polish-inhabited territories. The offensive was started by the Russian army, which attacked German Eastern Prussia. By the end of August the initiative was in German hands. On Polish territories, the Russians did not regain it again. By October, the German offensive had consolidated earlier victories and German troops moved towards Warsaw. The industrial town of Łódź was occupied but Warsaw was not captured. The second Russian thrust had been in the direction of Eastern Galicia, scoring victories against the Austrian Imperial Army. German assistance was vital in minimising the scale of the Austrian defeat. General Paul von Hindenburg took command of the Eastern Front. From the spring of 1915, the German and Austrian war effort was coordinated. After a notable victory at Gorlice, German troops occupied Warsaw on 5 August. Earlier, Austria captured Lublin. By the end of that year, all Congress territories were under joint German and Austrian control. Germany nominated Warsaw as the administrative centre of occupied Polish areas, while the Austrian occupation authorities settled in Lublin. Austria had suffered at Russian hands. There were inevitable consequencies to this and to the German military victories. Initially, the Austrians had hoped to have the freedom to determine the fate of occupied Polish territories. However, their dependence of the German war effort meant that they had to accept that the German military authorities would dictate future policies on the Polish question. Some plans were considered for post-war Poland. However, during the war, military considerations were more important in determining responses to the Polish question, rather than long-term political objectives.

Inevitably, Polish military and political leaders from the outset sought to ascertain whether the belligerent powers could be persuaded to make promises concerning the future of Poland. Most of ethnic Polish territories had been under Russian control at the outbreak of the war. Therefore the Tsarist governments' declarations were initially scrutinised most intensely. On 14 August 1914, Grand Duke Nicholas made a proclamation to the Poles. Its contents were disappointing. He used references to the 'resurrection of the Polish nation and its fraternal union with all Russia'. However,

Polish leaders could find nothing in the proclamation which could give them hope that the Tsar would reward Polish loyalty with autonomy within the empire.[1] This was a bitter blow to those who had hoped that Polish units could be formed to fight with the Tsarist army. Pro-Russian Polish patriots in the Congress Poland territories were swayed by strong anti-German feelings. These led them to hope that a Russian defeat of Germany would rid the Polish nation of, what they considered to be, its most important foe. But, still there was an uneasy awareness that Russia could not be counted on to support the Polish cause. In the meantime, Austria – Germany's ally – had been the least oppressive of the partitioning powers. In spite of the modest content of the proclamation, Dmowski and a number of like-minded Polish deputies to the Duma maintained that it would have been unwise at this stage to demand independence for Poland. Their view was that would have only caused irritation. To the national democrats the destruction of Germany remained a priority. If that meant biding their time until Russia achieved this end, they were willing to wait.[2] In the meantime, a group of conservatives established a national committee in Warsaw with which Dmowski associated. Local citizens' associations were formed in order to mobilise the community and to channel its efforts towards the war effort. Reluctantly, the Russian military authorities agreed to the formation of the Puławski Legion. This fell short of Dmowski's hope of raising a Polish army of several thousand men. The Russians continued to ignore Polish gestures of goodwill and support. The Tsarist regime had no intention of making concessions in return for help given during the war.

There were many who had initially pinned their hopes on Russia assuming a leading role among the Slavonic people. The result of Russian intransigence was that these hopes had to be reconsidered. Of those, Roman Dmowski was the most prominent. Polish industrialists, financiers were among those who had economically benefited from links with the Russian Empire and had supported the national committee. They had to accept that they would not be successful. In November 1915, Dmowski left Petrograd. He first went to Switzerland and from there travelled to London and Paris. He made London his base. There he focused on making contact with British policymakers. In Western Europe, Dmowski concentrated on

lobbying the French and British governments.[3] He had not abandoned his original commitment to the creation of a Russian-led
Slav unity of nations. What he had, nevertheless, come to realise
was that the Tsar was unwilling, or unable, to recognise Poland's
key role in Russia's fight against Germany. He therefore changed
his tactics and tried to persuade Russia's two powerful allies that
they should put pressure on the Tsar to address the Polish question
more seriously. He certainly did not want Britain and France to distance themselves from Russia. On the contrary, he wanted the two
Western governments to be more active in raising the issue, which
he believed was relevant to the conduct of the war against Germany
and to Europe's post-war plans.

As the German thrust proceeded East, the Russian authorities decided to remove much of the industrial capacity in Congress Poland
and the Baltic areas into the interior of the empire. Workers and
their families were forcefully evacuated with the plants in which
they had been employed. At the same time, when evacuating territories in advance of the German offensive, the Russian military
authorities destroyed everything that might have been of use to the
German war effort. This wanton destruction took place in May 1915.
Not only was the industrial infrastructure dislocated, but forests and
farms were burnt. This precipitated a flight eastwards, as the Polish
community succumbed to panic. It is believed that over 3 million
Poles ended up in Russia, frequently in tragic circumstances. As
German troops occupied territories of the former Polish Kingdom,
the economic situation was already dire.

In the Austrian Empire, at the time of the outbreak of the war,
Poles hoped that the Polish question could be addressed positively.
The community was united with Austria in its hatred of Russia and
appreciative of the cultural and political privileges which it enjoyed
within the empire. The least they hoped to achieve from the new
situation was the same status that was enjoyed by Hungary. Had
the Austrian war effort been successful and Austria were to extend
its control over Congress Poland, this could have resulted in the
reconstruction of the Polish Kingdom within the Habsburg Empire.
Piłsudski added an entirely new element to discussions taking place
within the Polish community in Galicia. On 6 August 1914, he
led a unit of volunteer riflemen from Kraków towards the Austrian

border with the Russian Empire, crossed it and proceeded to march towards Kielce with the aim of reaching Warsaw within three days. By marching into Congress Poland Piłsudski had hoped that the Poles would flock to the riflemen's unit. This would grow from a cadre structure to an army. His assumption had been that once news spread of a Polish army heading towards Warsaw, a civilian authority would emerge there and naturally bestow on Piłsudski the rank of commander-in-chief. The key to his thinking was the calculation that he could reach Warsaw in advance of the Austrian army and before the German units entered the city. This would lead to the creation of a fait accompli in the form of a Polish civilian authority and through that to the Central Powers' acceptance of the emergence of a Polish state.

The reality turned out to be very different. As the riflemen marched through Polish areas, peasants remained indifferent. Townspeople were equally passive. The vision of a new national uprising, on which Piłsudski had staked his reputation, did not happen. All attempts to stir the Congress Poles to action by declaring that a Polish authority could be established in Warsaw before the Germans entered were to no avail. Within days, the enterprise proved to be a failure. Piłsudski and his men were routed by the Russian army near Kielce.[4] In spite of the fiasco, there were positive consequences. Polish parties in Galicia came together and agreed to speak with one voice. They formed a Supreme National Council (Naczelny Komitet Narodowy – NKN), which was to direct all political and military decisions. At the same time, the Austrian authorities agreed to the formation of Polish legions, but this time under direct Austrian military control. The riflemen's units were thus reorganised and became the 1st Brigade of the Polish Legion. Piłsudski was put in command of that brigade, and this became his power base in future negotiations with the Austrian and later the German authorities.

The Polish military contribution to the Austrian war effort was small. The Polish question was not important enough to Austria, the Vienna authorities would not risk upsetting the delicate balance between the various national groups. This was a time when the Adriatic basin and relations with oil-rich Romania were increasingly important elements in Austrian considerations. It was therefore questionable whether Austria would invest heavily in extending its political influence in North and Eastern Europe. In 1915 the Austrians came to depend on German assistance in the war against Russia. In these circumstances, the Austrians were willing to allow the German military authorities to set the pace in determining both occupation polices and making long-term plans in relation to Polish territories captured from the Tsarist Empire.

On 5 August 1915, German troops occupied Warsaw. By the end of the year Congress areas, East Prussia, Courland, Lithuania, Latvia, Ukraine and most of Galicia were under the administration of the Central Powers. The first decisions made by the German occupation authorities inspired Polish leaders with confidence. The university and a polytechnic institute in Warsaw were reopened. The previous policy of Russification was abandoned and the use of Polish language was permitted in schools and state organisations. While under Tsarist control, Russian-appointed bureaucrats had governed towns and districts. The German authorities encouraged the emergence of local authorities and appeared to be willing to work with civil organisations which the Poles had established during the war. However, the goodwill which these policies had generated was quickly squandered when extremely harsh economic delivery quotas were imposed on the Polish areas. All resources which could be of use to the German war effort were confiscated, irrespective of the consequences that this had on the civilian population. This, in turn, made it impossible for factories and enterprises to continue production. Hunger and unemployment quickly followed German occupation. At the same time, it was generally noted that German policies towards the Polish territories went beyond utilisation for military purposes. Under the guise of maximum exploitation for the war, the military authorities were, in fact, making long-term decisions. These were to change the region's economic relations with Germany after the war. By selectively destroying chosen branches of industry in Congress Poland, the occupation administration was making sure they would not compete with German industry. Furthermore, they ensured that the latter retained that monopoly once hostilities ended. Textile and steel production, in particular, were identified as likely, in the long term, to compete with German industry and were therefore dismantled. German occupation of Polish areas resulted in heavy exploitation and wanton destruction. Some of this had a lasting impact on the ecology of the area. Employment fell to 30 per cent of pre-war levels. In spite of the introduction of food rationing, hunger became widespread. In 1915, attempts were made to persuade the Poles to work in Germany. When that proved unpopular, they were conscripted. At the beginning of 1916, shortage of manpower became an important factor in German plans for the continuation of the war. This, in turn, determined decisions in relation to the Polish question.

On 5 November 1916, the German and Austrian emperors jointly issued a proclamation in which they declared their intention to establish an independent Polish state once the war was ended. Although the frontiers were to be defined later, the new state's future political system was outlined. Poland was to be a hereditary monarchy with a constitutional government. Crucially, even before the independent state became a reality, a Polish army was to be formed. Somewhat ironically, the proclamation stated:

> The glorious tradition of the Polish armies of the past
> and the memory of the brave Polish comrades in arms in
> the great wars of our days shall continue to live in your
> own national army.[5]

In reality, the German High Command, having established control over Polish-inhabited territories, proceeded with their long-term plans. They did not approve of the Austrian solution for a Polish state within the Austro-Hungarian Empire, nor did they intend to return the occupied Polish areas to Russia. The German military leaders insisted on the emergence of an independent Poland. In this way, they reduced Austrian influence on the issue and, at the same time, proceeded to make plans for a weak Polish state. This would be economically and politically dependent on Germany. In the meantime, Polish manpower was to be used to fight Russia.[6]

The German and Austrian initiative failed in so far as the Poles heartily distrusted the German authorities. Far from flocking in numbers to the recruiting stations, they hung back awaiting further developments. The German authorities realised that there was a need to reinforce promises made earlier. Piłsudski was invited to

Warsaw for talks with the German military commanders, while a Provisional Council of State of the Kingdom of Poland was put together from a number of obliging Poles. Piłsudski was given responsibility of military matters. In spite of these initiatives, the situation remained far from clear. To start with, the precise function of the Council of State remained vague, as were the Central Powers' plans on the Polish question. Sensing their lack of commitment, Piłsudski was anxious not be compromised by collaboration with an organisation which might still turn out to be of no significance. He therefore maintained a secret military organisation throughout Polish areas, the role of which was to build up units and prepare for military action.[7]

However, by publicizing the promise to establish an independent Polish state, the Central Powers effectively opened what amounted to an international auction. All those who might benefit from the emergence of Poland or who could cause the enemy discomfort by promising support for the Polish cause, entered into the bidding. Britain, France and Italy were anxious that Germany would deploy Polish units on the Western Front. But long-term political considerations also played a part in the British and French leaders' determination to put pressure on the Russian Empire to make a positive declaration on the Polish question. Germany and Austria could make similar commitments to other national groups under their military control. Britain, France and Italy were only too well aware that this would make life very difficult for the Entente Powers, both during, and after, the war. Until then, they had tried not to be drawn too closely into supporting the national aspirations of the disparate European ethnic people. Naturally, the Russian Empire had a direct interest in events taking place in Warsaw. The first Russian response to the Central Powers' declaration of 5 November 1916 was a communiqué by the Russian prime minister. This stated that Polish areas would be united and would be granted autonomy within the Russian Empire. This was considered wholly unsatisfactory by most Poles and the Entente. The commitment was therefore reiterated on 25 December 1916 by Tsar Nicolas II. This position reflected the limits of the Tsarist authorities planning for a post-war Polish state.[8]

These declarations, in turn, obliged Britain, France and the USA to, likewise, make some pronouncements on the Polish question. Of those, undoubtedly, the one made by the President of the USA carried most weight.

Amongst all the Polish roving ambassadors – men who toured West European and American capitals, lobbying governments and raising public awareness of the Poles' desire for an independent state – none was more flamboyant than the pianist and composer Ignacy Paderewski. He was the son of a Pole who had been imprisoned by the Russian authorities for supporting the national cause. Paderewski was brought up in an atmosphere of deep patriotism. Before the war, he had already established a reputation as a romantic piano player. When war broke out, he, together with a number of prominent Pole residents in Switzerland, founded the Polish Victims Relief Fund. In April 1915 Paderewski went to the United States where, during a series of whistle-stop tours, he lobbied for support for the establishment of a Polish independent state at the end of the war. It is difficult to gauge the extent of his success. But he certainly attracted attention through his playing and public speaking. His wild romantic appearance and flamboyant hairstyle, which particularly attracted many women, left a lasting impression. His personality and behaviour conveyed the impression of a passionate Polish patriot, an image he was willing to use to the full. Paderewski was able to mobilise the large Polish community in the United States to lobby their representatives in the Senate and Congress. During a meeting with President Woodrow Wilson, he pressed his case for an independent Polish state. A number of charitable organisations were drawn into the campaign in which relief for the starving Polish people was linked to support for an independent Poland.[9]

The battle for American support for the Polish cause was not free from conflict. Paderewski had allied himself with Dmowski and his Polish National Committee. The aim was to gain the support of the Poles in the USA for Dmowski's interpretation of Poland's historic grievances and his vision of Poland's destiny. In the publicity materials prepared during Paderewski's tour, Germany and Austria were demonised and represented as responsible for the Polish Kingdom's tragedy. Furthermore, Paderewski propagated the idea that it was the world leaders' moral duty to reverse the injustice of the partition and to ensure that, at the end of the war, an independent Poland once more emerged. By 1917, Paderewski's campaign had led to the forging of a temporary unity within the Polish community. However, few were willing to go along with Dmowski's suggestion that Russia should be considered Poland's most likely ally.[10]

Woodrow Wilson's views on Polish communities in the United States changed throughout his political career. In his *History of the American People*, published in 1902, he described the Poles as uncouth and lacking energy. He subsequently came to regret making these sweeping and derogatory comments. Nevertheless, the Polish community never forgave him. During the course of the war and while the United States was neutral, Wilson came under strong pressure from his friend Colonel Edward Mandell House and from the Secretary of State Robert Lansing. They wanted Wilson to make a declaration on Poland. Both, and in particular House, had been deeply impressed by Paderewski. He had used all his wiles and charms, and delivered a number of highly impressionistic memoranda to persuade his influential interlocutors of the need for the USA to take up Poland's cause. His efforts were crowned on 22 January 1917 when President Wilson, in the course of a speech to the Senate, stated that the emergence of an independent Poland should be a war aim of the USA.[11] In April 1917, the USA entered the European war. The Polish case was one of the issues that Britain and France had to address so as not to be at variance with their new and very powerful ally. On 8 January 1918, President Wilson stated in Point 13 that the creation of an independent Poland was one of the Fourteen Points defining the US war aims. This assurance was the only one within Wilson's declaration in which a national group was given a clear promise that it would be guaranteed the right to statehood. It was, nevertheless, imprecise. For the Poles there was ground for optimism, since clearly the tactics of Dmowski and Paderewski had succeeded. But there was also reason for anxiety. No assurance was given as to when Poland would emerge and in what borders. Most obviously, Wilson referred to a Polish state which would include territories inhabited by the Poles, thus clearly making a commitment to borders based on ethnic grounds. This implied that Polish claims to Lithuanian, Ukrainian and Byelorussian territories might not be supported.

The outbreak of the February Revolution in Russia was the turning point in the war and beyond. On 12 March (in Russia, in accordance with the Julian calendar, the date was 27 February) 1917, strikes and riots led to the collapse of Tsarist authority in Petrograd. Numerous Poles were directly involved in these events, either as soldiers conscripted into the Tsarist army, or as residents and refugees living in the capital. Like other national groups, the Poles tried to evaluate the implications of the Tsar's abdication and the emergence of the dual authority of the Provisional Government and the Petrograd Soviet upon their national aspirations. The Russian revolutionaries regarded the Polish issue as outside their main areas of concern. However, the Poles tried to elicit from both authorities assurances that the collapse of the autocratic system in Russia meant that the Poles now had freedom to determine their fate.

The outbreak of the war and the support that socialist parties had given to their belligerent governments, spelled the end of the Second International. Nevertheless, many socialists were not happy with the failure of international cooperation and tentative efforts were made to build new links. The most important of these efforts was the meeting which took place in the Swiss town of Zimmerwald in September 1915. In exile in Switzerland, Vladimir Ilyich Lenin, the leader of the Bolshevik faction of the Russian Social Democratic Party, made contributions to that, and subsequent meetings. The Zimmerwald Conference discussed, among other subjects, the possibility of war leading to civil wars or perhaps revolutions. Although Polish, Karl Radek and Adolf Warski were part of the Bolshevik delegation, while Róża Luxemburg headed the German delegation. The questions of the primacy of the future revolution over that of national independence, and whether nationalism was evidence of state building or merely a cultural expression were central to the debates. These debates took place within the socialist circles before the war and continued to be discussed during the war. The European socialists, who met in these precarious circumstances, discussed nationalism. Polish participants made their contributions on this subject.

Due to the Russian Revolution, these considerations became linked in a much more practical way to the question of the future course of the revolution. The Polish community in Russia had grown during the war. The Poles had been part of the Tsarist bureaucracy, army and workers. In addition to them, workforce, workers and their families were evacuated into the interior as part of the reallocation of factories. When leaving the territories of Kingdom Poland in the face of the German offensive, political prisoners were also evacuated into Russia. They were released after the February Revolution. All this led to the emergence of a highly politicised Polish community in Russia. They were part of the workforce and had been directly involved in strikes and manifestations which overwhelmed Russia in 1917.

The more settled Polish community scattered throughout the Russian Empire, reacted with excitement to the collapse of the hated Tsarist regime. Some still thought in terms of remaining in Russia until the situation became clearer and the war ended. In any case, the German authorities tried to limit the movement of Poles into areas under their control, in particular after the February Revolution. The German authorities feared that the influx of the workers and activists who had been exposed to the revolutionary ideas would exacerbate unrest in areas now under German control. Thus, until 1918, most evacuated Poles were forced to remain in Russia. There, heated debates continued on the future of the revolution and on the possibility of the emergence of an independent Poland. Democrats and socialists wanted the Russian Provisional Government to declare that Poland would be free. Left wing Poles disagreed that freedom should be granted to the Polish people by a Russian government and proclaimed that freedom should be an expression of the will of the Polish people. It was not clear which of the two Petrograd authorities – the Provisional Government or the Petrograd Soviet – should make a declaration on the Polish question.

In the end, it was the Petrograd Soviet which came out with its first statement on the Polish issue by making a dignified Proclamation to the Polish Nation. In it, the Petrograd Soviet declared that the Tsarist regime had oppressed the Poles and Russians alike and that democratic Russia accepted the Poles' right to self-determination.

The proclamation ended with sincere fraternal wishes that the Poles succeed in their fight for an independent republican Poland. The Provisional Government had tried to avoid making any commitments about Russia's future borders. It had no choice but to follow up the Soviet's proclamation with one of its own. Thus, on 28 March, Pavel Nicolayevich Milyukov, the Minister for Foreign Affairs, called for the Poles to fight against the Central Powers. His declaration referred to the future free Polish state comprising all areas inhabited by Polish nationals. Milyukov, nevertheless, made changes to the borders of the Russian Empire, dependent on the approval of the government which would be formed after free elections had taken place.[12]

The Poles in Russia greeted the two declarations with mixed feelings. Generally, they were welcomed. But since the precise functions of the two authorities in Petrograd remained unclear, various Polish political parties took from them what they thought were the most telling points. The national democrats viewed the Provisional Government's proclamation as an indication that a future constitutional government in Russia would accept a free and independent Poland. SDKPiL and PPS-Lewica activists naturally viewed the Soviet's Proclamation as the more important of the two. Some associated themselves with the Menshevik line in the Petrograd Soviet. Those who took a more radical line supported the Bolshevik policy of non-cooperation with the Provisional Government. Their view was that the revolution was not yet complete. They had the choice of two options. In alliance with the Western democracies, they could fight for an independent Poland. Or they could support the revolution and, in particular, the Bolshevik line of transfer of power to the Soviet. In the latter case, the fight for Polish independence would be subordinate to the success of the revolution. Of all the revolutionary parties in Russia, it was the Bolsheviks who most consistently supported the right of national minorities to break away from Russia. They believed that national groups had the right to self-determination and only then would they make a conscious commitment to revolutionary internationalism. In the meantime, the Provisional Government established a special commission to deal with the consequences of Russian control of Polish territories. SDKPiL and PPS-Lewica would have nothing to do with the commission, declaring it to represent the interests of the Russian and Polish bourgeois.[13]

On 17 November (25 October per the Julian calendar) 1917, the Russian Provisional Government was overthrown by a combination of armed workers, Bolshevik revolutionaries and the Red Guards – the military wing of the Petrograd Soviet. Polish revolutionaries and workers, members of the Red Guards, participated in the turbulent events. The Council of People's Commissars assumed authority, as one of its first decisions. It issued a Declaration of the Rights of The People of Russia. Article 2 of the Declaration supported the right of the people to self-determination, including the right to secession and the establishment of an independent state. Interestingly, Luxemburg agreed with some of the points made by the radical section of the Polish social democrats. She believed Lenin's declaration weakened the revolution by encouraging national groups to seek independence. According to her, it would be better to stay united, in anticipation of the inevitable attack from the capitalist forces.

In the meantime, developments in Polish territories under German occupation, took their own course. What happened there determined both the manner in which the first Polish administration emerged and the way in which the borders of the new state were finally settled. Towards the end of 1916 and the beginning of 1917, German policies of cooperation with the Poles appeared to be stalling. The Provisional Council of State met on 14 January 1917. However, it remained unclear as to what would be its role. Piłsudski initially agreed with the idea of recruiting a Polish army under German command. Now he demanded that plans for an army should be postponed until a Polish government was established. In reality, Berlin had come to doubt the wisdom of proposals which had been put forward by General Beseler, the German commander of occupied Polish territories. The outbreak of the Russian Revolution and the effective end of fighting reduced the need for a force to fight in the East. German reticence was increased by the realisation that troops raised in Poland would be unwilling to fight on the Western Front.[14] By then, the Entente Powers were showing themselves as adept as the German authorities had been in encouraging the Poles to believe that their interests would be best served by agreements with Britain and France. The German authorities had come to doubt the wisdom of granting the Provisional Council of State real power and of expanding Polish military units. Piłsudski had also arrived at a similar conclusion. During the spring of 1917, his reservations about cooperation with the Central Powers' war effort increased.

The change in Entente's policies on the Polish question meant that decisions had to be made now on the future of the Polish military units. These units had already been raised and trained by the Central Powers. Initially, Beseler had agreed to the extensive recruitment in 1917. However, he now decided to limit that recruitment. In addition he assumed direct control over the Polish legions in German-controlled Poland. When Polish soldiers were required to take an oath of loyalty to the Central Powers, Piłsudski objected and insisted that a Polish army could only be formed under his command. The German response was to arrest Piłsudski and his close collaborator Kazimierz Sosnkowski. While Piłsudski was held in the Magdeburg prison, the German authorities tried to administer Polish areas using the Regency Council. This situation worked to Piłsudski's advantage. The Council consisted of loyal and obliging conservatives. During the following critical months, it floundered. Piłsudski was increasingly perceived to be a true patriot and leader of the nation.[15]

Nevertheless, discussion on the possibility of Polish independence was no longer confined to specific partition areas. Because of this, debates on the Polish question could not be suppressed by punitive actions. A conviction had taken root that the Poles everywhere had a common destiny. The Poles now held a shared belief that the war would result in the emergence of an independent Polish state. This belief held even if, in the summer of 1917, it was still far from clear who would win the war and just how Poland would emerge from the still unresolved military situation. Polish leaders were increasingly determined that the Polish question should be placed on the agenda of all and any international talks. Those leaders believed that it was their sacred duty to make sure that the European Powers did not discuss the future of Poland without reference to the Poles. If the European Powers were to make decisions by themselves, the inevitable result would be a weak recreated Polish state which would be a pawn in the changing European balance of power.

German policies were implemented in Congress territories under military occupation, in the summer of 1917. These caused Poles in the West to take the initiative in relation to the Entente governments. On 15 August 1917, the Polish National Committee (Komitet Narodowy Polski – KNP) was formed in Lausanne to coordinate the work of Polish organisations in the West. They built on already existing relief organisations and were encouraged by the entry of the USA into the war. The KNP sought to establish direct contacts with West European governments. Their support for the Polish cause was considered vital. KNP planned to make a direct military contribution to the war effort. This was a point which it used when it sought the French government's recognition. The first attempts to form Polish units in 1914 had not been entirely successful. The French authorities were only too happy to allow for the formation of two units. These were integrated into the French Foreign Legion. In July 1915, this brief initiative had come to an end. This was mainly due to Russian opposition and heavy casualties. In August 1917, the situation had changed sufficiently for the KNP to renew calls for recruitment of the Poles to fight with the French. The KNP hoped to make a direct link between the military contribution, which the Poles would be making to the war effort, and requests, which were made to the French government, to consider the restoration of an independent Poland as one of the Entente's war aims.[16] By February 1918, the KNP was a recognised official representative of the future Polish state. Together with the French government, they signed a military agreement. This led to recruitment to a Polish army, which was to fight with the French on the Western Front. General Stanisław Haller was appointed as commander-in-chief of the Polish Army in France. To Dmowski and the KNP these were very important achievements, confirming the Entente's commitment to the creation of a Polish state. But Dmowski knew only too well that the real test of strength would come during talks concerning the peace treaties at the end of the war. Nevertheless, the purpose of making a direct military contribution to the fighting was to secure for Poland a place at the negotiating table. In the meantime, Dmowski concentrated on preparing submissions and memoranda, in which he expounded his vision for a post-war Poland. Since he dominated the KNP, submissions made to the Entente governments reflected Dmowski's own analysis of the international situation and his plans for the future of Poland.

Throughout the war, Dmowski had been consistent in his distrust of Germany. Nevertheless, he altered his view of Russia. Initially, he felt that the future independent Poland would remain within the Russian sphere of influence. However, military failures and the outbreak of the February Revolution led him to review his ideas. During 1917 he increasingly spoke of a strong Poland which would act as a barrier to German expansion to the East and the Black Sea coast. Dmowski anticipated that Poland's role in post-war Europe would be pivotal in maintaining a balance between the still powerful German state and a Russia which he believed would succumb to anarchy. In the circumstances, he also changed his views on the future Polish borders. Until the beginning of 1917, he lobbied the French and British governments with requests that they support the restoration, to Poland, of the Poznan region, West and East Prussia and Upper Silesia. In the East, he was careful not to make references to areas beyond those which had been part of the Polish–Lithuanian Commonwealth. By July 1917, Dmowski changed his views and, henceforth, called for an independent Poland within borders which went beyond those defined by history and were not even justified on ethnic principles. Dmowski claimed that for Poland to act as a guardian of European stability it needed to be strong and economically viable. In addition to areas already mentioned, he asserted that the borders of the new Poland should include Minsk, Wilno, Grodno, Volhynia, as well as the Austrian held Cieszyn Silesia and Galicia.[17]

On 20 August 1917, the French government recognised the KNP as representing Polish interests. This was the first significant diplomatic breakthrough on the road to the establishment of an independent Polish state. The British and US governments followed suit within weeks. For the Poles, this meant that the objections of the Russian Provisional Government had been ignored. In effect, this strengthened their hope that any Polish government they would form in the future would be granted full recognition.[18] The matter, nevertheless, was far from clear. On 8 January 1918, President

Wilson, as part of the Fourteen Points American declaration war aims, gave an assurance that one of the war aims would be the creation of an independent Polish state with access to the sea. However, the Entente Powers did not declare this to be one of the war aims until 3 June 1918.

The Russian revolutionary government had come to power in the October Revolution. On 3 March, they signed the Brest-Litovsk Treaty with Germany. The Bolsheviks from the outset dominated the new government. They pressed for a swift end to fighting. Lenin, in particular, insisted on the absolute necessity of ending the war. These had not been circumstances in which the Russians could have insisted on their objectives. Facing further German military action, they had to accept punitive conditions. As a result of the treaty, Russia relinquished claim to territories which were already under German control. These included all Polish-inhabited areas. Additionally, Russian troops were to evacuate Estonia, Livonia and Finish areas, where in due course, local administrations would be established with German assistance. The Ukraine was to be guaranteed independence. Notably missing from the treaty was any reference to Poland. Indeed, only Article 3 of the treaty could have generally applied to Poland. The article stated that Russia was to refrain from all interference in the internal relations of territories, previously Russian, now held by Germany. Germany and Austria-Hungary were to 'determine the future status of these territories in agreement with their population'. To the Poles this could only mean that Germany would not countenance the emergence of a genuinely independent Polish state.[19] The signing of the German-Russian Treaty marked a dangerous point in the final months of the war. However, the Poles benefited from the anxiety of the Entente Powers that Germany would turn the full force of its military capacity to the Western Front dominate Eastern Europe. The Entente governments hastened to make clearer commitments to the restoration of a Polish state.[20]

In 1918, the fight for the restoration of a Polish state was fought on several fronts. The diplomatic battle took place in Paris. There, the KNP tried to make the most of the Entente's willingness, at last, to make plans for a post-war balance of power. Nevertheless, the KNP was a narrowly based organisation. Dmowski realised that he had even failed to bring together Polish leaders in the West.

Politically, the KNP was entirely dependent on the national democrats. For it to become a provisional government, it needed to link up with the Poles under German occupation and to draw into its ranks the Socialist Party. In this objective Dmowski failed and developments in Congress Poland led many Poles to believe that it was more realistic to base hopes for an independent Poland on the Central Powers.

In the summer of 1918 Dmowski went to the United States. There he reached an accommodation with Paderewski and met President Wilson. For the first time, Dmowski came face to face with Jewish lobby groups. These groups drew attention to his anti-Semitic rhetoric and publicly raised doubts as to whether, under his leadership, a Poland restored onto the map of Europe would respect the rights of the Jewish community. American Jewish groups demanded that the government of the USA support the KNP only if assurances were given that the Jewish communities, as well as other national minorities, would not be discriminated against in independent Poland.

After the Brest-Litovsk Peace Treaty, the German authorities were free from the need to maintain a front against Russia and proceeded with their own plans. They clearly intended to ignore the Polish committee established in Paris. Popular anger over the Central Powers' treatment of the Polish issue led to strikes and widespread protests. All political parties and groupings participated in these. At the same time, radical workers established workers' councils and took over factories and enterprises. This was an expression of revolutionary fervour. It was equally a reflection of the wish to wrest control over all forms of production from the hated Germans. The desire for independence grew. At this stage, the German and Austrian authorities were still able to retaliate by taking action against the Polish population. Troops, which were no longer needed on the Eastern Front, were brought into the Polish areas and were deployed against Polish workers. In Polish areas and in regions which were contested by the Poles and Germans, the German population participated in these military actions. These frequently took the form of bloody confrontations between the two communities.

On 21 March, a new German offensive started on the Western Front. At this point, for the first time during the course of the war, Polish politicians in occupied areas turned against the Central Powers and started looking to the Entente governments for support. An idea was held by some conservatives, that Germany and Austria would allow for the emergence of a truly independent Polish state. This idea had been discredited. The Regency Council, nevertheless, continued trying to find a way forward by putting together a government, while at the same time negotiating with the German authorities. The plan was to extend its authority until a fully functioning government was established. This was unsuccessful because most Poles held the Regency Council in contempt for its excessive subordination to the Germans. This sharpened the conflicts between political parties which were already positioning themselves to assume authority in an independent state.

By October 1918, the Poles knew that the Central Powers had been routed and that their withdrawal was merely a matter of time. German troops were being moved out of Polish territories even before the signing of the armistice on 10 November. In areas under Austrian control, self-proclaimed Polish authorities filled the vacuum created by the departure of the imperial administrators. In several cities, attempts were made to put in place a Polish administration. These were often spontaneous and uncoordinated initiatives, frequently gaining momentum from the revolutionary fervour which affected industrial workers and soldiers.

In 1917 the prospect of the end of the war had become a reality. The Entente Powers were far from assured of victory. However, the entry of the USA into the conflict made it more likely that they, rather than the Central Powers, would be victorious. As the end of the conflict came closer, debates on post-war territorial revisions were extended. The issue of Poland's future political structure was one that had not been discussed during the course of war. The restoration of an independent state was a matter of such gravity that it tended to overshadow, if not outright stifle, any debates on the question of Poland's future internal structure. Nevertheless, initially with the exception of SDKPiL and PPS-Lewica, all other parties generally assumed that Poland would be a monarchy based on an Austrian prince who would begin a new royal line. The last hereditary Polish monarch of the Jagiellonian line had died in 1572. In the years leading up to the destruction of the Polish – Lithuanian

Commonwealth in 1795, Poland had been ruled by a succession of elected monarchs. But monarchism, in particular a political system based on a strong royal authority, had no historic precedent in Poland. On the contrary, the Polish nobility took pride in the Commonwealth being described as a 'republic of the nobles'. Some South European states emerged from the progressive weakening of the Ottoman rule before the First World War. In all these states, the establishment of monarchist rule, initially by German lesser princes, was seen as building the foundations of the future state. Thus, while the Poles thought this might still be the most obvious model, they rarely expressed genuine enthusiasm for Poland emerging as a kingdom. By the end of the war it appeared that monarchism was at best irrelevant, at worst discredited. Nevertheless, as the fighting came to an end, various political groups became clearer as to what sort of government they expected to establish.

The Russian Revolution clearly emboldened left-wing parties and gave rise to hopes for a revolutionary government in Poland. SDKPiL and PPS-Lewica started thinking in terms of a dictatorship of the proletariat. In 1909, the main sections of the socialist movement in areas under Russian control had made the decision to abandon the name of PPS-Frakcja Rewolucyjna and instead simplified its name to Polska Partia Socjalistyczne (Polish Socialist Party – PPS). The critical decision was made at a party conference which met in Vienna in September 1909. The leaders of the increasingly reformist PPS, distance themselves from the Russian socialist movement. They declared that if war were to break out between Russia and Austria, Polish socialists would support Austria. The Tsarist government was seen as Poland's main oppressor and this justified future support for its enemy. This formulation indicated the increasing separation from the Russian socialist movement. With that, they affirmed the need for an independent Polish state.[21] During the course of the war, PPS had hoped that the Central Powers would support the Polish cause. But, when this turned out not to be the case, the party moved more forcefully towards formulating plans for the emergence of an independent Polish state. In 1897, Polish socialists in Austria had broken away from the Austrian organisation and formed the Polska Partia Socjalno-Demokratyczna Galicji i Śląska (Polish Social-Democratic Party of Galicia and Silesia

– PPS). In accordance with the instructions of the Second International, PPS and PPSD were supposed to try to form a single Polish party. However, until the war, there was no natural unity between the two Polish socialist parties.[22] During the course of the war the two parties were increasingly drawn together through their joint plans to defend the interests of Polish workers. They also distanced themselves from Piłsudski's plans for military cooperation with the German authorities. The Russian Revolution accentuated the reformist elements in both parties and the main focus became that of securing independence for Poland. Both parties were anxious about the rise of revolutionary activities and Soviet intervention in the Ukrainian and Byelorussian regions. Polish socialists had assumed that, when Poland would be reconstructed, these areas would be incorporated into its borders. They therefore had little sympathy for the national aspirations of these ethnic groups which had in the past been part of the Polish–Lithuanian Commonwealth.[23] In the autumn of 1918, the two socialist parties embraced and declared their support for the establishment of a republican government in which they would form an alliance with the peasant movement. Peasant parties, nevertheless, had made it clear that their minimum programme was for a Polish state in which elections to a national assembly would be on the basis of a universal franchise.

The debate extended to the question of whether an independent Polish state would be economically stable. Moreover, whether it would be able to develop an industrial base. All economic debates invariably addressed the issue of wider regional unity. These touched on the issue of whether an independent Poland would be in a position to withstand economic marginalisation and exploitation by its powerful neighbours. Ideas put forward by Zofia Daszyńska-Golińska were interesting contributions to these debates. She developed her thesis in 1916. The starting point of it was the assertion that it would not be beneficial to Poland to continue economic links with the Russian Empire. According to her, this had been an unequal relationship. Russian industry had developed high-quality production which could be exported. Polish production was mainly small-scale and underinvested. It only supplied the Polish markets. The solution was to form a Central European economic bloc, which would include Germany, Poland, Austria, Bulgaria and Turkey. The key to her thinking was the belief that it would be in Germany's interests to encourage industrial development in Poland. She believed that Germany would not be Poland's rival, but an economic ally. In the plans for regional economic expansion, Daszyńska-Golińska and another economist, Klaudiusz Angermann, anticipated that Poland would act as a bridge between the West and East and would benefit from trade moving in both directions. Proponents of close cooperation with Austria put forward a slightly less ambitious economic model in 1917. They thought in terms of Poland being an autonomous part of the Hapsburg Empire and, through that, benefiting from the empire's internal market.

The emergence of Polish administration was not something Polish leaders had been able to either anticipate or prepare for. All depended on the way the occupation forces withdrew and on the authority of the Polish leaders in the key town. In areas under Austrian control during the war, a national committee functioned to consolidate all Polish activities. The main conflict within that committee was between the conservatives, and the alliance between the peasant party and the socialists. The conservatives thought in terms of regional autonomy within Austria. The peasant party and the socialists, on the other hand, had come to distrust the Austrians. By 1917, the peasant movement became active. Its leader Wincenty Witos put forward a programme for the establishment of an independent Polish state, radical economic reforms and, critically, land redistribution.[24] In October 1918, the Polish Liquidation Commission was established in Kraków. Its first aim was to secure the loyalty of the Polish soldiers and then form a national government. Until then, the Polish soldiers had been under Austrian command. The second aim of the Polish Liquidation Commission was to prevent the breakdown of law and order. Its final aim was to indicate to the parties in Warsaw that the peasant movement would be taking a direct interest in the process of state building. This was already taking place in Polish areas from which German troops were withdrawing.[25] At the same time, fighting broke out between the Poles and Ukrainians in Eastern Galicia. In the industrial centres of the Dąbrowa Basin, soviets emerged.

Polish socialists in Austria and in Germany were strongly committed to a democratic path to socialism. They did not approve of the much more radical line. This was the line taken by some of the comrades from Polish areas that had been part of the Russian Empire. They believed that there would be an attempt by the PPS-Lewica and the SDKPiL to stage a revolution and establish a workers' state. At the end of October, moderate socialist leaders first sought to prevent this by planning to take power. On 3 November, the Austrian Governor of the town of Lublin announced that he was handing all authority to the Regency Council. PPS leaders decided to go into action. They established the Provisional Government of the Peoples' Republic of Poland. This only functioned for four days. It was, nevertheless, indicative of the determination of sections of the PPS which believed that a workers' government could be established by means of a ballot. Rejecting collaboration with the revolutionary left, the PPS advocated an alliance with the peasant movement. Its programme spoke of nationalisation of key industries, communication and all natural resources. Furthermore, it advocated land reform. Land was to be put into the hands of those who cultivated it. In private enterprises, workers were to be given the right to participate in decision making. The Lublin government's social programme spoke of access to education and the protection of citizens' right to work. Ignacy Daszyński acted as the leader of the Lublin government. He had hoped to link up with workers who were striking in other parts of German-occupied Polish areas and thus to extend the Lublin government's authority.[26]

Events in Warsaw intervened. Piłsudski had been incarcerated in the Magdeburg prison for sixteen months. His authority among Poles remained undiminished and increased. The German authorities agreed to release him from prison. His arrival in Warsaw on 10 November sidelined all earlier attempts to form a Polish provisional government. The Regency Council had no authority and were frightened by the possibility of a revolution engulfing Polish areas. They were only too willing to hand over to Piłsudski the responsibility of forming the first government. The German military authorities received assurances that troops would be given safe conduct out of Poland. They therefore allowed the soldiers to be disarmed by the Poles. Piłsudski, with the full approval of all but the SDKPiL and the PPS-Lewica, took the title of Head of State.[27]

Piłsudski returned to Warsaw. The military units had earlier been willing to take orders from the Lublin government. However, they now turned their attention to Warsaw. There, more important events attracted the attention of most Poles. What had happened in Lublin had not been unusual. Polish civil authorities in other towns had spontaneously assumed responsibility for maintaining law and order. Especially as it was rapidly becoming clear that German and Austrian soldiers were being withdrawn. The threat and fear of revolution seemed very real. Workers in several industrial areas of the Kingdom formed workers' councils modelled on the Russian revolutionary example. In reality, the government in Warsaw appeared to establish its authority. Thus councils and local administrations generally, either dissolved themselves, or collaborated with it.

On 11 November 1918, Dmowski was in Washington. There, he had been able to secure a critical victory. The Entente Powers had intended to demand, as part of the armistice, that all German and Austrian troops withdraw from occupied territories. Were this to happen, Germany would have abandoned Congress Poland. Dmowski feared that this would have allowed the Red Army to enter into Polish territories. He therefore strenuously lobbied the Entente Powers not to force the Germans to withdraw their occupation units from areas East of Germany. Clause 12 of the armistice specified that they were to remain there until the Entente governments decided that they should go home. Thus Dmowski and the KNP were diplomatically successful in so far as the KNP was increasingly treated as a provisional government. It was less clear whether it would be able to establish its authority in Polish territories. For that, the KNP had to contend, in the first place, with Piłsudski. It also had to contend with left wing parties. These had gained strength and confidence from events taking place in Russia.

When the National Government was formed in Warsaw, it was agreed that the first general elections in the independent Polish state would take place on 26 January 1919. Piłsudski's personal authority was reflected in the popular support given to him by the people of Warsaw. His strength lay in this. Morevoer, he was able to articulate the wishes of most political leaders. Dmowski, and most of the leaders of the national democratic movement, were abroad. This allowed Piłsudski to assume authority, unchallenged by them. The myth of Piłsudski being a patriot and the father of the nation was one he chose to cultivate from the outset. In November 1918, the Kraków Commission and the Lublin government abdicated their claims to govern and decided to support the National Government being formed in Warsaw. This therefore reduced the potential for internal conflicts.

At this early stage, the KNP in Paris was the only authority which could still have challenged Piłsudski. This was because of the importance of the forthcoming international conference to the process of defining Poland's borders. Nevertheless, Piłsudski sent an official note to the main European governments, informing them of the emergence of an independent Polish state. In this way, he minimised the Paris groups' influence. For the time being, only Germany recognised the authority of the government which was being formed in Warsaw. Washington, Paris and London hesitated. They were still considering the possibility that the KNP might still return to Poland and assert its authority over the administration formed there. The national democrats continued to stand aloof. Piłsudski gave the task of forming a provisional government first to the socialist Ignacy Daszyński. When he failed, Piłsudski asked another socialist, Jędrzej Moraczewski. Piłsudski retained control of the military forces and appointed himself as Head of State. This was a function no one was willing to deny him.[28]

The road ahead promised to be very turbulent. There was still the unclear issue of the new state's borders. In addition to this, there were many questions which needed to be answered before the romantic idea of Poland could be translated into statehood. Poles from the three partition areas had been part of very distinct political traditions. All socialist parties from the three partitions belonged to the Second International. But little united Polish socialists from the Kingdom area with those who had lived in the German Empire. The peasant movement and the nationalists were equally, if not more, divided. At the same time, expectations exceeded true possibilities. It was inevitable that many would find independence a disappointment, as real economic problems bedevilled state building attempts.

# 3  Independent Poland in Interwar Europe

As Piłsudski assumed the role of Head of State, his initial preference was to ignore the KNP in Paris and to establish direct relations with West European governments. Although Britain was not committed to supporting the KNP, the French government was less willing to ignore it. The presence of Polish military units on French soil under the command of General Haller, called for reflection. As a result, even though the French government was hesitant in opening talks with Piłsudski, it did not give Dmowski too much encouragement.[1] The two Poles were left to sort things out. In Polish territories, Piłsudski's authority was undisputed. But in Paris and in dealings with European governments, Dmowski was better placed to speak on Poland's behalf. To the two men's credit, although exchanges between them were acrimonious, they realised that the authority of the young state would be undermined and its interests would be ill served if they were they to continue their quarrels in public. Uneasily, both compromised. As a result, the KNP recognised the authority of the government in Poland. In return, Dmowski became head of the Polish delegation to the Paris talks. Paderewski, in the meantime, left for Poland. There he became Prime Minister and Minister for Foreign Affairs. When a delegation from Poland joined Dmowski, there was a need to clarify precisely what vision of a future Poland was to be put to Britain, France and the USA. These were the three powers which would have the final say over all matters discussed at the conference. When Piłsudski's instructions were put to Dmowski, it became clear that the former had a vision of a federated state within the borders of the previous Polish–Lithuanian Commonwealth. Dmowski, on the other hand, believed in the outright incorporation of non-Polish ethnic groups into Poland's borders. This debate specifically related to Poland's eastern borderlands, where the Ukrainian, Byelorussian and Lithuanian communities showed no desire to be included in a new Polish state. The KNP and the delegation from Poland finally decided to submit Poland's case on the basis of Dmowski's programme. While the Polish delegation conducted long-drawn-out discussions throughout the spring in Paris, events in Poland were far from static. In fact, in Poland, Pilsudski led military campaigns. These resulted in the consolidation of Poland's eastern borders. This situation gave rise to two parallel policies. One of these was fought on the diplomatic front, the other was determined by military action.

The Paris Peace Conference opened in January 1919 and ended with the signing of the Versailles Peace Treaty on 28 June. It was ostensibly meant only to address the German issue. In reality, it became a forum where key issues were thrashed out and to which aspiring and hopeful national leaders and groups presented their claims and memoranda. Decision making was confined to the Council of Ten. This which included the leaders of the USA, France, Italy and Britain, together with their foreign ministers and some additional advisors. Two Japanese delegates were also admitted to the Council of Ten. By March, the main decision-making body was reduced to the US President Woodraw Wilson, the British Prime Minister David Lloyd George, the Italian Foreign Minister Vittorio Orlando and the French Prime Minister Georges Clémenceau. When discussing the future of Germany, only Poland's borders with Germany should have been the subject of the committee's deliberations. But inevitably the discussion extended to consideration of Poland's future place in Europe.

Defining and agreeing to Poland's borders with Germany caused endless problems. When it became apparent that the information on which to base key discussions was lacking, the Council of Ten despatched a fact-finding mission to Poland. In the meantime, Dmowski was asked to put Poland's case. This he did confidently. Although he impressed his listeners with his command of detail,

## The borders of Poland after the First World War

Poland's expectations concerning its future borders were bound to cause anxiety. The right of national groups to self-determination was accepted as a guiding principle at the conference. Nevertheless, the Paris decision makers were only too well aware that this could not be done without balancing the needs and aspirations of different national groups who lived in the same areas. Too often, these aspirations proved impossible to reconcile. At the same time, the long-term viability of territorial changes had to be considered. Post-war governments were under pressure to demobilise and to reduce further military commitments outside their borders. Thus, from the outset, the Paris negotiators tried to avoid making decisions which would require the further deployments of troops in Europe.[2]

After some deliberations, the Polish case was finally handed over to the specially assembled Polish Commission. This was to feed facts and relevant information to the Council. As it turned out, some matters could not be resolved by the time of the signing of the Versailles Peace Treaty and were left to the League of Nations to investigate and to make final recommendations. In the meantime, developments took place in Eastern Europe without regard for decisions being reached in Paris. In reality, Poland was never a major issue for the Paris negotiators. Although, at the end of the war, the USA, Britain and France were committed to the creation of an independent Poland with access to the sea, all decisions relating to the new state's borders, depended upon their own long-term European policies. To France, the collapse of Russia, the much-needed eastern ally, raised questions of future strategy. This, in turn, hinged on the likelihood of a democratic government emerging in Russia. The calculation made in Paris was that if Russia were to succumb to turmoil, a string of pro-French states East of Germany could substitute for Russia. During the Paris Peace Conference, Russia was engulfed by civil war and this made it impossible for French politicians and military leaders to anticipate what role they might require Poland to play in a possible future eastern front. The British government was more concerned with stability and a viable European balance of power. A large Polish state, incorporating disaffected people of other nationalities and at loggerheads with its neighbours, spelled trouble for years to come. Furthermore, Britain and France were anxious about instability in Germany. They therefore would not unconditionally support Polish demands in East Prussia, Danzig and Silesia. Both British and French governments and their delegations, which led the talks in Paris, considered various options and continued to investigate new ideas throughout the course of the conference. This explains their frequently confused responses to the Polish question.

The US delegation, headed by the President, inevitably carried most weight during the Paris discussions. The Poles were encouraged by Paderewski's earlier success, when he gave a concert at the White House, and Dmowski's recent trip to the USA. As it turned out Wilson's 14 Points programme contained an explicit commitment to the establishment of an independent Poland with access to the sea. However, in spite of this, the issue of the borders had not been considered by the US government. Wilson had only a vague idea as to what the establishment of a Polish state would entail and what would be its impact on regional politics.[3] In March, when Wilson returned to the USA, his aides had not kept up to date on discussions on Poland. The result was that the committee's responses to Polish demands evolved gradually and acrimoniously. Lloyd George was opposed to the incorporation of Eastern Prussia into Poland and determined to deny Poland the port city of Danzig. Many Poles were, and still are, only too ready to believe that Lloyd George's attitudes can be traced to the malign recommendation of Lewis Namier. Lewis Namier was an academic who acted as an advisor to the Foreign Office. Namier was of Polish-Jewish origin. He had cautioned against supporting Poland's excessive territorial demands. However, other considerations determined British policy on the issue of Poland's borders. Similarly, the US was unwilling to approve Poland's extensive territorial demands in the West and East. This was attributed to the influence of the Jewish lobby. All these factors played a role in the extensive discussions which took place in Paris. In reality, Poland's western border was discussed as part of the German issue and the question of how to stabilise Germany in Europe, and not as a Polish border issue only. Anxiety about revolutions breaking out in Germany and the still unresolved civil conflict in Russia, likewise, affected the negotiators' judgement insofar as France took an active interest in both. Britain and the USA were wary of allowing France to benefit unduly from Germany's moment of weakness.[4]

Polish submissions to the Polish Commission were discussed by the Council in the course of long debates and became the subject of disputes, primarily between the French and British delegations. When the Versailles Treaty was signed on 28 July 1919, it appeared to satisfy the Polish delegation's minimum demands in relation to Germany. It also obliged the Polish delegation to accept the deferral of decisions on a number of unresolved issues.

The borders of the new Polish state were consolidated as a result of complex and frequently contradictory developments. The fall of the three European Empires created the preconditions for the Poles to stake a claim to independence. Nevertheless, just how and where the final border was drawn depended on a number of factors. Poland's border with Germany created problems because of the mixed population in the border areas. As the war drew to a close, German troops were no longer willing to remain on Polish territories as an occupation force. In the regions where both states were likely to lay claim, the two communities fought to establish their authority.

In the case of Poznań (Posen), and the surrounding district, the Polish and German communities tried to determine the course of events without waiting for instructions from either Berlin or Warsaw. In November 1918, Polish paramilitary organisations were formed. Conflicts between the two communities and the initial unwillingness of German troops to defend the town led to a Polish uprising, which broke out on 27 December. The Poles then formed a council. By then, German troops were brought back into the city and district. Their presence led to regular military confrontations with the newly formed Polish units. The result was that the Poles were able to retain control of the town of Poznań and of Pomerania along the lower reaches of the river Wisła. The initiative, as many similar ones in areas of mixed Polish-German population, had not been directed or instigated by the Polish authorities in Warsaw. Ultimately, by presenting this as a fait accompli the Polish delegation in Paris was able to make a forceful case for Poland retaining the areas.

In some cases, decisions made by the Paris negotiators prevented the Poles from claiming disputed areas. Thus, contrary to Polish demands, the ancient Hanseatic port town of Gdańsk (Danzig), with its majority German inhabitants, became a Free City. Its status was guaranteed by the League of Nations. Lloyd George refused to agree to Poland's claim to territories which contained a majority German community. Because of this, a plebiscite was sanctioned in Kwidzyń (Marienwerder). The plebiscite took place in 1920. The inhabitants opted for the region to remain in Germany. Polish access to the Baltic coast was secured through a strip of land along the river Wisła. Having been denied the port of Gdańsk, the Polish state, in due course built a new port of Gdynia. The corridor linking the Polish state to the coast became a symbol of the limitations of Big Power intervention in border settlements. Successive Polish governments resented the League's presence in Gdańsk and clung to the few prerogatives they had there, namely, use of some port facilities, control of the postal system and customs duties. To the Germans, the separation of Eastern Prussia from Pomerania by the so-called Polish Corridor was a constant reminder and symbol of the unfairness of the Versailles Treaty. It was realised that the situation could not be altered without a major conflict. This prevented the Polish and German states from taking military action to reverse what both sides considered to be a series of monumental injustices.[5]

In the case of Upper Silesia, the local Polish community tried everything possible for the areas to be included in the Polish borders. Silesia had distant historic links with the medieval Polish Kingdom. These claims were not accepted at the Paris Conference. Most Silesian coal mines were owned by German capital. In Paris many inhabitants defined themselves as Poles. In reality, their links with Polish culture were tenuous. France would have preferred to see the areas incorporated into Poland. But British concerns about Germany's ability to pay reparations and anxiety about economic conflicts between Poland and Germany, played a role in the final decision.[6] In August 1919 the Silesian Poles staged an uprising. This was brought to an end with the aid of Entente troops. The German administration retained control of the region. In February 1920, the Poles staged a second uprising. Once more, peace was restored by negotiations and the presence of British, French and Italian military detachments. The compromise solution of a plebiscite did not resolve the issue. The plebiscite took place in March 1921. In spite of acrimonious accusations of fraud, the League of Nations upheld the majority decision for Upper Silesia to remain in Germany. The local Polish population then staged a third uprising in May. The Poles were against incorporation into Germany. The French supported Polish demands. This led to a compromise solution, whereby the towns of Katowice, and Chorzów were granted to Poland.[7]

Poland's eastern border was defined in a series of skirmishes, wars and military campaigns. Only in March 1923 did the Conference of Ambassadors give its approval to the final border. What happened between the German armistice with the Entente Powers in March 1923 had a lasting impact on Poland's relations with the European Powers. It also affected Poland's relations with its neighbours and the internal politics of the new state. Most Poles, nevertheless, believed that Poland could have claimed more territories. The Lithuanian, Ukrainian and Byelorussian communities nursed resentment and a desire for revenge. They believed that they had been denied the right to self-determination. Relations with the Soviet Union, likewise, were affected by these actions throughout the interwar period.

The resolution of Poland's eastern frontier depended on a number of factors. Of those, the fate of Eastern Galicia proved most complex. At the root of the problem lay the diverse ethnic and religious population. The town of Lwów (Lemberg, Lviv) and the area surrounding the town, contained a Polish majority. But outside the enclaves, the peasant community was Ukrainian. Most Ukrainians belonged to the Uniate Church. A minority were Orthodox Christians, while the Poles were nearly entirely Catholic. The towns contained sizeable Jewish communities. Before the First World War, Eastern Galicia had been ruled by Austria. During the war, Ukrainian nationalist leaders thought of forming a Ukrainian state, to include Western and Eastern Ukraine. By 1918, the situation became very complex indeed. On 20 November 1917, a Ukrainian Central Council (this authority is also variously described by historians as the Rada or the Directorate) based in Kiev proclaimed the establishment of a Ukrainian People's Republic. At Germany's invitation, the council sent a delegation to the Brest-Litovsk peace talks. This ended the German-Russian war. In due course, German relations with the council collapsed and its leaders sought the support of the Entente Powers for Ukrainian aspirations.

In the meantime, in Eastern Galicia, a separate Ukrainian authority emerged. This called itself the West Ukrainian People's Republic. Troops led by it captured the city of Lwów on 1 November 1918. The Poles in the city, unprepared for this military action, were able to call on military units from Kraków. The Ukrainians were forced out of the city. However, fighting between the two communities continued, with Lwów remaining in Polish hands. In the meantime, the fate of Eastern Galicia became the subject of enquiry by the Polish Commission to the Paris Conference. After the signing of the Versailles Peace, this matter was handed over to the Conference of Ambassadors. Britain and France viewed the issue from their, arguably, larger interests. They attempted to settle the Ukrainian question in accordance with these interests. Both governments favoured the Russian claim to Ukraine as long as there was the hope of the White forces winning any civil war in Russia. The British Foreign Office was partly influenced by Lewis Namier's suggestion that Polish claims to Eastern Galicia were excessive. They feared that a Polish state in conflict with Russia would act as Germany's Trojan horse. France, on the other hand, vacillated between supporting the White General Anton Denikin and strengthening the new Polish and Czechoslovak states. They hoped that the Denikin would head a Russian government after he overthrew the Bolshevik government. However, the new Polish and Czechoslovak states would act as a barrier against the revolutionary government. A factor in French considerations was their growing interest in the oil reserves in Eastern Galicia.[8]

The Polish delegation in Paris repeatedly tried to put the case for the region to be included in Poland. As long as the issue of Poland's western border was not resolved, Piłsudski had to proceed warily. Britain and France accused and suspected the Poles of trying to pre-empt the decisions of the Polish Commission. The Poles gave the appearance of accepting the arbitration of the Paris negotiators. In November 1919 the Red Army effectively defeated Denikin. The French sought to find ways of allowing the Poles to retain Eastern

Galicia, even if the British continued to oppose Polish demands. In the meantime, on 14 May 1920, Piłsudski authorised an attack on Eastern Galicia. The Poles were successful in their fight against the Ukrainians. However there was considerable French anger at the use of the Polish units, which had been brought from France to fight against the Bolsheviks. Piłsudski consistently claimed that his actions were intended as an attack on the Red Army and not an attempt to consolidate control over Eastern Galicia. This found favour with some of the Western diplomats. They saw the advantage of allowing the Poles to capture Ukraine just at the time when the Red Army was poised to move into the region. Piłsudski was able to secure a military convention with Semen Petrula, the head of the Directorate of the Ukrainian Peoples' Republic. There was only one issue uniting the two, namely anxiety about the Red Army and Soviet aspirations in the Ukraine. These had manifested themselves in the support for a Ukrainian Soviet Socialist Peoples' Republic. On 8 May Polish troops and units loyal to Petrula entered Kiev. They were expecting that the population would support them. This did not happen. In fact, they were met with hostility. During the brief period when Kiev had been in Soviet hands, the peasants benefited from land reform instigated by the Soviets. Polish control meant the reversal of the land redistribution and the return of Polish landowners. The East Ukrainian population viewed the Poles as enemies and Petrula as a traitor. More worrying was the fact that the Soviet troops had not been defeated, they merely abandoned Kiev and regrouped. This posed a danger to the Polish army in Byelorussia. At this point, the future of Eastern Galicia was linked to the Allies' willingness to help the Poles in their negotiations with the Soviet Union. In July, the conditions of the armistice between the two sides were agreed in Spa. The future of Eastern Galica was therefore made dependent on arbitration. For the time being Poland retained control of areas up to the river Zbrucz.[9] In any case, the future of Eastern Galicia was just one chapter in the evolution of Polish relations with the Soviet Union.

Piłsudski had hoped to extend Polish borders eastward. He was driven by a desire to reconstruct the Polish–Lithuanian Commonwealth of the Jagiellonian period. He thought of a federal Polish state. The eastern ethnic groups (the Ukrainian, Byelorussian and

Baltic people) would be included in this. The problem with that reasoning was that, like the Poles, these national groups had hoped for independence. Federation with Poland was viewed as aggression and an attempt to deny these national groups the right to self-determination.

At the beginning of 1919, Piłsudski's main worry was the possibility of the counter-revolutionary White forces defeating the Soviet government in Russia. The Whites insisted on the restoration of the Russian Empire in its pre-war borders. This threatened Poland's newly established independence. Not surprisingly, in spite of British pressure, Piłsudski refused to aid the Whites' fight against the Red Army. First contacts between the Polish and Soviet governments were made through the Red Cross at the beginning of 1919. These were aimed at the exchange of prisoners of war. However, they also led to a tacit understanding that neither side would take action against each other.[10] By autumn of that year, the situation had changed. Denikin had operated in Southeastern Russia. In June, he unsuccessfully tried to launch an attack on Moscow. By October, his forces were defeated. Admiral Alexander Kolchak had established control over Siberia. He was likewise losing ground by the end of 1919. In October, General Nikolai Yudenich tried to capture Petrograd with British assistance. He was routed. This meant that the Red Army stood poised to move West and was likely to confront the Polish forces.

Piłsudski hoped that Polish forces would hold their own in the East. He knew he could count on Polish military units which had emerged in the eastern regions. He was also able to continue the build-up of the Polish army, since the newly elected assembly, the Sejm, was willing to provide finance for his expansionist plan. Poland's thrust eastwards at the end of 1919 and during 1920 was not determined by the government. Instead, it was determined by the military leadership, primarily by Piłsudski and those close to him. This, in turn, had an impact on Poland's foreign policy. Through the creation of faits accomplis, Poland was embarking on a policy of confrontation with the Paris negotiators, the Soviet regime and its neighbours, Lithuania and Czechoslovakia.

By April 1920 the Soviet authorities had become anxious about the extent of Polish intervention in Ukraine, while the Poles, seeing the collapse of the White offensive, came round to the view that military action against the Red Army was feasible and desirable. On 25 April 1920, the Polish offensive against the Soviet Union started. Initial victories in the Ukraine were followed by defeats. The Red Army's victories brought it closer to ethnically Polish territories. In June, Semion Budyonny's Red Cavalry forced the Poles out of Kiev. In July, General Mikail Tukhachevsky defeated the Poles in Byelorussia. He forced them to abandon Minsk, Wilno, Grodno and, finally, Białystok. In Warsaw the government decided to seek the assistance of the heads of the Entente governments, who were attending a meeting in Spa. When the Polish delegation arrived there on 6 July, they were left in no doubt as to what Britain expected in return for undertaking to mediate. The conditions for brokering talks with the Soviet government were clear. The Poles were to commit themselves not to go beyond the Curzon line. The British considered this to be Poland's ethnic border in the East. Furthermore, they were to give up claims to Danzig, Wilno and the coal-mining Teschen region, the subject of disputes with the Czechoslovak state. The Polish delegation appeared to accept these conditions, but the Soviet government rejected British mediation. The Poles had to open direct talks with the revolutionary government.[11]

In Warsaw, the military crisis led to the formation of a new coalition government headed by Witos. Anxious about the consequences of Soviet revolutionary propaganda, the government approved a number of reforms, most notably land reform. The Poles were united in their opposition to Soviet entry and viewed Soviet attempts to form local revolutionary administrations with hostility. Soviet hopes that the entry of the Red Army would precipitate a revolution proved illusory. Such hopes were really a way of legitimising a war of aggression. The perilous military situation caused the military leadership to review its tactics and carry out a root and branch reform of the army. In August, the Red Army reached the Wisła and threatened the capital. During the following weeks, the Polish army successfully defended Warsaw. What is known as the Battle of Warsaw, even now, invokes strong passions. Some see this as a prophetic victory over the Bolshevik forces and a crucial defence of European civilisation.[12] By October, both sides were exhausted and agreed on an armistice. The Riga treaty, signed on

18 March 1921, defined Poland's eastern border beyond the Curzon Line. This irritated the British, but it was a line which the Polish and the Soviet governments were willing to accept for the time being. Piłsudski's concept of a federal state, including Poles, Lithuanians, Byelorrusians and Ukrainians, could no longer be pursued. The Byelorussian- and Ukrainian-inhabited areas were now divided between Poland and Soviet Russia. Lithuania retained independence, deeply resenting Polish claims to reconstitute the previous Polish–Lithuanian Commonwealth.[13]

The way in which Poland's eastern border was defined is best illustrated in the case of the town of Wilno (Vilnius) and the surrounding countryside. At the root of the problem lay the incompatibility of Polish and Lithuanian aspirations. To Lithuanian leaders, Poland was an enemy, likely to stand in the way of their claim to national self-determination. Theirs was a vision of a state based on the extended borders of the Grand Duchy of Lithuania in 1569, with Wilno as its capital. At the end of the war, most Poles refused to accept that Lithuanians had the right to determine their own future. This attitude was variously justified by suggesting that most of the Lithuanian nobility had been Polonised; that Lithuania could not exist as an independent state and would therefore become a satellite of Germany; and finally that Wilno was a centre of Polish culture. Both Dmowski and Piłsudski expressed such views. Dmowski firmly believed that Lithuania, together with Ukraine and Byelorussia, should be incorporated into the Polish state. Piłsudski favoured a federalist approach, in line with progressive thinking on the rights of national groups. He accepted that the Lithuanians might choose to form a separate state. However, he still advocated the inclusion of Wilno into Poland's borders as a precondition for a settlement with an independent Lithuania. In January 1919, German troops withdrew from Wilno. A Lithuanian Soviet Socialist Republic was proclaimed with the help of the Red Army. German troops had been stationed in the region in accordance with the terms of the armistice signed with the Entente Powers. These continued to be a factor in determining developments. German interest in these areas was confirmed with the establishment of German militias, the Freikorps, in Lithuania. In the meantime, in Paris, Dmowski tried to persuade France and Britain to support Polish claims and his vision to incorporate Lithuania into Poland. During the course of 1919 fighting raged in the area. Poles fought the Lithuanians. They were, in any case, divided along political lines. Some allied themselves with the revolutionary Russian forces. Others, hoped to establish a democratic state, separate from Poland and Russia. In April 1919, Polish troops fought the Red Army to take over Wilno and Grodno. Piłsudski visited Wilno and promised its inhabitants that they would be given the right to decide the town's fate.

During the following months, the Poles held on to Wilno. Its future and that of Lithuania was closely linked to the course of the civil war in Russia. British and French views of the desirability or otherwise of allowing the Poles to dominate Lithuania were dominated by considerations relating to the future of Russia. The Polish delegation in Paris disagreed on the Wilno case that they were to put to the Commission on Poland. Ignacy Paderewski voiced his dissent from Dmowski's line. During the summer, Polish and Lithuanian troops confronted each other. The collapse of the Whites only further complicated the issue of Lithuania's future. Britain became a champion of the Baltic states' independence against Poland. As Poland and the Soviet Union fought each other, the Lithuanians allied with the latter. This was in return for Soviet agreement that Wilno should be incorporated into Lithuania. The Red Army, on arrival in the town, refused to relinquish control. In August 1920, the Poles pushed the Soviet army out of territories which had previously been held by the Poles. The Lithuanians then stepped into the military vacuum and took control of the city. Under the guise of pursuing Soviet troops, Polish units pushed into Lithuania. In September, they confronted the Lithuanian army. British and French condemnation of Polish actions led Piłsudski to change his tactics. In October 1920, the Poles ostensibly agreed to leave Wilno in Lithuanian hands. On 9 October, General Lucjan Żeligowski led a division of Polish soldiers into the town. Piłsudski pretended that Żeligowski's actions had not been authorised. He claimed that Żeligowski and his unit had mutinied. The elated Sejm agreed to establish a local administration in the town. Its future was all but decided. On 8 January 1922, the city's elected assembly voted for the incorporation of Wilno into Poland. Lithuanians broke off diplomatic relations with the Poles, refusing to accept the loss of the city. Diplomatic relations were not restored until 1938.[14]

In the South, Poland found itself the victim of Czechoslovak aggression. When Austrian rule collapsed, the Poles and the Czechs could not agree on the ownership of a coal-rich area of Cieszyn. The Polish population was in a majority. However, the Czechs argued that the Poles were not local but an incoming population attracted to employment in the mines and that the indigenous population had been Czech. The issue was taken by both sides for arbitration in the Paris talks. In January 1919, when the Poles were fully preoccupied with fighting in the Ukraine, the Czechs took over the district. The Poles appealed. However, the question of the ownership of the region became tangled up with France's anxiety about coal supplies. From this perspective, the Czechoslovak state seemed a potentially important economic partner. The result was that the Polish claim was rejected and Czechoslovakia retained the region.[15] Throughout the interwar period, the Poles refused to relinquish their claim to the lost region.

The issue of Poland's borders reflected a complex transition from the previous domination of the area by the three empires, to the principle of self-rule and nation states. The definition of borders was ultimately based on ethnic and historic grounds. This was particularly difficult for Poland. There was a visible lack of natural borders. In addition to this, the borderland had always been inhabited by a mixed population. At the same time, there was a lot of disregard prevalent among the Poles for the national aspirations of other national groups. This caused friction and ultimately led to military conflicts. The emergence of an independent Poland inevitably led to local conflicts. With the passage of time, these were not set aside. Instead, they acquired a deeply symbolic meaning. This had an impact on regional politics and with that on Poland's future foreign policy.

The nationalist Polish leaders recreated the multi-ethnic empire like the ones they had fought to destroy. Nationalism prevented them from acquiring an understanding of how such an empire might function. This understanding could have been gained from fuller engagement with these empires. Nationalism undermined the multinational empires. In Poland's case, nationalism led to

the recreation of a multinational empire, though in a reconfigu-
rated form. The political and economic problems facing the new
state were formidable. Its territories had been administered by three
European Empires, each with distinct political traditions. This had
been the case for over a hundred years. During this period, a strong
sense of Polish national consciousness developed. It was one that
transcended the frontiers of the three partition powers. The Polish
state had to build state institutions; establish a single legal code; a
national economy. Finally, it had to foster a consensus. This would
be a prerequisite for a viable democratic system.

Paradoxically, the new Polish state was anything but a national
state. During the interwar period two censuses were conducted in
Poland. The first took place in 1921. It did not include the Wilno
and Upper Silesian regions. These were not formally part of Poland.
Those conducting the exercise struggled when trying to identify the
communities in the eastern borderlands, in accordance with strict
national definitions. Some people merely responded by stating that
they were 'local'. In these cases, an attempt was made to categorise
their nationality in accordance with religious criteria. At times this
merely confused rather than clarified the matter. During the 1931
census, an additional question on the mother tongue was introduced. Even then, the figures were unreliable. It is now believed
that the Polish government forged returns relating to the eastern
borderlands to make it look as if the Ukrainian community was
neither compact nor distinct in those areas.

The first census revealed that 69 per cent of Poland's inhabitants
defined themselves as Polish nationals. The largest national minority were the Ukrainians (16%); 3.9% defined themselves as Byelorussians. This was about the same number that defined themselves as
Germans. 9.8 per cent defined themselves as Jewish. Thus, one third
of the population were defined as non-Polish nationals. Even this
did not convey the full picture, since it can be assumed that there
were those who either did not know how to define their nationality
or were reluctant to do so because of anxiety about persecution. This
has led some historians to suggest that in reality over 40 per cent of
Poland's inhabitants belonged to a non-Polish national minority.[15]

The Ukrainian community formed the largest national minority.
Nevertheless, in spite of them being defined as Ukrainian, this group

was far from uniform. The majority of Ukrainian nationals in East Galicia belonged to the Uniate Church. This was a section of the Orthodox Christian Church which subordinated itself to the Church of Rome. Ukrainians in the Volhynia region usually belonged to the Orthodox Christian Church. The Ukrainians' attitude to the Polish state depended on their past political experiences; the state of the local economy and, finally, the degree of national awareness. Four basic political trends manifested themselves within the community. The Ukrainian National Democratic Party supported the establishment of an independent Ukrainian state. The Ukrainian and Galician communist parties sought unity with the Ukrainian regions incorporated into the Soviet Union. The third group, mainly agrarian parties, accepted incorporation into Poland. But they campaigned for autonomy within the Polish state. The final group hailed from the military organisations active during the 1918–19 period. These took an ultra-nationalist programme. This group focused on training youth organisations and paramilitary units, which were to be ready to fight for Ukrainian independence. Despite numerical strength, the Ukrainian community was not successful in parliamentary politics. This was because of the divisions between the groups. During the 1921 elections, most Ukrainian parties called for a boycott of the elections. When Ukrainian soldiers took military action against the Poles, the state responded by sending General Haller's units into the Ukrainian-inhabited areas. The pattern was thus set, with the Ukrainians boycotting recruitment drives and Polish state organisations. In the meantime, the state did all in its power to undermine the communities' cohesion. The right to education in the Ukrainian language was restricted. Land reform gave Polish war veterans farmsteads in Ukrainian areas, while denying the local community the right to land. In 1930, the Ukrainian areas were brutally pacified. Police and army units were sent in, arresting and beating up Ukrainians. Ukrainian cooperatives, cultural centres and schools were closed down.

Ukrainian communities in rural areas were severely hit by the economic slump of the early 1930s. This, along with the actions of the Polish state, led to the radicalisation of the Ukrainian community. Some sections sought an accommodation with the Polish government in the 1930s. However, this accommodation proved elusive. Attempts to build bridges between the Polish state and the Ukrainian community were made on the basis of a shared anxiety about the Soviet Union. This had limited appeal to nationalists. They increasingly saw the Polish state as the main enemy of Ukrainian nationalism. In 1934, Poland was condemned by the League of Nations for its mistreatment of the Ukrainian community. Colonel Josef Beck, the Minister for Foreign Affairs, responded by declaring that the Minorities Treaty no longer bound Poland. This, in turn, focused the international spotlight on Poland. When the Nazi Party came to power in Germany, it was able to undermine the Polish state by supporting the Ukrainian minority.

If the Ukrainian community was numerically the largest minority, the Jewish community was seen as a matter of utmost gravity, requiring radical solutions. From the outset, national democrats sought to portray Jews as hostile, if not outright dangerous to Polish nationalism. As a result of such reasoning, there were calls for the Jewish threat to be counteracted. The nationalist movement took the view that the Jewish presence in independent Poland should not be tolerated. This was not an unique view. Some sections of the peasant movement and the Christian parties, agreed with this analysis. The tactic of the national democrats was to attack political opponents by accusing them of tolerating the Jewish presence within the body politic. This led to debates on the perceived Jewish threat. These formed the core of arguments used by most political parties during the interwar period. The main differences between the nationalists, on the one hand, and the peasant and Christian parties on the other, amounted to the question of how to counteract that threat. The Endecja advocated the outright expulsion of Jews from Poland. The moderates' suggested limiting the Jewish influence on Poland's economy, education, culture and politics.

The Ukrainian community lived in compact groupings in the eastern borderland. Unlike them, Jews were scattered throughout Poland. Only in some areas did they form distinct groups. In others, they coexisted with other national and religious communities. Jews lived nearly entirely in urban areas. Only 1 per cent derived their income from farming. A minority defined Hebrew as their language, while most stated that Polish was their mother tongue. No other community was divided by such a diversity of political ideas. Jews were divided on religious, social and cultural lines. Religious obser-vance, likewise divided the community.[16] The orthodox commu-nity was numerically the strongest. The zionist parties dominated the political life of Polish Jews. As a result of the 1922 elections, 35 Jewish deputies joined the Sejm. Of them, 25 represented zionist parties. The Jewish community of the eastern regions was usually extremely poor and belonged to orthodox strands of Judaism. In the big urban areas of what had been Congress Poland, Jews could be found among the intellectual and professional classes. Neverthe-less, the majority of Polish Jews derived their income from working as artisans, employed in small-scale production or at home. Anti-Semites claimed that Jews controlled large industry and banking. However, this was clearly not the case. During the depression in the early 1930s, the Jewish community suffered pauperisation. This was due to their concentration in small trade activities and production. This brought to the fore conflicts with the Polish community. The national democrats benefited from the situation. They continued to draw attention to what they alleged was the parasitic presence of Jews within the body of the nation.

Emigration was one way out of poverty and persecution. For Jews, the USA had been the obvious destination. During the 1930s, US im-migration restrictions limited the settlement of Jews from Poland. Despite this, during the interwar period, over 50 per cent of Jews leaving Europe, came from Poland. In the late 1930s, Palestine be-came the main destination for Jews. Some refused to leave, either on religious grounds or because they believed that assimilation was the correct way of responding to the complex economic and political situation in Poland. However, economic factors also played a large role in persuading Jews to migrate. In the mid-1930s, the nationalist movements and the Polish Maritime and Colonial League openly spoke of forcing Jews out of Poland and into overseas territories. There was a call for Poland to be granted the island of Madagascar, where it was hoped to settle the 'surplus Jews'.[17] This was evidence of the attitudes certain Poles had towards the Jewish community.

The Byelorussian community formed the second largest national minority in Poland. It was concentrated entirely in the northeast. This was the poorest and most economically and culturally back-ward region of Poland. The Byelorussian communities lived in rural areas dominated by large estates owned by the Poles. Ethnic conflict was increased by settlement drives. The aim of these was to increase the presence of Poles in the borderlands. Land reform transferred land into the hands of the incoming Poles. Byelorussian peasants therefore had no way of benefiting from land reform. This led to mass protests. The government responded to this by arming Polish settlers and sending in troops. They ignored the expectations of the Byelorussian community and made it difficult for legitimate peasant organisations to function as representatives of their grievances. In this way, the Polish state made it easy for the communists to gain support in those areas.

The Polish state was obliged to act in accordance with the Minorities Treaty, signed by Poland in June 1919. This affected their treatment of the national minorities. Representatives of the East European Jewish communities had been instrumental in the formulation of the treaty. This was a point that was ultimately held against them. The Jews, in common with all minorities, experienced difficulties in the exercise of all rights, supposedly guaranteed by Poland's commitment to the Minorities Treaty.[18] The Poles deeply resented the treaty. In due course it became clear that the League had no effective means of compelling a member state to protect and facilitate the cultural life of its national minorities. The Polish state was obliged to ensure that minorities had access to schooling in their own language and that state funding was available for these basic educational activities. In reality, this was always difficult to enforce. The emergence of a Polish state generated intense national sentiments. This meant that the rights of the minorities were subordinated to the political demands of the Poles. The constitution guaranteed the rights of all citizens. In practice, however, the rights of the national minorities were subordinated to the demands of the state. The state saw itself as the defender of Polish national interests. Furthermore, successive governments had to balance the needs of various communities against the demands of the national democratic Party. This party's rowdy campaigns criticised the government for its supposed laxity in defending Polish interests and the security of the state.

Inevitably, the state of the economy presented the largest single challenge. The establishment of the independent state caused the separation of Polish areas from large, integrated economies. This, in turn, caused long-term disruption. Nevertheless, the main task in the first few years was to create a unified infrastructure. The three railway systems needed to be linked. A Polish currency had to replace the pre-war and wartime currencies. Schooling systems had been established to integrate the Poles into the empires. These had to be replaced by a Polish curriculum. These were immediate issues. However, in the long term, the Poles had to build a modern state system which its citizens would uphold through their willingness to pay taxes; their consent to military service and their participation in its democratic institutions. Their willingness to act in this way varied. It depended on their previous political experience, wartime agreements and their commitment to the national cause.

The economy was the biggest obstacle to the building of a modern Polish state. Inflation hit Poland in several waves. The first wave was in 1919–22 when production was still below pre-war levels. However, uneven economic development made it difficult to arrive at a clear picture of what was happening. In 1921, over 75 per cent of the population lived in rural areas. Only 14.5 per cent worked in industry. Employment in small-scale retail, workshops and family production predominated. Levels of development between the three partition areas varied.[19] During the war, Polish-inhabited areas had been affected by military activities. Russia, Austria and, most of all, Germany had exploited the industrial capacity and the natural resources of the Polish areas under their control. Severe deforestation, among others, was the result of ruthless German exploitation. However, the Russians too had contributed to Poland's economic difficulties. They evacuated industrial plants, together with the workers employed in them, into the interior. This stripped Congress areas of machinery and skilled labour. Before any plans for industrialisation could be considered, a long period of reconstruction was necessary. In agriculture, land reform was the most pressing issue. For it to be successful, the vested interests of the still powerful landed gentry had to be broken. This had to occur in areas previously under Austrian and Russian administration. To do so, the first governments had to be bold and determined to modernise both sectors of the economy.

The first elections to the national assembly, the Sejm, took place in January 1919. The so-called Small Constitution was approved on

20 February 1919. This outlined the future political profile of the new Polish state. Poland was to be a republic. But the precise details of the relationship between the legislature and the executive were still to be agreed by a constitutional commission. Piłsudski remained the Head of State, even though he was involved in dispute with the Sejm. The government focused on the need to build state and regional administrative structures. In the meantime, political parties concentrated on the constitutional commission. They hoped to influence it in order to ensure control of the future legislature. In the meantime, Piłsudski was fully preoccupied in reforming and building up the new army. He was then able to deploy it in the eastern borderland. This gave him a patriotic aura. At the same time, it elevated the military leadership and the army to an apparent position above politics. He clearly appropriated a critical role in defining Poland's borders. However, while doing this, the military leadership was also determined to have a say on future relations between the legislature and the military. In effect, the leadership tried to limit any attempts to restrict military budgets and to control the activities of the new Polish army. The military leaders were usually Piłsudski's close collaborators and fellow legionnaires. During these conflicts, they established an unchallenged political position. They were aided by the Sejm's dedication of over 58 per cent of the national budget to military reforms. The military's power during this period was enhanced by its direct control over munitions production and armament industries. The government committed extensive funds, in anticipation of the need to defend the new state.

The final draft of the constitution was adopted on 17 March 1921. It was based on the French example. It was the result of extensive manoeuvring between parties dominating the first Sejm. The conflict between Dmowski and Piłsudski had not subsided. On the contrary, their disagreements continued by other means. The national democrats hoped to use the legislature as a counter balance to Piłsudski's presidential ambitions. Thus, they ensured that the presidency was weak and that the legislature was strong.

The emergence of the Polish state and the establishment of proper constitutional procedures were accompanied by the process of forming parties. Before the First World War, each party needed to address specific problems, which arose in a given partition zone.

Efforts were made to broaden the debates. However, the character of parties and organisations had been moulded differently. With the emergence of independent Poland, parties needed to form national organisations. This, in turn, opened up debates on ideological and doctrinal issues. Where unity was achieved across former partition borders, it was frequently fragile. The basis of such unity was often just personality or ideology, rather than a political programme.

During the first elections, the socialists' showing was very low. They only polled 9 per cent of votes cast in the previous Congress areas, in comparison with 45 per cent secured by the national democrats. Thus, the unity congress of the socialist parties of the three partition areas consolidated the movement into a national party. In addition, it defined its objectives with reference to the most pressing issues of the time. By then, the radical left had largely parted company with the socialist movement and formed a Communist Party. Nevertheless, during the interwar period, Polish socialism embraced a wide spectrum of ideas.

The socialist movement fully supported Piłsudski's policies of extending Poland's borders in the East. Initially it formed a provisional administration in Lublin. The socialists accepted Piłsudski becoming the Head of State. He entrusted the task of forming a government to the socialist Jędrzej Moraczewski. After this auspicious start, relations between Piłsudski and the socialists deteriorated. Instead, Piłsudski sought to sideline the party. Even though Moraczewski supported the Piłsudski coup, no socialist was again to head a government during the interwar period.[20]

The congress met between 27 and 28 of April 1919. The socialist movement was dominated by members from the Congress areas. Over one third of the Congress socialists supported the radical left wing call for the destruction of the bourgeois government and establishment of a revolutionary authority in the form of workers' councils. In the course of debates, the left wing was defeated. Most socialists supported a non-revolutionary programme of collaboration with the state. The final programme of the Polska Partia Socjalistyczna (Polish Socialist Party – PPS) was agreed at the XVII party congress. They met in May 1921. In the intervening period the party moved towards the right. It instructed its members to leave the workers' councils which had sprung up in the industrial areas. Instead, they were to support the creation of socialist trade unions. The councils either disbanded or were destroyed as part of the government's attempt to break workers' strikes. These flared up in industrial areas.[21]

An important factor in the socialists' move towards a parliamentary road was the strength of the national issue. The new state embarked on what was seen as a fight to defend its independence and define its borders. Whilst this happened, socialist leaders had to be clear on their and the party's attitude to Poland's relations with its neighbours. Poland's unwillingness to accept the wishes of the Ukrainian and Byelorussian communities to independence was in stark contrast with their claims to self-determination. Leaders of the PPS uneasily supported Piłsudski's military campaigns. At the same time, they tried to find a formula which would define their own policy on the rights of national minorities forcibly incorporated into the borders of the new Polish state. The national issue became an important topic in party debates, particularly as PPS branches in Upper Silesia and Cieszyn demanded support for the inclusion of these regions into Poland. During the fighting with Russia, the Red Army advanced towards Warsaw. At this point, defence of the state took priority over any doctrinaire debate of the role of the revolutionary state.

The PPS programme developed in a varied and complex way in response to these challenges. On the one hand, Polish socialists rejected the dictatorship of the proletariat as their immediate aim. Instead, they committed themselves to supporting the democratic parliamentary system in Poland. On the other hand, radical social and economic objectives remained important elements of the PPS programme. Thus, the party expressed its hope that the army and police would in due course disband and be replaced with people's militias. Equality of access to education, to work and state-funded retirement were to be important pillars of a new just society in independent Poland. In the economic sphere, the PPS referred to workers' councils assuming a managerial role in factories and enterprises. Control of economic resources for the common good was an important guiding principle of the PPS. The party programme referred to the socialisation of key industries as well as expropriation of large landed estates. The party, nevertheless, distinguished immediate objectives from these ultimate goals. They were defined as the need to gain seats in the Sejm and to enter into electoral arrangements with other parties in order to be able to participate in coalition governments. In the long term, the party would strive towards the establishment of a society based on socialist principles. In its desire to secure its immediate objectives, inevitably, the radical aims became a dead letter. The party leadership would moved to the right during the interwar period. During the 1922 elections, the PPS increased the number of deputies in the Sejm from 35 to 41. Together with the PSL and the ND, it dominated the political life of interwar Poland.

From the outset, relations between Polish socialists and other European socialist parties were strained. The international socialist movement expressed disapproval of Poland's occupation of Wilno and military action against Russia. This was something which most Polish socialists supported. In 1921, the Second International was reconstituted. The PPS found itself outmanoeuvred by the German and Czech socialist movements, which dominated the Second International. The question of Poland's claim to Upper Silesia and the Polish-Czechoslovak conflict over Cieszyn soured relations between the PPS and the Second International. In 1921, the Poles left the Second International. In 1923, the PPS rejoined the International. In spite of this, relations between the Poles and the International, remained bad throughout the interwar period. Though they approved fully of its move towards an active anti-fascist policy after 1933.[22]

On 16 December 1918, the Komunistyczna Partia Robotnicza Polski (Communist Workers Party of Poland – KPRP) emerged from the unification of the SDKPiL with the PPS-Lewica. This was not an unexpected development. The emergence of the KPRP was a logical conclusion of debates and divisions. These had manifested themselves before the war. However, they were intensified during the war by the question of the socialist movement's support for the war effort. The outbreak of the Russian Revolution drove the final wedge between the moderate and radical wings of the socialist movement. The Bolshevik seizure of power in October drove this wedge further in. Militant workers spontaneously formed workers' councils in industrial parts of Poland. When this happened, SDKPiL and PPS-Lewica decided to act in unison and guide the revolutionary

workers. The Menshevik belief was that capitalist democracy was
the inevitable next stage in history. SDKPiL and PPS-Lewica took
the Bolshevik line and distanced themselves from this belief. The
two left wing parties came together to direct the militant workers
towards an immediate objective of a proletarian revolution. Lenin's
policy allowed national groups the right to self-determination. The
KPRP disagreed with this. Instead, true to their Luxemburgist roots,
the KPRP rejected the call for an independent Poland. The party
continued to manifest what Lenin described as an 'infantile left
wing disorder'. They rejected cooperation with the peasants and
advocated the socialisation of land, rather than its redistribution.
This had been the Bolsheviks' policy during the early stages of the
Russian revolution.[23] The KPRP was so confident of the inevitability
of the revolution in Poland, that it decided not to stand in the first
elections. This was because an independent Poland was seen as a
transitory stage. During the Polish conflict with the Soviet Union,
the KPRP advocated support for the Red Army. This inevitably alienated the militant workers with whom the KPRP had collaborated
in the early stages in the formation of the workers' councils. The
Red Army entered ethnically Polish areas and formed a revolutionary committee in the town of Białystok. No attempt was made to
appoint Polish communists to this or other regional committees,
which the Red Army military commanders tried to establish in the
wake of their success.[24] Thus, from the outset, relations between the
Soviet Union and the Third International (Comintern) on the one
hand, and the Polish communists, on the other, were fraught. The
Poles took an ultra-leftist position.

The KPRP was in due course, renamed Komunistyczna Partia Polski (Communist Party of Poland – KPP). It remained a small party. It
had only limited appeal in a society in which nationalist sentiments
were a strong element of political life. The party was unwilling to
associate with the new Polish state and supported the Red Army.
In addition to this, the demise of the workers' council had briefly
offered the Communists a platform for their activism. All of this
reduced the KPRP's membership. Throughout the interwar period,
the KPP failed to build a base within the Polish working class. Party
calls for general strikes tended to go unheeded. They had qualified
successes in attracting Jewish membership and were popular among

the Ukrainian communities. However, these were of limited value, and tended to confirm perceptions that the party was an alien political force in Poland. The party failed to gain support within the working class. One of the factors was its continuing ambiguity on the nationality issue. The party supported the German minority's call for the inclusion of the disputed areas in the Corridor, Danzig and Upper Silesia, into Germany. This puzzling policy came about because of the Comintern's view that Germany was more important in plans for a future European revolution. In the circumstances, Polish communists were expected to advocate policies which would increase the German communists' popular appeal. However, these also undermined their own standing in Polish society.[25]

During the period after 1934, most European communist parties moved to the popular frontist line of forging anti-fascist collaboration with socialist parties. KPP remained reluctant to commit itself to this policy. There were earlier attempts made by the PPS and PSL, to build unity on the basis of opposition to the post-May 1926 government. However, these were unsuccessful. The leadership of KPP remained wedded to its doctrinaire view that the PPS and the peasant parties were 'social-fascists'. They failed to note the PPS and peasant parties' efforts in the defence of democracy. The rank and file in many cases did not follow the party line and allied itself with striking workers and peasants. This was especially the case during the general strike in March 1936.[26]

In August 1937, Stalin authorised the liquidation of all KPP leaders who were in exile in the Soviet Union. This purge was extended to the murder of Polish communists who were taking part in the Spanish Civil War. Sixty-nine per cent of the members of the Central Committee were thus murdered. Those who survived, owed this to the fact that they were in Polish prisons and were not able to heed the call to present themselves in Moscow. By September 1938, all KPP cells in Poland were dissolved. The precise reasons for this action still remain unclear. The official accusations levelled against the Polish comrades, varied from the suggestion that the party had been infiltrated by the Polish police, to statements that the party had succumbed to doctrinaire deviation.[27]

When independence was regained, 76 per cent of Poland's population lived in villages. The pattern of land ownership had both economic and political implications. Sixty-four per cent of farms were described as smallholdings or dwarf holdings. In areas previously under Austrian control, rural poverty was endemic. The western regions, which had previously been under German control, were most advanced. Considering Poland's agrarian base, the peasant parties should have dominated the Sejm during the interwar period. Land reform was the key demand from the villages. The singular importance of this demand should have further focused the loyalties of the village community. Unfortunately, the peasants' representatives in the Sejm were divided along economic and regional lines. The two main peasant parties were PSL-Wyzwolenie and PSL-Piast. They represented the two main strands of the debate until 1931, when a decision was made to unite. PSL-Wyzwolenie was established in 1915. It advocated cooperation with the socialist movement and was generally seen as a left wing party. PSL-Piast was dominated by Witos. They preferred to ally themselves with the national democrats. The first elections were in 1919. The peasant parties jointly secured 118 deputies. These represented one third of the Sejm. Forty-four deputies represented PSL-Wyzwolenie. 70 were from PSL-Piast. An additional four deputies were from the Radical Peasant Alliance. All the peasant parties supported land reform. The PSL-Piast, represented landowners and wealthy peasants. They spoke of compensation and proper use of land. The other two, however, advocated that land should belong to those who toil it.[28]

When it came to implementing land reform, successive governments baulked at approving wholesale land redistribution. This was not only due to strong opposition from within the community of landowners. Redistribution of land raised the spectre of destruction of large surplus-producing estates and their replacement with small inefficient farms. The first Land Reform Act was passed by the Sejm on 10 July 1919. It was limited. Only in the borderlands were the authorities robust in expropriating landowners. They were especially robust when the landowners belonged to the non-Polish minority. Land freed in this way was distributed to Polish colonists. Many of these had been demobilised soldiers. In this way, the authorities hoped to strengthen Polish presence. In addition to this, they hoped to increase the security of the Polish state in areas where loyalty to the new state was weak. These solutions did little to alleviate local land hunger. However, they contributed to the deterioration of relations with the Ukrainian community. The Ukrainian community was not allowed to benefit from the land redistribution. On 15 July 1920, the Red Army moved into Polish territories. The government was fearful that the peasant community might not support the Polish government. They therefore approved a seemingly radical land reform package. When the national emergency ceased, the landowners and politicians were unwilling to implement it. The peasant parties increasingly allied themselves with the national democrats. They too were less willing to champion the cause of poor and landless peasants. During the following years, the land reform momentum was lost. Landowners disputed the peasants' right to land. In many cases, they called in troops to evict peasants from land they had taken over during the war and the turbulent post-war years. By 1925, a new law extended the rights of the landowners. This, in essence, ended any hopes of a future radical land redistribution.[29]

Three were peasant parties in 1919. The two largest were the PSL-Piast and PSL-Wyzwolenie. They were cautious about collaboration. Both parties appreciated the need to overcome their differences and to speak with one voice in the Sejm. Nevertheless, in the politics of interwar Poland, parties still defined themselves in terms of their regional origins. This proved near impossible as parties were therefore dominated by personality cults. Regional particularism played a role in the two parties' failure to cooperate. In addition to this, their different political programmes and specific membership played a role. PSL-Piast clung to its roots in the Austrian Empire and its leader Witos could not overcome his hostility to Piłsudski. PSL-Wyzwolenie emerged during the war in Warsaw and supported Piłsudski. PSL-Wyzwolenie advocated radical land reform and an egalitarian social policy. This was a genuine peasant party, which had an antagonistic attitude towards large landowners.[30] PSL-Piast, on the other hand, supported an evolutionary process of transformation. They believed that the village community could cooperate in implementing necessary land reforms and the party emphasised national unity. In 1924, the party was to see a move towards right wing policies. This was especially the case when Witos advocated the strengthening of the executive against the legislature. On economic questions, he called for the lifting of the ban on export of grain. This, which he believed, would increase peasant income. The government, however, feared that this would increase the price of food in Poland.[31] Many of PSL Piast's members belonged to the middle peasant strata. Agronomists and intellectuals were also among its members. In addition, the party also attracted poorer peasants. In spite of disunity within the peasant movement, the peasant parties played a pivotal role in the coalition governments of the period up until 1926. Witos acted as Prime Minister on three occasions. He notably formed the centre-right government on 12 May 1926. This was overthrown by Piłsudski's coup.

During 1926–27, Poland's economic situation had improved because of increased demand for Polish coal. This had been caused by the General Strike in Britain and the rising prices of agrarian products. This, in turn, improved the standard of living of middle class and wealthy peasants who formed the majority of the PSL-Piast base.

The dominant political grouping of the interwar period was the alliance of national democrats with a number of Christian parties. Dmowski remained the leading figure of the nationalist right. During the latter stages of the Paris Conference, his role had been eclipsed by the arrival of Ignacy Paderewski. He was Poland's Prime Minister and Minister for Foreign Affairs. He took over the chairmanship of the delegation. When Dmowski returned to Poland in May 1920, he was an aggrieved man. Piłsudski was determined to sideline him and diminish his contribution to the Paris Peace Talks. In the meantime, he made sure that his own military leadership, in the conflicts that defined Poland's eastern borders, was kept in the public eye.[32] Dmowski and his followers believed that they had been denied their right to form the first government by Piłsudski's alliance with left wing parties. The nationalist group was the largest political grouping in the Sejm. Therefore their claims were not without foundation. Nevertheless, during the period 1920–22, Dmowski believed the situation was not ripe for the nationalists to challenge Piłsudski. At the same time, the nationalist bloc experienced problems in adjusting to the establishment of an independent Polish state. This had been the main point of the nationalists' programme. Dmowski was convinced that the national democrats still had to gain enough political experience before they could go on the offensive. However, to some, he appeared to be holding back his followers. This, in turn, irritated the younger generation of nationalists. They were increasingly moving towards radical right wing ideas. Dmowski found it difficult to work within the framework of a parliamentary democracy, while not understanding the new currents within the nationalist movement. He felt detached from the new political realities. At times, he even felt alienated from the very movement which he had created. It was now increasingly being led by new men. The nationalist camp assumed the name of Związek Ludowo-Narodowy (National Populist Union – ZLN). During the 1922 general elections, it secured 98 seats. This was the largest showing by a single party. However, it was not enough to form a government. In November 1922, the second elections in the newly formed Polish state took place. The national democrats allied with the christian democrats and a number of other small right wing parties. Jointly, they won 169 seats. However, they were not able to form a government. The right-Christian grouping came to be known as Chjena. They opened talks with Witos, the leader of the Peasant Party – Piast faction. They had 70 seats. The result was that in May 1923, the national democrats and the Peasant Party – Piast agreed to talks on forming a government. With the success of the talks, they succeeded in achieving their aim in October, though the result was a highly unstable coalition government.[33]

In 1922, the election results signalled the potential importance of the national minorities. These combined to form the Blok Mniejszości Narodowej (Block of National Minorities – BMN). They secured 87 seats in the Sejm and 25 in the Senate. In this way, the Block became the second largest parliamentary grouping. Nevertheless, throughout the interwar period, the national minorities failed to arrive at a common programme. This was inevitable as the Ukrainian, Jewish, Byelorussian and German communities were only united in their anxiety about the Polish government's policies on the nationality question.

Political life, during the interwar period, continued to be characterised by extreme instability. This, in turn, made it difficult to address very real economic problems. The picture was complex. Lack of political experience and the leading parties' failure to arrive at a working consensus, blighted all attempts to achieve any political aims. The 1921 Constitution was a compromise. It did not provide for a strong executive. Successive governments had been put together as a result of prolonged negotiations. They had little chance of finding solutions to problems which faced them all. A next round of negotiations predictably followed each government's inevitable fall. Piłsudski manoeuvred to reduce the political power of the national democrats. The national democrats later made sure the presidency was weak. The numerically strong peasant parties failed to speak with one voice. This reduced their effectiveness on a national level. PSL-Wyzwolenie and the smaller radical peasant parties hoped to enter into coalition agreements with the PPS. In the meantime, Witos manoeuvred to lead the largest peasant party towards an agreement with the nationalists. The PSL-Piast played a pivotal role between the two options. Because of this, successive governments were unstable. In the meantime, hyperinflation and failure to implement land reform, caused economic distress and anger.

The November 1922 elections to the Sejm and the Senate were followed by presidential elections in which Piłsudski refused to stand. Witos conducted extensive negotiations with a view to forming a government with the national democrats. In the meantime, their candidate to the presidency was defeated. The peasant and left wing parties were joined by parties representing national minorities in voting for Gabriel Narutowicz to become Poland's president. As a result, the Endecja started a vicious campaign against Narutowicz. On 16 December 1922, a fanatic, belonging to the nationalist movement, assassinated the President. The nationalists and their opponents took to the streets. The internal situation was stabilised by the appointment of a military man, General Władysław Sikorski, as Prime Minister and Stanisław Wojciechowski as President. They restored order by means of emergency laws. The peasant parties had jointly supported Wojciechowski's candidacy.

Nevertheless, in 1923, PSL-Piast and the nationalist bloc reached an agreement to form a government. The centre-Christian coalition resulted in some degree of social and economic stability. But this came at a price. Dmowski briefly took the post of Minister for Foreign Affairs and was able to put into effect his policies of rapprochement with the Soviet Union. He considered these to be but a transient phenomenon. The nationalists continued to view Germany as the main enemy of the Polish state. Dmowski was generally judged to have been a failure in parliamentary politics. He effectively withdrew from active politics and concentrated on developing a long-term strategy for the nationalist bloc.

The Weimar Republic's policies of economic warfare against Poland, bode ill for the future. Nevertheless, participation in the centre-Christian coalition, discredited PSL-Piast. The army was deployed against striking workers who had been hit by the 1923 inflation. Peasants fared little better. Progress made with land reform had stalled earlier, when landowners challenged the legislation in the courts. The deadlock was broken and compulsory redistribution of land went ahead. Although this was with full compensation for the landowners.

A brief period of stability came with the formation of a government of specialists. Headed by the economist Władysław Grabski, it was supported by parties on the left and right of the political spectrum. It was given the authority to implement long overdue currency reforms and to pass further land reform legislation. The period of economic stabilisation coincided with a tariff war waged by Germany. This was supposed to weaken the Polish state. When Grabski resigned in November 1925, economic and political instability followed.

The instability of successive governments suited Piłsudski. In spite of his ostensible retirement to his villa in Sulejówek, he was determined to highlight the governments' apparent failure to defend national interests. He and those around him encouraged the emergence of the Piłsudski myth, in which he was portrayed as the father of the new Polish state and a man above party politics. In reality, he strengthened his power base within the army and fought off all attempts to reform it and reduce his influence within the military organisations. Another government appeared likely. This time it was to be led by Witos, and included the national democrats. When this happened, Piłsudski decided to stage a military coup d'état against the civilian authorities.[34]

At the time, parliamentary democracy appeared ill prepared to deal with the growing economic problems. During the latter part

of 1925, unemployment increased, prices rose and banks faced liq-
uidity problems. The government appeared unable to put forward
solutions. Other European states had faced similar difficulties. Italy
and Spain had replaced weak parliamentary governments with a
dictatorship dedicated to what was perceived to be the search for
solutions. These were often used as examples of what would benefit
the nation as a whole. Thus, a common currency within political
circes was the idea of replacing inefficient and corrupt elected governments, with either a government of specialists, or a nationally
accepted leader. In October 1922, Mussolini marched on Rome. In
September 1923, Primo de Rivera staged a military coup in Spain.
These two events suggested a way out of the morass in which Poland
appeared to find itself. There were several assumptions that these
two examples had in common with Piłsudski's own plans. Firstly
was the assumption that the army would not remain loyal to the
government and that it would support the leader of the coup. Sec-
ondly, that the community as a whole, including most political
parties, would tacitly, if not openly, support the overthrow of the
weak government. Finally, that a process of national regeneration
would form the main plank of the post-coup political platform.

The excuse for the coup was provided by the resignation of the
government. It was precipitated by the National Bank, refusing to
offer further loans to support the budget. After extensive negotiations, the President had to accept the only viable coalition. This
was the coalition of PSL-Piast with the national democrats. Piłsudski
made the decision to overthrow the newly formed government. In
doing this, he knew he could count on popular support. There were
economic problems and successive governments had been obviously unable to assure stability. This had led to criticism of party
politics. At the same time, the formation of a government based on
two controversial parties was something he hoped to turn to his advantage. On 12 May Piłsudski, supported by troops of whose loyalty
he was assured, went to Warsaw. They hoped to confront President
Wojciechowski with a statement of a demand by the army that the
recently formed Witos government should be dismissed. The two
men missed each other and instead troops were massed on the two
key bridges. The President was known to be unhappy with the newly
formed government. Nevertheless, he refused to accept Piłsudski's

demand. Furthermore, not all military units abandoned the government. Several high-ranking military leaders also disapproved of Piłsudski's actions, most notably his colleague, General Kazimierz Sosnkowski. In the early evening, Piłsudski met the President in a theatrical stand-off on the bridge. Conflict was inevitable. The government and President withdrew from the capital. In the meantime, 379 people died during fighting between troops loyal to the government, and those under Piłsudski's command.[35] All left wing parties, notably the PPS, but also the peasant parties, with the exception of PSL-Piast, declared their support for Piłsudski's actions. On 14 May, the government and President resigned. Piłsudski successfully presented the army's actions as above politics and in support of the stability. This played a decisive role. His own image was that of a man unsullied by the corruption, which supposedly characterised parliamentary politics. His rhetoric of moral regeneration also played a role in reducing and disarming the opposition. During the months preceding the May coup, a carefully orchestrated propaganda campaign had prepared the public for the acceptance of what was presented as a moral crusade.[36] The appearance of legality was completed when, in the hastily prepared presidential elections, Piłsudski won an outright majority against the national democrat candidate. He then refused to assume the office of president. He instead nominated Ignacy Mościcki. He became a compliant President, not one to challenge either Piłsudski or the army.

Piłsudski's own aspirations appeared to be limited. He neither disbanded the Sejm, nor did he establish a personal dictatorship. Initially, repression was minimal and the main focus of official policies was the restoration of economic stability; cleansing of government organisations of corruption and focus on national interests. Before the coup, and certainly in the years that followed, those associated with Piłsudski sought to portray the coup as an act of moral renewal. Successive governments had failed to deal with pressing economic and political issues. This was put down to the party leaders' corruption, moral failures and self-interest. In contrast, the image of the army and of Piłsudski was of men who would selflessly dedicate themselves to rooting out these failures and, through that, bring about a healing process. Much of the public believed the propaganda generated by the Piłsudski camp. They felt that few politicians had shown genuine interest in larger social and political reforms in the period since Poland had gained independence. In the process of renewal, it was promised that justice and social issues would be addressed as well as principles governing political decision making.[37]

Piłsudski's policies were undoubtedly very confusing to party leaders. This explains their failure to anticipate the way the ruling coterie gathered power into its hands. By not dissolving the Sejm and supporting the formation of a new government, Piłsudski's coup had initially appeared not to challenge the existing party and democratic structures. While the nationalists had good reasons to be anxious, Piłsudski's socialist past led the PPS and peasant party leaders to hope for radical reforms. In reality, Piłsudski had no intention of promoting radical reforms. Nor was he clear as to what economic policy to pursue. His own ideas on governance were initially limited to ensuring that legislation was introduced which redressed the relationship between the legislature and executive, in favour of the latter.[38] A Bill for Constitutional Changes was approved by the Sejm in July. This increased the power of the presidency, vesting it with extensive powers. On two occasions, Piłsudski became Prime Minister. But even when ostensibly not in office, his authority was unchallenged. His power base remained the army, which was purged of those who disagreed with the coup. Until his death, Piłsudski held the Ministry of Defence portfolio and occupied the newly created post of General Inspector of Military Forces. In 1926, there were attempts by Sejm deputies to challenge the army. These were resolved through the use of premeditated brutality. Officers invaded the Sejm, disrupted the meetings and beat up a prominent deputy who criticised attempts to increase the army budget. During the 1928 general elections, Piłsudski and his supporters consolidated their position. They first formed a ruling party and then extended the army's control over all aspects of civilian life. The Bezpartyjny Blok Współpracy z Rządem (Non-Party Block for Co-operation with the Government – BBWR) was in reality no more than a means of consolidating the military's control over the political life of Poland. It won a majority in the 1928 elections.[39]

The 1926 coup initially divided the main political parties. PSL-Wyzwolenie approved of the coup. They saw it as a means of preventing the national democrats from gaining power. Only when Piłsudski failed to appoint socialists to the new government and when the post-May government approved attacks on strikers did the party face up to the full implications of what had happened. By that time PSL-Piast had realised that the main thrust of Piłsudski's attack was the national democrats. They shifted from initial condemnation of the coup to a conciliatory line. This shift occurred in 1928. The first moment of reflection came after the general elections. In these, the peasant parties' representation in the Sejm was reduced to one fifth of the number of deputies. Government policies, aimed at limiting the importance of the legislature, led to further soul-searching. During that year, the peasant parties came to realise that the defence of democracy required them to close ranks. Anxiety about the Piłsudski regime forging alliances with large landowners and the consequences of the burden of taxation falling onto the rural community were factors in the peasant parties' assessment of the situation. However, the conviction that democracy was under attack and that it was up to the toiling people to defend it, motivated the peasant leaders to speak out against the government. In 1929, against a background of increased attacks on the Sejm and its deputies, left wing parties combined together with the peasant parties and Christian Democrats to form a centre-left (in Polish – Centrolew) Sejm opposition grouping.[40] In 1930, the economic crisis gripped Poland. The government's response was the launch of an attack on the Centrolew parties, mainly the PPS and PSL-Piast. During the night of 9–10 September, leaders of the opposition were arrested and incarcerated in the fortress of Brześć. A show trial was staged during the following year. In this, all were accused of having planned to overthrow the government. Following a disastrous showing in the general elections of September 1930, the peasant parties made the critical decision to unite. The Stronnictwo Ludowe (Peasant Movement – SL) marked a high point in the development of that movement. As its main objective, the new peasant party put forward the defence of democracy and the fight against the dictatorship. During his imprisonment, Witos had had time to reflect on the reasons why Piłsudski had been able to undermine the Sejm. It was a bitter moment for political leaders like him, who had dedicated their lives to the fight for a proper representative political system, to see it challenged on grounds that this had led to establishment of institutions incapable of dealing with real economic problems.[41] Unity within the peasant movement represented an impressive organisational achievement. However, the Piłsudski military regime was firmly in control. Witos fled to Czechoslovakia. From there, he continued to direct the peasant movement, which organised waves of peasant strikes, most notably in 1937.

The 1930 elections were conducted in an atmosphere of intimidation. In these elections, BBWR won a majority. Centrolew secured 17.7 per cent and the nationalist bloc 7.1 per cent. The Piłsudski camp could consider changing the constitution. By then, what had started with hopes for a process of renewal had become a corrupt military-dominated regime, with no ideology other than a desire to maintain a grip on power. In this, Piłsudski was assured of the support of the large landowners, with whom he had sought reconciliation after the May coup. An assurance was given to the landowners that the government would not implement further land reform legislation. The industrialists were confident that the government would not support the PPS. They called for extending protective legislation and lent their support to the BBWR.

On 23 April 1935, the regime succeeded in changing the constitution. Introducing presidential rule, it reduced the prerogatives of the elected assembly. It should have been a legal framework for Piłsudski's vision of the rule of a strong man. However, it came too late. On 12 May Piłsudski died. He left a coterie of military henchmen to continue governing Poland. The so-called rule of the colonels was characterised by the increased process of militarisation of state and economic institutions.[42]

The Polish economy showed the first signs of emerging out of the depression only in 1933. This late date was due to the economy being based on agriculture. This continued to be in recession for longer than the industrial sector. A further factor which influenced the late recovery was dependence on foreign capital. This continued to shun Poland. Nevertheless, 1935 witnessed the first solid signs of recovery. This was a period associated with the policies of Deputy Prime Minister Eugeniusz Kwiatkowski. He worked on a wide-ranging national economic programme. His Four Year Plan and the following plan were approved in 1938. In these, he envisaged the development of an internal economy and an industrial takeoff based on armament industries. Thus, his economic vision had two objectives – to lift Poland out of economic backwardness and to establish it as a regional power. The central plank of his Four Year Plan was the creation of a Central Industrial Zone (Centralny Okręg Przemysłowy – COP). This envisaged the development of mainly munitions- and armament-related industries in the triangle between the rivers Dunajec, Wisła and the San. COP was developed in an area which, it was believed, would be beyond the range of German and Soviet military planes. Assisted by extensive government funds and French loans, COP did indeed promise to form the basis of Poland's industrial takeoff. At the time of the outbreak of the war, Polish economic performance appeared to be improving. Its basis, however, was not sufficiently solid to assure the army of a victory.[43]

The years 1935–39 were a time when the military regime appears to have degenerated into no more than a gravy train for Piłsudski's coterie of military men. He initially portrayed itself as a force for regeneration and renewal. However, ultimately, the colonels presided over financial mismanagement and oppression. In 1926, the officer core commanded the nations respect. However, in the late 1930s, this was no longer the case. Both in the left and the right, as in all other parties, younger leaders were untainted by support for the coup in 1926. They voiced disaffection and anger with the government's policies.

Poland, in common with many European states, experienced a deep political polarisation. On the right, the national democrats found that radical elements within the nationalist movement wanted to see action and were weary with parliamentary politics. Of the splinter groups which emerged during this period, the Falanga was modelled on the Italian Fascist Party and led by Bolesław Piasecki. It was noted for its violent anti-Semitic action within universities. The national democrats called for a boycott of Jewish businesses. In effect, they blamed the Jewish community for Poland's economic difficulties.

The Peasant Party and the socialists watched the nationalists and the extreme right with deep anxiety. They were, in particular, fearful that the nationalists would be able to appeal to the peasant

community and disaffected workers through their policy of direct
action and stage-managed events at universities and against Jewish-
owned shops. Thus, briefly in 1937, the two discussed the formation
of a peasant left alliance. This came to nothing. Although the peasant movement did briefly threaten the government. In August 1937,
peasant strikes virtually cut off food supplies to the cities. The peasants called for a moratorium on debt repayments and for economic
aid to help with high levels of indebtedness caused by payments
for land obtained under the land reform acts. As the result of a
split within the SL leadership, the decision was made to attack the
government. Witos called for an all-out attack on the ruling military coterie. Maciej Rataj, the chairman of the SL, had doubts about
the effectiveness of strikes and was anxious about the likely consequences of relations. In the end, the decision was made to call for
a peasant strike. This led to Rataj resigning.[44] The government's response was to send in troops. In battles which followed, 44 peasants
were killed and thousands were arrested.

Under the patronage of the pianist Igancy Paderewski, several political leaders in exile met in Switzerland to discuss forming a united
opposition to the post-Piłsudski regime. This came to be known as
the Front Morges, from the place where Paderewski resided. The
leading light of this grouping was General Władysław Sikorski. He
was an opponent of Piłsudski and a bitter critic of his successors.
Witos and Herman Lieberman took part in the talks in Morges.
Witos represented the peasant movement. Lieberman was a socialist and a victim of the Brześć trials. In the end, these meetings, took
place far away and were cut off from the reality of what was happening in Poland. They were of little more than symbolic importance.

The Piłsudski led coup resulted in confusion within the Socialist Party. Many hoped that he would turn to the PPS. This did not
happen. Instead, Piłsudski established closer relations with leading
landowners. The army remained his main power base in the gradual
process of reducing the authority of the elected assembly. By 1928,
PPS decided to ally itself with a number of centre parties, most notably the two peasant parties. In 1930, the opposition parties, united
in the Centrolew, went into attack. The regime retaliated by arresting all the leaders, including those from the PPS. Norbet Barlicki,

Adam Pragier, Herman Lieberman, and Stanisław Dubois were all incarcerated in Brześć. Here, most were severely beaten and tortured.[45] During the following years, the party was in disarray. Some advocated an outright fight against the Sanacja regime. Others suggested a moderate response, remaining within the law. The latter trend dominated the leadership, through the party rank and file. They increasingly appeared to want to take the battle against the government, to the streets. During the mid-1930s, the PPS agreed to limited cooperation with the KPP, the Jewish Socialist Party, the Bund and with trade unions. This was mainly in order to form a popular front opposed to the post-Piłsudski regime. One of the options considered by the PPS was unity with the peasant parties. Before the outbreak of the Second World War, these ideas found a ready echo within the PPS leadership. Nevertheless, there were always those who preferred not to commit the party to any cooperation which would have limited the party's freedom of action.[46] The growth of German threat in 1938, meant that the PPS leadership was reluctant to challenge the government. This, in effect, allowed the government to present its policies as the defence of national interests. This was a formulation which made it difficult to criticise the government's internal and foreign policies.

# 4  The Outbreak and the Course of the Second World War

The 1930s was dominated by concerns over the rise of the radical right in Europe. In 1933, the Nazi Party came to power in Germany. Feelings of foreboding gripped European capitals. In their propaganda statements, the Nazis made it clear that they would seek the revision of the Versailles Treaty. Their hostility towards Poland and Czechoslovakia was known and was not unique to the Nazi Party. Thus, few European observers doubted that the security situation in Europe would change dramatically. In Poland, there was an awareness that throughout the Weimar period, successive German governments had consistently refused to accept the loss of previously German territories to the new Polish state. This compounded the sense of anxious anticipation. In September 1939, Poland faced the full might of the German attack. In spite of the inevitability of this attack, the country was badly prepared for war. Furthermore, in spite of having earlier signed agreements with France and Great Britain, neither state provided military support to Poland.

Following the First World War, France formed the cornerstone of Polish security plans. In spite of the shared anxiety about Germany, relations between the two states proved difficult. On the Polish side, frustrated expectations cast a cloud over dealings with Paris. The Poles had hoped that France would treat Poland as its key eastern ally. The Polish ruling elite were Francophiles, along with the strata of the landed gentry from which officers in the armed forces were recruited. Indeed, the Poles were under the impression that a restored Poland would replace Russia in French military plans. This was encouraged by French military support for Poland during the war with the Soviet Union. In the years that followed, military contacts between Poland and France remained strong. The Polish military academy was established by the French and most military leaders looked to France for up to date doctrines and equipment.

French governments did not reciprocate these sentiments. Independent Polish and Czechoslovak states emerged and, at the end of the First World War, a revolutionary government was established. This required the West European Powers, most notably France, to reassess their previous foreign policy. Before and during the war, Russia formed the cornerstone of the military and political concept of an eastern front. The purpose of this was to maintain effective security on two fronts against Germany. Immediately after the war, the future of Russia appeared unclear. There was some hope that, in due course, a liberal government would be established there. French foreign policymakers kept this option open. At the same time, they investigated the possibility of building up a pro-French bloc, based on Poland and Czechoslovakia. It later became clear that the revolutionary government in Russia would not collapse swiftly. This reduced support for the White Russian forces. Poland's position in French thinking continued to be subject to a number of contradictory considerations. Most importantly, it was believed that Poland did not have the military and economic capacity to form a durable eastern front. Throughout the interwar period, France, in principle, had been willing to support Poland as a possible barrier to German expansion to the East. However, in the new circumstances, France was willing to consider other options. This made Polish politicians uncertain as to the extent to which they could count on France's support.[1]

As a result, successive Polish governments were always disappointed with what they considered limited French support. Initially, Polish leaders had hoped that France would take a direct interest in Poland's economic and military development. When this did not happen, they became frustrated at France's apparent unwillingness to make large-scale commitments to Poland. In February 1921, the Franco-Polish Political and Military Convention was signed. This did not stop France from entering into agreements with Britain and

Germany to secure France's western border. The latter initiatives resulted in the conclusion of the Locarno Treaty. This offered France
security, in the event of an unprovoked German attack. Nevertheless, France still felt it prudent to reaffirm its agreement with Poland,
by signing the Treaty of Mutual Guarantee in October 1925. At the
same time, the French government remained interested in Russia
and the option of a treaty with the Soviet Union was maintained.
This was a source of constant irritation to the Poles. Poland was
Germany's most likely object of attack. This decreased the French
governments' willingness to underwrite Poland's security. In any
case, there were many unresolved territorial conflicts between
Poland, the Soviet Union and Czechoslovakia. This made it impossible for France to bring the three states together to build a regional security bloc. Efforts to strengthen and define France's commitments
to Polish security were strained. This was due to Franco-German relations throughout the 1920s. The other element in Polish security
calculations was the belief that the Soviet Union was the other most
likely aggressor. Attempts were thus made to build up an anti-Soviet
bloc.[2]

In 1932, Colonel Josef Beck, one of Piłsudski's trusted wartime
comrades, became Poland's Minister for Foreign Affairs. Beck had a
reputation of being anti-French. His foreign policy was a reaction
to France's continuing search for agreements with the Soviet Union
and Czechoslovakia. However, he was determined to establish for
Poland, an independent position in Central Europe. One of his proposals was a regional pact. This would extend from the Baltic to
the Mediterranean. Unfortunately, his ideas proved to be too ambitious. The Scandinavian countries shared Poland's interest in the
Baltic region. However, a closer association with Poland had little to
offer them. Beck attempted to establish a leadership role for Poland
in relation to the Baltic States. This yielded limited results. Estonia,
Latvia and Lithuania, all in varying degrees feared the Soviet Union
and Germany. Despite this, unity between the three only had a
narrow foundation. Critically, Poland had a conflict with Lithuania
over the Wilno region which had been incorporated into Poland in
1920. This precluded the development of a regional pact. Nor was
Beck able to impose Poland's authority on Hungary and Romania.
Other attempts were made to forge unity between states which were

equally determined to remain independent of Germany and the Soviet Union. However, these required the resolution of intractable regional conflicts. Of these, the Romanian-Hungarian conflict was the most difficult. Relations between Polish and Romanian governments were good largely based on the shared anxiety about the Soviet Union. Polish relations with Hungary also appeared to be constructive, even though no agreements were signed between the two governments. But, neither the Romanian, nor the Hungarian government, was willing to overlook their own territorial disputes, in favour of a Polish-dominated regional bloc. Polish-Czechoslovak relations were always strained throughout the interwar period. This was due to Czechoslovak occupation of Teschen and support for the Ukrainian irredentist movements. These relations deteriorated dramatically with the first signs of German intention to destroy Czechoslovakia in 1937.[3]

In 1934, soon after Hitler came to power, Józef Lipski, the Polish ambassador in Berlin, appeared to have made a critical breakthrough. He secured a German commitment to a non-aggression agreement with Poland. The advantages of this treaty were very obvious. Until then, successive German governments had refused to accept the post-war border with Poland. This implied that Germany might take action, including military intervention, to redress this grievance. The Baltic port city of Danzig had been granted the status of a Free City under the protection of the League of Nations. There were conflicting German and Polish claims to Danzig. These risked the possibility of Poland losing its precariously secured access to the sea. Finally, the German tariff war had directly affected the Polish economy. But, it had indirectly frightened off West European investors from Poland. This therefore decreased its governments' hopes for economic recovery and industrial takeoff through securing foreign loans. The Non-Aggression Agreement was signed in January 1934. It indicated that, although none of these problems had been resolved, both sides had made a commitment to their peaceful resolution. At the same time, diplomatic and military links with France were maintained, although these were increasingly strained.

In 1938, Beck played a dangerous game. German aggression towards Czechoslovakia offered the Polish military regime an opportunity for a diplomatic coup, or so it seemed at the time. The crisis developed, the Nazi regime assuming the role of protector of the allegedly mistreated German community in Czechoslovakia. In the meantime, Beck coordinated Poland's demands for the reopening of the Teschen issue with the Nazi propaganda campaign. The Polish Minister for Foreign Affairs had calculated that the weakening of Czechoslovakia, would allow Poland to regain the Teschen region. More importantly, it would also affirm Poland's authority in the region. However, France and Britain took the lead and, ultimately took responsibility for forcing Czechoslovakia to accept German demands, for the cession of the Sudeten borderlands to Germany. This was something the Polish Minister for Foreign Affairs had not anticipated. The Munich Conference took place on 30 September 1938. There, Italy, France, Britain and Germany determined the future of Czechoslovakia. The exclusion of its government from this diplomatic settlement proved to be a bitter blow to Poland. Czechoslovakia lost territories to Germany and suffered the abrogation of the 1924 alliance with France. This allowed Poland to claim the Teschen region. However, it quickly became apparent that Germany's influence in the region was dramatically increased. This was of direct interest to Poland. At the end of 1938, Poland was dangerously exposed, both diplomatically and militarily.[4]

The full extent of Poland's perilous situation should have become apparent on 24 October. Lipski had hoped that, with the removal of the Czechoslovak problem, relations between Poland and Germany could be improved. He was informed, by Ribbetrop, that Germany now intended to pursue its demands towards Danzig. The Poles saw the issue as a touchstone of German goodwill. An attempt had been made to strengthen German control over the city. This was followed up by an indication that, in the long term Germany would seek to reclaim the town. This indicated a dramatic change in the Nazis attitude towards Poland.[5]

It is difficult to be precise about when the Polish Minister for Foreign Affairs, realised the enormity of the German threat to Poland's security. Nevertheless, in January 1939 he undertook an informal trip to France. He was clearly aiming to probe French willingness to support Poland. At the same time, enquiries were directed towards London. This was firstly in order to mend fences with British politicians. They had felt slighted by Poland's earlier pursuit of its territorial claims to Czechoslovakia. This had occurred when Neville Chamberlain, the British Prime Minister, was trying to broker an agreement between Germany and Czechoslovakia. Beck's diplomatic initiatives, in relation to the Western democracies, were unsuccessful. However, in March 1939 a new crisis forced Britain and France to assess the long-term implication of the growth of German influence in Eastern Europe.

During the night of 14/15 March, German troops marched into Prague. The destruction of Czechoslovakia contradicted the terms of the agreement signed at Munich. Developments elsewhere gave the British and French governments further cause for alarm. There were rumours that Romania was being pressurised to grant Germany absolute control over its oil production. There was also anxiety that Germany was planning to attack the Low Countries. These factors combined to create an atmosphere of anticipation. The Poles refused to divulge any details. However, British politicians suspected that Germany was putting pressure on the Poles to hand over Danzig. London was faced with a quandary over this particular issue. It was suspected that the Poles would rather fight than succumb to German pressure. It was feared that this would lead to the outbreak of a Europe-wide war. On the other hand, if the Poles bowed to German pressure, Poland would become a vassal state. German expansion to the East would irrevocably destroy the European balance of power. The British Cabinet reasoned that it might also cause a European War.[6]

The British prime minister investigated the possibility of Britain acting as patron to the creation of an East European bloc of states, committed to opposing Germany. This investigation was inconclusive. After this, on 31 March 1939, the British prime minister declared that Britain intended to defend Poland. The guarantee was to operate, even if Germany only moved to incorporate Danzig in the Reich. The British gesture was badly thought out. In the course of the following months, its hollowness was fully exposed in the British-Polish military talks; the French-Polish political and military talks and, most conclusively, the British-French military talks. Neither the British nor the French politicians knew what action they might authorise in the event of a German attack on Poland. Militarily, little could be done, unless preparations were put in place beforehand. Most damningly, the role of the Soviet Union, in any possible war with Germany, was not thought out. Prolonged talks took place, first with Soviet politicians, and later with top military leaders. However, the role of the Soviet Union still remained unclear in any potential war with Germany. This remained the case even as German troops marched into Poland in September.[7]

To the Polish government the German attack was a time of reckoning. The full extent of the lack of military preparedness had not been addressed. Successive governments, in particular those connected with the Piłsudski regime, exonerated themselves from responsibility for the army's lamentable performance. They instead accused the French and British of failure to support Poland in the face of German aggression. In reality, the Franco–Polish Political Agreement and Military Convention of 1921 and the Treaty of Mutual Guarantee did not provide for unambiguous and automatic military support, in the event of a German attack. In April 1939 General Tadeusz Kasprzycki led a Polish delegation to Paris. The aim of this was to secure precise French support for the increasingly likely military German attack on Poland. After nearly a month of negotiations, the Polish general was left in no doubt that France was unlikely to take any military action to relieve Poland. Behind the facade of supporting Poland, the French government was fast reducing its commitment to fighting Germany. Instead, they preferred to hide behind political pronouncements, which had no military backing.[8] The British guarantee of March 1939 to Poland and the British-Polish Guarantee of Mutual Assistance were signed on 25 August 1939. They did not state what Britain's response would be in the event of a German-Polish war. Article 1 of the latter, indicated that if either party were to find itself under attack, the other party would give 'all support and assistance'. The Secret Protocol made it clear that the agreement only applied in the event of an attack by Germany.[9] Were another European state to be the aggressor, there would be no commitment to assist the victim state. Thus, in reality, Poland had no prior assurance that Britain or France would automatically take any military action in support of Poland. Polish politicians and military leaders also knew that, if the Soviet Union were to take action against Poland, the two Western commitments to defend Poland, would not apply.

The situation was, in fact, much worse than the government of colonels was willing to accept. There was a conviction that the maintenance of an independent Poland was of critical importance to the European balance of power. However, French and British chiefs of staff admitted in the course of military talks that, unless Poland could form the basis of a viable eastern front, its fate would depend on the ultimate outcome of the war. In 1939, neither Britain nor France could build up an effective front against Germany. Therefore, Poland's fall was assumed to be a foregone conclusion. During the final stages of the Franco-British-Soviet talks in August, the Red Army commanders quickly realised that neither side intended to commit resources to fighting Germany in the East. They instead hoped that the Soviet Union would do something. It was unclear what that "something" was to be. Military talks with the Western democracies failed. This drove Stalin and his generals to seek an accommodation with Germany. The Ribbentrop-Molotov Non-Aggression Pact was signed on 23 August. As a result of this, Germany was assured of Soviet neutrality, in the event of an attack on Poland. The Secret Annex to that agreement stated that if Germany were to attack Poland, the Soviet Union would occupy the eastern regions of Poland. The fate of Poland was thus sealed.[10]

The Germans attacked Poland in the morning of 1 September. This followed a summer of mounting tension. In the Free City of Danzig, the Nazi Senate introduced para-Nuremberg Laws and demanded the removal of Polish customs police. There were disputes between the Nazis, determined to see the incorporation of the city into the Third Reich, and the Poles, who insisted on defending their prerogatives in the Free City. These led to confrontations between the two communities and attacks on Polish institutions. The Polish government took this as a sign that Berlin, rather than the local Nazis, sought a conflict with Poland. Beck, to the end, made efforts to reopen a dialogue with the Nazi government. These were to no avail. Belatedly, it was realised that Poland was ill prepared for the possibility of an outright German military attack. It proved too late to remedy production shortages. Attempts were made to obtain loans from the British and French governments in order to purchase military supplies in the West. The French government was sympathetic. However, they were reluctant to take on the burden

of financing the Polish war effort. The British Treasury responded
with hostility. A complex evaluation was taking place, of all possible scenarios, in which Germany, Italy and Japan were all likely
to take military action against Britain's imperial interests and supply routes. The events unfolding in Poland were not a priority. In
London, it was realised that once Germany attacked Poland, it
would be impossible to supply Poland with military equipment.
However, the final decision was still not to allow the Poles to purchase from Britain supplies, which British military forces would
need.[11]

The German attack on Poland was relentless. The German air
force bombed bridges, railway lines and strategic points, as well as
civilian objects. In the meantime, the Wehrmacht attacked from
three directions. From the North, West and South, German units
moved into Polish territory. Within two weeks, the Polish war effort was defeated. Though in some areas, fighting continued until
the beginning of October. On 17 September, the Red Army entered
into Eastern Poland. This hastened the already inevitable collapse of
the Polish defence. In Poland, the sense of isolation and abandon-
ment was absolute. Britain and France declared war on Germany
on 3 September. However, no military action was taken to attack
Germany in the West, or to hinder German progress into Poland.
The British and French governments confined their actions to verbal
protests. They rejected all Polish requests that they should deploy
their air forces over Germany and that they should also declare war
against the Soviet Union. Optimistic evaluations had been made,
that the Western democracies would have to support Poland's war
effort. Belatedly, Poland's rulers came to realise that this was not going to be the case. Beck's faulty reasoning that Hungary and Romania would look to Poland, further weakened Poland's position. Hungary allowed the safe passage of Poles through its territory, while
Romania initially allowed the fleeing Polish government the right
of entry, only to intern it for the duration of the war. Nevertheless,
both states ultimately sided with Germany.

German occupation of Poland lasted six years. The pre-war government was interned in Romania and had no realistic hope of
returning to lead the struggle for liberation. The social and political leadership of the nation was decimated by brutal occupation

policies. Nevertheless, the Poles in the occupied territories, and in exile, always believed that the Polish state would be restored. Thus, from the moment of defeat, supporters of the interwar government and its critics anticipated the end of the war and the formation of first post-war administration. For the political and military elites of the interwar period, the question was how to make sure that the war ended in such a way that would enable them to return to Poland and to prevent power from falling into the hands of those whom they had sidelined earlier. In the eyes of these men, the national democrats, the socialists and the revolutionary workers and peasants, all posed a threat to their plans to rule Poland, once it had been liberated.

It could be argued that the battle for authority in post-war Poland, started even before the German and Soviet forces established control of Polish occupied territories in September 1939. On 4 September, the government decided to evacuate Warsaw. As the German military effort proceeded, the government and the High Command moved closer to the Romanian border. where, evacuation points were kept open. This precipitated a flight of the civilian population. On 17 September, the final decision was made to cross into Romanian territory. The entry of the Red Army into Polish territory, hastened the President's departure from Poland, along with most of the ministers. The exodus included the Minister for Foreign Affairs, Marshal Edward Rydz-Śmigły, the Commander-in-Chief of the Polish Army and Cardinal Hlond, the Catholic Primate of All Poland. Military units and government employees were encouraged to depart too.[12]

The next stage of their plan was to reconstruct a government in exile and to establish control over Polish resources abroad. France appeared to be the obvious place to continue the fight for the liberation of Poland. The Polish Embassy in Paris was under the control of Ambassador Łukasiewicz. He was a staunch Piłsudski supporter. The Polish Embassy became the focal point of intrigues and dealings, the purpose of which was the appointment of a Polish government. The Romanians, acting on German instructions, interned the Polish Government. News of this allowed politicians from other parties to assert themselves. Demands were made for the formation of a broadly based exile government, rather than a successor to the pre-September government. The French became party to these decisions, mainly because of their dislike of Beck and a desire to make sure that the Polish government formed in Paris would be pro-French. There was a possibility that the Germans would establish a collaborationist government. The Poles in exile therefore hastened to complete the legal transfer of power to an exile authority. They acted in accordance with the 1935 Constitution. This allowed for the President to appoint a successor in circumstances of national emergency. The President, interned in Romania, resigned and appointed a successor. That successor, in turn, had the authority to form a government.

The composition of the Polish government in exile was announced on 30 September. In due course, a National Council was appointed to act as a quasi-parliament. In forming the government, the Polish leaders who had managed to make their way to Paris, arrived at an uneasy compromise. Representatives of the pre-war government reluctantly accepted that they could not hold on to power. Leaders of the parties which had been sidelined during the Piłsudski period were not strong enough to form a government on their own. The military leadership remained committed to the Piłsudski legend. Critically, Władysław Sikorski, the Prime Minister, was acceptable to the French and had the support of all the parties, bar the pre-war loyalists. These had sided with President Władysław Raczkiewicz, a Piłsudski man.[13]

Until his death in an air accident off Gibraltar on 4 June 1943, Sikorski was uneasily able to keep the exile politicians together. His main aim was to make a visible Polish military contribution to the war effort. Through that, he hoped to secure a place at the anticipated post-war conference. There, the future of Europe, would be discussed. Sikorski was determined that the exile government should remain allied to France and Britain. In this aim, he faced strong opposition. This opposition came mainly from within the ranks of the officers who had fled from Poland, and who had enrolled in military units formed in France. They were highly politicised and refused to accept his pragmatism. They insisted on earmarking the Polish exile military units for action on Polish territory only. The socialist, peasant party and national democrat leaders who had also managed to get to France were included in the government and the National Council. They continued to distrust supporters of the pre-war regime.[14] Unity between these groupings was always fragile and this, in turn, prevented them from arriving at any agreement concerning post-war Poland. Initially, the obvious problem was that neither France nor Britain was willing to write off the Soviet Union. The Soviet Union cooperated with Nazi Germany until June 1941. Despite this, the Western democracies knew that, in due course, German plans for the defeat of communist Russia, would lead to war. With that would come the possibility of the Soviet Union allying itself with France and Britain. To the Poles this meant that they would have to face the prospect of being allied to a government which had attacked Poland in September 1939, and re-fused to relinquish claims to territories occupied during the period of cooperation with Nazi Germany.

At the same time, Polish political leaders in France were anx-ious that no national leaders should emerge in occupied territories to challenge the exile government's monopoly of political decision making after the liberation. Throughout the war the government in exile sought to build up a strong resistance movement in Poland, one that could coordinate its actions with the Western Powers at the moment of Germany's defeat. In that, it was important to subordi-nate that movement to the authority of the exile government. The resistance movement that emerged in the occupied territories came to be known as the Home Army (Armia Krajowa – AK). In princi-ple, they accepted the authority of the exile government. However, most of the underground military leaders of the AK belonged to and supported the old Piłsudski regime. Therefore, the government in exile was always anxious, lest the underground military leader-ship sought to establish a post-war administration and, with that, replicate Piłsudski's success after the First World War.[15]

The German attack on France and France's capitulation dealt a bitter blow to the Poles. In June 1940, the Polish government in exile moved from France to Britain. Nearly 28,000 Polish men were evacuated, mainly from the coast of Brittany, and conveyed to mil-itary camps in Scotland. A nucleus of a Polish air force had already been established in Britain. Some Polish naval and merchant ships had evaded capture during and after the September campaign. They had also made their way to Britain. In addition, nearly 6,000 Polish soldiers were formed into a unit named the Carpathian Brigade. They fought with the French in Syria and then moved to join the British command in the Middle East. Initially, the Polish contribution to the war effort was modest, but distinct. Lack of manpower was the main reason for its modesty. Nevertheless, Sikorski was determined to see the expansion of units in the West. He made a direct and unconditional contribution to the war. In doing this, he sought to establish a position of influence for the exile government. For this, he had to balance the need to dedicate all Polish manpower to fighting under British command against the desire to hold some back for the final stages of the war. He hoped that in the final stages, they would establish control over liberated territories and secure it for the return of the government from exile. Sikorski completely dedicated himself to supporting first the French war effort, and then the British one. He faced criticism from the President and the officers. They accused him of excessive subordination to British interests.[16]

In June 1941, Sikorski had to simultaneously silence his critics, while maintaining control. When Nazi Germany attacked the Soviet Union, the British Prime Minister Winston Churchill, committed Britain to supporting the Soviet Union. The USA faced the Japanese threat. Churchill believed that Britain, together with the USA, had to cooperate with the Soviet Union if they were to survive. This attitude undermined the precariously maintained position of influence which the Polish government-in-exile had built up in Britain, and which it hoped to extend to the USA. Sikorski, nevertheless, reasoned that, without a major injection of manpower, the Polish war effort would decrease. In addition, his government's insistence on being treated as Britain's major war ally, would be undermined. He therefore entered into direct negotiations with the Soviet side. He did this even though Stalin refused to make commitments to the restoration of Poland's pre-war eastern border after the war. This was a tactical decision. Sikorski hoped that this would enable him to expand the Polish fighting forces in the West by recruiting the Poles trapped in the Soviet Union. These were people who had found themselves in the Soviet-occupied areas after the Soviet advance into Eastern Poland in September 1939.[17]

In July 1941, Sikorski and Ivan Maisky, the Soviet ambassador to London, signed an agreement. As a result, during the following months, the Poles released from Soviet camps were incorporated into Polish units. These were formed under the command of General Władysław Anders in Russia. Stalin, nevertheless, changed his mind and, by the beginning of 1942, imposed limits on the size of Polish units. The British command in the Middle East was short of manpower. So Anders agreed to the removal of already formed units. These numbered approximately 44,000 men, from the Soviet Union. They were placed under British command in Iran. All Polish civilians, who could attach themselves to the evacuation, were assisted in leaving the perilous situation in which they lived in the Soviet Union. These units were retrained, reorganised and deployed in fighting in Italy. There, they had, in particular, distinguished themselves in fighting around the monastery of Monte Casino. Polish families who had left the Soviet Union with Anders were settled in camps in British dependencies in Africa and India. After the war, they were allowed to come to Britain. Here, they formed the biggest Polish diaspora outside the USA.

Sikorski died on 4 July 1943. He had failed in his main objective. This was to create a debt of gratitude, which the British government would discharge by unconditionally supporting the Polish cause after the war. Due to British dependence on the Soviet war effort, the Churchill government first sought to persuade and then intimidate the Polish government to stop raising with the Soviet Union, the issue of the eastern border and the fate of thousands of Polish officers. It was known that these officers had been held in Soviet camps. Early in 1943, relations between the Sikorski government and the Soviet Union, deteriorated. On 13 April, German radio broadcast news that mass graves containing bodies of executed Polish officers had been found in the Katyń forest in what had been Eastern Poland. The Soviet government denied responsibility. They claimed that Germans occupying the region in the autumn of 1941 were responsible. The Polish government in exile called for the International Red Cross to investigate. Stalin chose to interpret this as a hostile act and used it as an excuse to brake off relations with the government in exile.[18] The breach was then used as an excuse to foster pro-communist groupings among the Poles in the Soviet Union, with a view to them forming the first post-war government. Soon after, an announcement was made by the Soviet authorities that a unit called the Polish Kościuszko Division was formed to fight with the Red Army.

When Sikorski died, the government in exile fractured. Internal disputes and political intrigues, some dating to the interwar years, reduced the Poles' ability to negotiate with the British government. This was at a time when the importance of the Soviet Union was increasing. In 1944, Churchill effectively blackmailed the then Polish Prime Minister Stanisław Mikołajczyk, to accept the creation of a provisional government in liberated Polish territories. This turned out to be a Soviet-sponsored group, which had been established in July 1944, in the town of Lublin. The compromise proved unacceptable to most Polish politicians and military leaders in Britain, who refused to return to Poland after the war. In July 1945, Britain, soon followed by other states, recognised the Lublin authority as the provisional government. For the government in exile, this spelt the end of its plans to influence events in post-war Poland. The recognition of the Lublin government also ended hopes, which the pre-war politicians had fostered, for a return to Poland and the resumption of political life on the basis of parties which had been active during the interwar period. In Polish areas freed from German occupation, Soviet control was established without reference to the exile government.

The government in exile and the resistance movements, which had emerged in occupied territories, tried very hard to maintain unity and to focus on the main objective of liberation. This proved difficult. In principle, throughout the war, all parties except the communists accepted the authority of the government in exile. The reality proved considerably more complex. This was because the experiences of the underground and the exiled leadership, proved to be very different. As a result, they came to attach importance to different issues. The government in exile focused its efforts on international diplomacy. However, in Poland, survival under Nazi occupation and then relations with the incoming Soviet authorities had a more dramatic impact on plans for the end of the war. The underground resistance remained loyal to the government in exile. However, the underground leaders were much more aware of what had gone wrong during the interwar period. The exile politicians focused on the need for unity and chose not to dwell on the past. In occupied territories, that unity proved more difficult to maintain. Within each of the underground political organisations and parties, the future envisaged for post-war Poland was more radical. In effect, it was bolder than the prospect considered by the party leadership ensconced in London. The government in exile was only too aware that references to the interwar period, in particular the Piłsudski period, would prove divisive. They were therefore reluctant to publicise a radical programme of reforms. The only commitments they made were to the restoration of Poland to its pre-September 1939 borders and to the establishment of a democratic system. In Poland, the debate went beyond these obvious principles.

German and Soviet entry into Polish territories had opened a deeply tragic chapter in Polish history. The Polish state and its resources were under attack. In addition to this, the very existence of the Polish nation, its culture and all those forms of national self-expression that had so recently been legitimised were also under attack. On 28 September 1939, Nazi Germany and the Soviet Union, finalised the border between the two occupation zones of Poland. This ran along the lines of the three rivers, the Narew, Bug and San. Each power determined its own occupation policies, with no interference from the other. In June 1941, Germany attacked the Soviet Union. Polish territories, previously in Soviet hands, were occupied by Germany.

In September 1939, the Polish army was defeated. The areas under Soviet control had contained a mixed population of Poles, Lithuanians, Byelorussians, Ukrainians and a high proportion of Jews. Polish nationality policy had been to create military settlements with the aim of consolidating Polish control in the disputed borderlands. They did this particularly in the Ukrainian inhabited regions. The result of this was that when the Polish army was defeated. There was, in the region, little sympathy for its plight. Soviet occupation policies drove a further wedge between the Polish and non-Polish communities. Soviet propaganda proclaimed the eastern parts of Poland to be 'liberated'.[19] Polish soldiers and military men were treated as enemy prisoners and incarcerated in military camps. Here, unsuccessful efforts were made to recruit pro-Soviet elements. Polish community leaders were arrested and transported into the interior. During the winter, the Polish civilian population was forced onto trains at short notice and dispersed throughout the Soviet Union. To the Poles, Soviet actions amounted to no less than an attempt to deny their right to nationality, because they were forced to accept Soviet citizenship.[20] In July 1941, Sikorski signed an agreement with the Soviet Union. It was from among these Poles, that he hoped to be able to recruit the manpower to expand the Polish fighting forces in the West. The army was recruited in the Soviet Union, under the command of General Anders. It was seen as a lifeline for the Polish civilians. They flocked to the recruitment centres, seeking support and shelter. When those units moved to Iran, the Poles who remained in the Soviet Union had to wait for the end of the war before they were allowed to leave the Soviet Union for Poland. The repatriation of Poles dragged on for years. Some only returned to Poland in the 1950s.

Some political refugees were ex-members of the Polish Communist Party, which had been disbanded on Soviet instructions in 1938. They formed a separate group among the Poles in the Soviet Union. Many foreign communists in the Soviet Union, perished during the purges. Those who survived, fully accepted Stalinist polices. Stalin's future plans for Poland were unclear. In the meantime, these Polish Communists lingered on the fringes of the organisations of the Communist International. They hoped that, in due course. They would be put in charge of Polish territories, liberated by the Red Army.[21]

German policies towards occupied Polish territories were driven by Nazi racial ideology. This defined the Poles as a race capable of working for the superior Germanic race. On 12 October, Hitler ordered that no Polish administration should be formed in occupied territories. Some Germanophile Poles were mindful of the way the German authorities had governed Polish areas during the First World War. They put themselves forward as willing to form an occupation administration. The Polish areas were of military importance to the Germans in their plans for a future war against the Soviet Union. Therefore Hitler forbade the use of these offers.[22]

The port city of Gdańsk including surrounding areas, Northeastern Mazovia, Pomerania, Łódź and Silesia, were defined as areas having historic links with Germany. They were therefore incorporated into the Third Reich. The areas of Central and Southern Poland, including the cities of Warsaw, Radom, Kraków and Lublin, a Generalgouvernement (GG), was formed. This was under German administration. The reorganisation of ex-Polish territories required the removal of thousands of people. This, the Germans did with speed and indifference to the suffering of those being forced from their homes. Germans from the Reich were settled in the Polish territories incorporated into the Third Reich and some further designated districts. Poles were expelled from here, to the Generalgouvernement. Other German communities from Hungary, Romania and the Baltic states, settled as colonists on the newly acquired territories.

The fate of the Poles in the GG was tragic. The occupiers pillaged national libraries, museums, galleries and state buildings. Throughout this, schools and universities were closed. Poland's mineral and economic resources were used to Germany's benefit. Arbitrary acts of brutality were followed by actions intended to cower the population. Public executions reinforced the new laws. These laws decreed collective punishment, for acts of sabotage and attacks on Germans. The actions were ways of intimidating the Poles. Delivery quotas, imposed on villages, led to food shortages and hunger. Underlying these policies was an ideologically motivated contempt for the Poles. In addition to this was a desire to destroy the nation and its accumulated cultural and intellectual achievements.[23]

In relation to the Jewish communities, Nazi racial principles led to genocide. Initially, Jews were forced to wear a cloth badge in the form of the Star of David on their outer clothes. In addition, they were tormented by restrictive measures. Their property was confiscated. Finally, all Jews were obliged to move to defined ghettos, under threat of death. Throughout 1940, larger ghettos were established. Moved into these were Jews from Germany and Austria as well as local Polish Jews. Life in these ghettos was deeply tragic. In theory, they were administered by the Jews, through Judenrats, and policed by a Jewish police force. Nevertheless, these organisations were forced to implement German decrees. There was no doubt that the Nazis intended the Jews to die of starvation.[24] In July 1941, German troops occupied what had previously been Polish eastern territories. They faced a large local Jewish population. In a policy of planned genocide, these communities were usually killed and buried in mass graves within days of German entry. In a number of instances, the local communities either took action against the Jews, or assisted the Germans. The Warsaw Judenrat came to know of this. It was only too painfully aware that, in due course, the same fate would befall the Jews of the GG. From the spring of 1942, mass extermination camps were established and the transport of Jews, commenced. This occurred first from Polish ghettos, and then from all over Europe. Of those, Treblinka, Majdanek and Oświęcim (Auschwitz) were the largest.

On 19 April 1943, during the last stages of the removal of Jews to the extermination camp, young Jews in the Warsaw Ghetto started an uprising. They were doomed. The Germans put down the uprising using reinforcements and foreign troops. These were mainly Ukrainian units. It is difficult to know precisely how many Jewish people died in extermination camps established in the occupied Polish territories. By the end of the war, possibly no more than 210,000 Polish Jews survived. This was usually because they had managed to disguise the fact that they were Jewish or because they had been hidden by the Poles out of pity, or for payment. The number of survivors is imprecise because many continued to be anxious about their personal security after the war. Poland had been a society riven with anti-Semitism. So the sheltering of Jews was a dangerous undertaking. Anyone aiding Jews, if caught, would be summarily executed, along with all those living in the building. The attitude of the underground resistance to the plight of Jews was ambivalent. Only the extreme nationalist Narodowe Siły Zbrojne (National Armed Units – NSZ) was actively involved in hunting down and killing Jews. When the Jews tried to fight back, they found it difficult to obtain arms. Resistance groups were reluctant to share scarce military equipment and ammunition. When aid was given, this was incidental rather than a policy of helping the Jewish community.[25]

Owning and listening to radio broadcasts was an offence punishable by death. However, information penetrated through to the occupied Polish territories. The government in exile kept in contact with the underground movement by couriers. These people worked at great risk to themselves. They moved along various routes to neutral countries. From there, they could be transported to Britain, to hand over information and microfilms of documents. By 1942, the flight range of airplanes had increased. This enabled flights from

Britain to Poland. where, planes landed at prearranged, secret land-
ing strips and picked up information, or dropped off or picked up
people. Thus, the government in exile continuously fed the allied
governments with intelligence information. This included information on the production of the V1 and V2 flying bombs and on
German troop deployments and movement of equipment. They also
had direct information on the German genocide policy towards the
Jewish communities. This was then handed over to the British and
US governments.

Contacts between the government in London and the resistance
movement in Poland, allowed the government to exercise a greater
degree of control over the underground resistance movement in
Poland, than might be expected in the circumstances. The government in exile had, from the outset, determined that it would form
the first post-war administration. In anticipation of possible revolutionary activities, it had trained a Polish unit. This would be
parachuted into Poland at a critical stage. A delegate was appointed
to act as liaison officer with the resistance in the occupied territories. The role of the delegate was to make sure that the resistance
movements did not try to usurp the government's role. Additionally, a skeleton of the future government was set up in Poland. The
underground resistance did not seek to establish its own political
authority in occupied territories. This was because of German brutality and the AK's dependence on the government in exile, for
supplies. That is not to suggest that unity between the underground
and the exiled government was ever easy. On the contrary, the AK
commanders found it difficult to bring all armed resistance groups
and political organisations, into its fold. The nationalists distrusted
the ex-army officers dominating the AK. Units loyal to the peasant
parties also viewed the AK with unease. They recalled the officers'
role in the destruction of democracy during the interwar period.
The PPS splintered. Its main leaders in London and in occupied
Poland supported the government in exile and the AK. However,
radical socialists moved to create their own political organisation
and to form armed units. These were mainly based on the industrial working class around Warsaw. Throughout the war, a sense of
lawlessness prevailed in Poland. The underground resistance tried
to maintain unity at all costs and reduce sources of tension and

fratricidal conflict. In the meantime, this unity was threatened by debates about post-war reforms and the role of the state.[26]

It had always been the government-in-exile's plan that Poland be liberated by joint British-US military action. This would be assisted by Polish units coming from the West. In its final stages, this action was to be coordinated with the AK. This was going to stage a national uprising, codenamed 'Burza' (Storm). This would allow units, loyal to the government in exile, to establish control over liberated territories. Unfortunately for the Poles, already at the beginning of 1943, Britain and the USA had assumed that the Soviet war effort would be successful in pushing the Germans out of Russian territories. Not only this, but that it would defeat the Germans in the East. In London and Washington, this led to the acceptance that the Red Army would liberate Poland. The government in exile, nevertheless, continued to plan for a national uprising. They hoped to persuade the Combined Chiefs of Staff, that the uprising in occupied Polish territories, would make a key contribution to the defeat of Germany. In making those plans, they sought to play down the importance of the Soviet war effort, and to ensure that the entry of the Red Army into Polish territories, would be forestalled by US and British troops. The hope was that they would reach Poland first. Unfortunately, neither the US nor the British governments were interested in these plans.[27]

The purpose behind the planned national uprising in Poland had been to forestall the establishment of a puppet authority, by the incoming Soviet army. At the end of 1943 and in 1944, the Poles in the West continued to lobby for British and US military assistance to the AK. In the meantime, in occupied Poland, the various underground resistance movements realised the implications of the evolving military situation. Because of this, they had to reassess their plans.

The Home Army subordinated to the government in exile. This prevented it from putting forward a political programme of its own and meant that all efforts were focused on planning the uprising. This was not a situation easily accepted even by parties which supported the London government. The London leadership of the peasant party had always cooperated to a certain degree with those hostile in the interwar period. This made the rest of the peasant

**Figure 1. Rejtan in the Sejm 1773 painted by Jan Matejko in 1866.**

The painting shows the moment when the speaker of the Sejm approved the First Partition of Poland. Rejtan, portrayed in the dramatic pose of barring the traitors way to the room where the partition agreement was to be signed, did indeed try to prevent the act from being concluded. Matejko clearly indicates Poles bore some responsibility for the partition. Note the way in which he portrays the scheming nobility, the distracted ladies and the shrewd churchman.

**Figure 2. Battlefield in the Forest. Artur Grottger 1863.**
Grottger became famous for his painting and drawings which were inspired by the failure of the January Uprising. The image thus conveyed
is romantic and full of pathos. Only later would more perceptive questions be asked as to whether independence could be restored through
insurrections led by the nobility. At the same time women authors
would speak of the suffering endured by women while the men had
perhaps recklessly focused entirely on conflicts which had little chance
of success. © Muzeum Narodowe w Warszawie.

**Figure 3. Roman Dmowski (1864–1939) a politician and ideologue.**
In his numerous publications Dmowski elaborated his programme of National Democracy in which he defined the Polish quest for independence in quasi-Darwinist terms, namely the fight for survival against the German and the Jewish races.

**Figure 4. Signatures of the Polish delegation to the Paris Peace Talks.**
Jan Paderewski and Roman Dmowski, the two towering personalities which steered the talks on the subject of Poland's border, saw their involvement at the negotiations as the culmination of their life's achievements.

**Figure 5. Józef Piłsudski on the Poniatowski bridge on the day of the May coup in 1926.** This was the strategic point to the town centre where Piłsudski met the President.

**Figure 6. General Władysław Sikorski, Prime Minister of the Polish Government in Exile in the United Kingdom during the Second World War (second from the left) photographed with Prime Minister Winston Churchill and General Charles de Gaulle, leader of the Free French.**
Sikorski was very much in agreement with Churchill's vision of the need to cooperate with the Soviet Union. He nevertheless cultivated all exile governments and administrations in London in order to establish for Poland an independent role after the war. © Bettmann/CORBIS.

**Figure 7. Communist leaders celebrating Walter Ulbricht's 70th Birthday, East Berlin, June 1963.**
Władysław Gomułka Polish party Secretary third from the left with Khurshchev next to him at the table. A year later, when Khrushchev was removed from power after the Cuban Crisis, Gomułka would complain to Brezhnev that Khrushchev had exploited Poland economically; had not been frank about his plans for German reunification and had risked a third world war over an issue as small as Cuba.

**Figure 8. Lech Wałęsa, the charismatic leader of the free trade union Solidarity speaking to fellow workers in August 1980.**

The establishment of a genuinely free workers' organization marked the first stage in, what became the gradual process of the dismantling of the Communist regime in Poland. © Bettmann/CORBIS.

party uneasy. In occupied territories, pre-war hostility between the peasants and the landowners persisted. Although the quest for independence took precedence. The landowners were not averse to asking the commanders of the local AK units to rough up peasants who, they believed, had shown an excessive interest in politics. In some cases, the AK disarmed peasant units. The Bataliony Chłopskie (Peasant Battalions – BCh) were underground resistance units loyal to the Stronnictwo Ludowe. In principle, they accepted the authority of the AK. However, many AK commanders appeared to be on friendly terms with local landowners. This caused unease. The peasants' expected that land reform would be implemented at the end of the war. However, the government in exile did not want to discuss this. The debate did not stop there. In fact, the peasant party leaders felt it their duty to draw attention to their party's unblemished commitment to upholding democracy. Their plans for a future, just Poland went beyond land reform, anticipated state control of national resources and equality of opportunity. The peasants were unwilling to side with the communist resistance. Though there were similarities between some progressive elements of their programme and those put forward by the radical sections of the socialist movement and the reconstructed communist Party.[28]

The PPS was disbanded during the September campaign, in circumstances which were unclear. Fear of reprisals and anxiety, lest the Germans attempted to create a pro-German Socialist Party, were cited as reasons for this unusual decision. In its place, a temporary organisation was formed. This took the name of Wolność, Równość i Niepodległość (Freedom, Equality and Independence – WRiN). It was to function only as a temporary organisation during occupation. Those on the radical wing of the PPS, suspected that the leaders of the moderate wing, wanted to prevent the left, from taking the initiative. WRiN had been created for the duration of the war. Its leaders refused to address long-term issues. The Polish socialist movement was further handicapped. The PPS leaders in exile supported the exile government. However, those in occupied Poland, disagreed over which wing, the moderate or the radical, represented the movement's true direction.[29] The result was, that in March 1943, a left wing section broke away forming a new party. This took the name of Workers' Party of Polish Socialists

(Robotnicza Partia Polskich Socialistów – RPPS). Its membership was small and nearly entirely confined to the militant workers of the Warsaw factories. However, the programme they put forward was a direct challenge to the surprisingly moderate one publicised at the same time by the communists. The RPPS programme for the future gave the peasants land for cultivation. The workers would control the means of production. Equality of opportunity would be guaranteed to all, including women. This programme was interesting because the communists had, in the meantime, chosen not to lead with a radical revolutionary plan for a post-war future.[30]

In December 1941 a group of Polish communists was parachuted from the Soviet Union into Poland. They acted on strict instructions from the Comintern and formed a new organisation called the Polska Partia Robotnicza (Polish Workers' Party – PPR). This dissociated itself from the disbanded, pre-war KPP. Its initial objectives were to be limited to the building of left wing unity.[31] In June 1942, the PPR leadership tried to prepare an outline of its post-war objectives. In carrying out this task, the PPR leadership felt it was necessary to obtain the Comintern's approval. These were too weighty issues for the newly formed Polish Communist Party to put forward, without Soviet agreement. To their surprise, they found that Georgi Dimitrov, the head of the Comintern, forbade them to make any references to the nationalisation of land and workers' control of enterprises. The final programme was disseminated in November 1943. It only advocated the nationalisation of key industries and mines. It referred to workers' committees having a say in management decisions. This fell short of the expectations which many of the Nevertheless, they bowed to the Comintern's instructions. As a result, the PPR's main wartime objective remained that of building anti-fascist unity within the underground resistance. Polish communists had had, for the post-war state. In that objective, it failed. This was because the communists did not succeed at building a power base, either within the working class or the peasant communities.[32] Internal conflict within the leadership was caused by the unresolved issue of the disbanding of the KPP, and the murder of Polish communists in the Soviet Union. These issues troubled the new party. Moreover, the party's effectiveness was reduced by quarrels between Polish communists in the Soviet Union and those in Poland. In November 1943, the PPR announced the formation of the Krajowa Rada Narodowa (Homeland National Council – KRN). The purpose of this was to bring the other parties into the first provisional post-war government. Not surprisingly, none of the other underground parties, would have anything to do with this proposal.

The RPPS refused to abandon its critical attitude towards the Soviet Union. Stalin had implemented policies of rapid industrialisation and bureaucratisation of decision making. The RPPS saw these as a betrayal of the achievements of the Russian Revolution. Nevertheless, throughout the war, underground resistance units loyal to the PPR were supplied with arms from the Soviet Union. These underground resistance units operated side by side with the AK. The PPR units, initially called the Gwardia Ludowa (People's Guard – GL), were later renamed the Armia Ludowa (People's Army – AL). It is difficult to evaluate how effective they were in fighting the Germans. It is worth nothing that they refused to accept the AK's policy of avoiding military confrontation with the Germans. The AK's view was that military confrontation could lead to retaliation against the civilian population. In any case, the AK focused its activities on preparing for the national uprising. The more active resistance of the AL and its arms supplies did attract people to its ranks. This, in turn, lead the AL to cooperate with the BCh. In reality, the AL never rivalled the AK's organisational or numerical strength.[33]

In the spring of 1943, Stalin allowed a number of Moscow-based communists and socialists to form a new organisation. This was perceived as apparent disregard for the PPR's plans within occupied areas and the Comintern's attempts to build a new communist organisation in occupied Poland. The Związek Patriotów Polskich (Union of Polish Patriots – ZPP) announced its existence through radio broadcasts. Relations were deteriorating between the Soviet government and the Polish government in exile. There was also a diplomatic breach between the two governments. In view of this, the ZPP was meant to be a nucleus of a Soviet-sponsored future Polish government.[34] Nevertheless, Stalin appears to have considered several options, before finally allowing the Moscow-based communists to take the lead in forming a provisional administration. The Red Army liberated the first large city in ethnically Polish territories. Because of this, the Polski Komitet Wyzwolenia Narodowego (Polish

Committee of National Liberation – PKWN) was proclaimed. This came to be known as the Lublin government, from the city where it was first established. The PKWN was dominated by Polish communists, who had spent the war in the Soviet Union, with the addition of a few compliant socialists and peasant party members. Later, on Stalin's insistence, communists from occupied Poland were added and a splinter group from the RPPS. This did not change the fact that the PKWN was no more than a Soviet-imposed administration. It had no authority and only limited popular support in Polish territories.

In the summer of 1944 the Red Army approached Warsaw. German withdrawal appeared imminent so the leaders of the AK, in Warsaw, decided to launch an uprising. The idea of a national uprising had been first put forward during the early stages of the war. It was assumed that its outbreak would be coordinated with the Allied military effort. The Allied military leaders were interested in these plans. However, the final decision was not to support an uprising in Poland. This was because it was clearly going to be a Soviet operational zone. In August 1944, it was known that Britain and the USA were in no position to take military action east of Germany. The defeat of the German forces on Polish territories was a task left to the Red Army. By then, the AK knew that the Red Army would not tolerate the presence of any Polish units within its areas of operation. When the Red Army had first entered previously Polish areas, some degree of cooperation with the AK took place. However, once military action was completed, the AK units were disarmed and their leaders were arrested. This happened in the Wilno region. Plans for the uprising were changed and its purpose was altered. In the circumstances, the uprising became an attempt by the AK to establish control over the capital of Poland, and to pre-empt the Soviet authorities' design of putting in place a puppet authority. As it turned out, the strategy failed. This was mainly because the German forces had regrouped and decided to hold Warsaw. In the meantime, the Red Army halted its progress on the banks of the Wisła.

The uprising started on 1 August. The decision was unexpected. Though the city community and the Germans knew something was afoot. The uprising was hastened on by news from London, that Prime Minister Mikołajczyk had decided to go to Moscow. He had done this in order to try to reopen a dialogue with the Soviet Union. At the same time, news had been coming in from areas already under Soviet military control. This news indicated that the Red Army commanders were disarming AK units and arresting their leaders. On 1 August, the order was given for the uprising to start. Many local commanders and fighters were not forewarned. The fighting engulfed the city and throughout the fighting, the civilian population fully supported the insurgents. The Germans had anticipated the uprising and brought units back into Warsaw. These included the brutal Ukrainian units, the Vlasov Russian units and battle-hardened German units. Progressively, the insurgents' control over the town was narrowed down to the central districts of Śródmieście and Starówka. The AK had no control over the bridges and were unable to break the German encirclement. The AK units from outside the city were therefore unable to aid their comrades in Warsaw. The Warsaw AK commanders had made a critical miscalculation. They had hoped to prevent the Soviet Union from taking control over the capital and bringing in the PKWN. At the same time, the AK leadership had assumed that the Soviet military campaign against the Germans would continue. This would thus weaken the latter's ability to reclaim Warsaw. What happened, instead, was that the Red Army came up to the Wisła and then stopped. The official explanation has always been that the Red Army had outrun its supply lines and needed to regroup. But it is clear that it was in the interests of the Soviet command to allow the Germans to destroy the uprising. The uprising would have complicated the situation, both military and political, by establishing AK control over the city. This also explains why the Soviet military authorities refused to allow British planes, to land and refuel on territories under their control. These planes flew from the United Kingdom with supplies for the insurgents. This was the largest urban insurgency of the war and it continued until 2 October, when the commanders of the AK surrendered. One of the conditions for the end of fighting was that the insurgents should be treated as prisoners of war. Nevertheless, German retribution was brutal and merciless. While fighting was taking place, no distinction had been drawn between combatants and the civilian population. All were treated as criminals. Flame-throwing equipment, aerial bombing and artillery shelling were used to destroy the town. After the AK capitulated, the remaining civilian population was marched out of the city and the city was razed to the ground.

The Warsaw Uprising remains one of the most painful episodes in recent Polish history. Many, including a number of historians in the West, view it as a heroic manifestation of the Poles' will for independence. The subsequent communist regime wished to play down the uprising's significance. This has contributed to the general desire to view it as a positive episode in Poland's recent history. Undoubtedly, the Soviet unwillingness to assist the insurgents, contradicts the avowed aim of anti-Nazi unity. It also highlights the premeditated desire to see the AK sidelined and replaced with a puppet pro-Soviet government. Nevertheless, the AK was instrumental in starting the uprising in circumstances where there was little hope of it succeeding. Ultimately, in spite of the heroism and sacrifice made by the population of Warsaw, the insurgents were badly prepared for the fighting which followed. Calculations had been made of the likely fate of the civilian population, trapped amidst the fighting. These calculations did not sway the AK commanders in their decision to start the uprising. The Soviets decided to stand by while the uprising was defeated and the city was destroyed. However, this does not change the fact that it was the Germans who fought the Poles, and who rained fire and explosives upon the city. This resulted in over 200,000 casualties in just 63 days. The responsibility for the savagery and subsequent retribution lies squarely with the Germans and their allies.[35]

For the AK, the Warsaw Uprising spelled more than just the defeat of a hope for a national uprising, that would free the city from German occupation and put in place a Polish authority. The uprising meant the end of organised resistance and with that, the end of hopes that the underground state structures would assume authority in post-war Poland. In the months following the end of the uprising, attempts were made to rebuild the AK. This proved too difficult and local commanders had to make their own decisions as to how to continue the fight against the Germans and the incoming Red Army. For the Soviet leaders, the road to Berlin stood open. Although Polish territories were described as liberated areas, to many Poles it seemed as if German occupation had been replaced with

Soviet occupation. In September 1944, the Soviet offensive, stalled off the right bank of the Wisła. In January 1945, it was resumed. Within the following months, the remaining Polish territories and German areas east of the Oder-Neisse line were freed from German troops and put under the jurisdiction of the PKWN. These areas were originally going to be incorporated into Poland. Previously Polish territories east of the river Bug were incorporated into the Soviet Union.

In March 1945 the Soviet Security Services (the NKVD) arranged a meeting with the leadership of the AK, the delegate of the government in exile in Poland and leaders of parties which supported the government in London. All the Poles were arrested and spirited off to the Soviet Union. The Soviet authorities then denied any knowledge of their whereabouts. In June, the Soviet authorities staged a show trial in Moscow during which the arrested underground leaders were accused of having engaged in subversive activities behind the Soviet military lines. All the accused were sentenced to long spells in prison. The leader of the AK died soon after, while still in Soviet custody.[36] The unmistakable signal was that the Soviet authorities would not tolerate any organisations other than those which supported the Lublin authority. During the coming years, military courts were set up to try members of the wartime AK and supporters of the London government. These sentenced many Poles to death and imprisonment. In some cases it was possible to prove that they had indeed attacked representatives of the new government and Red Army units. However, in reality, many, if not most, were punished for having supported the wartime resistance organisations. These were hostile to Soviet control of Poland. Until 1948, scattered units in the outlying districts in the borderlands and in dense forests, continued the fight for an independent Poland.

In the meantime, the battle for post-war Poland had continued on the diplomatic plane. This was nearly entirely conducted between Churchill and Stalin. Mikołajczyk was increasingly left in no doubt by the British, that he had only one alternative. This was to accept the incorporation of previously Polish territories in the East, into the Soviet Union. During a joint visit to Moscow on 13–16 October 1944, Churchill forced Mikołajczyk to accept the new borders. This had, in any case, been already decided by the Soviet authorities. This was disputed within the government in exile. As a result, Mikołajczyk resigned. He had earlier hoped that the British government would defend Polish interests in dealings with Stalin and that, even if they did not do so formally, they would undertake to act as custodian of Polish sovereignty. In October, this increasingly looked less likely. Reluctantly, and in the full realisation that Churchill would not allow Polish issues to blight British-Soviet relations, Mikołajczyk, with a small group of like-minded émigré politicians, accepted the loss of Poland's eastern territories to the Soviet Union.[37] Within the émigré community, opponents of this policy grouped around President Raczkiewicz and General Anders. They rejected the need for any compromise. Instead, they pinned their hopes on a third world war, this time against the Soviet Union. This, they believed, would give Poland a uniquely strong position as a bridgehead to Russia. They would also be able to deploy up to 400,000 battle-hardened troops. These were demobilized and therefore remained in the West. In spite of all the recent painful disappointments, these men still clung to the hope that by, making a military contribution to the future war, they could ensure that Britain and the United States would repay the debt of gratitude by freeing Poland from Soviet control.

Stalin, in the meantime, determined the course of developments in Polish territories freed from German occupation. Not only were AK units disarmed, but all underground resistance was systematically destroyed. On 31 December 1944, the Soviet Union recognised the Lublin authority as Poland's Provisional Government. The heads of the allied state met at a conference in Yalta in February 1945. At this conference, many principles concerning the future of Poland had been already decided, most notably during the earlier Teheran Conference in November 1943. The Polish question was the most contentious and difficult issue discussed during the course of both conferences. Britain and the US were dependent on the continuing Soviet military contribution to the defeat of Germany. They also started to realise that they were equally reliant on Stalin declaring war on Japan. This would assist them in the Pacific war. These thoughts made them reluctant to support Polish interests. The result of the Yalta Conference was that Churchill, Roosevelt and Stalin, agreed that the Polish provisional government would be enlarged by the inclusion of representatives of democratic parties from the West. Henceforth, until the elections in 1947, it would be called the Tymczasowy Rząd Jedności Narodowej (Provisional Government of National Unity – TRJN). Poland was guaranteed the right to hold free elections. The Curzon Line was accepted as Poland's eastern ethnic frontier. The three heads of state decided that this was to be the future border with the Soviet Union. In principle, the extension of Poland's territory to the West was accepted. Eastern and Western Prussia, Gdańsk and Lower Silesia were to be incorporated into Poland. However, the precise border was to be the subject of further post-war discussions. Stalin spoke of Poland being rewarded by being given the Baltic port of Szczecin and a border which would run along the Oder and its upper tributary, the Neisse river. Neither Roosevelt nor Churchill were at this stage prepared to agree to this becoming Poland's permanent border with Germany, since this would have predetermined decisions concerning the future of Germany.[38]

On 30 June 1945 the British and US governments recognised the TRJN as the provisional government of Poland. Recognition was withdrawn from the exile government and its activities were wound up. In reality, already since the Yalta Conference, the British military authorities and the Foreign Office, increasingly restricted the operational independence of the Polish commanders and limited their use of radio communication with Poland. In spite of the apparent lack of gratitude towards the Polish solders, Churchill did have some reservations about the course of British relations with the Soviet Union. No Poles were forcibly removed from Britain and areas under British jurisdiction, back to Poland. All Polish servicemen who had fought with the Allied forces in the West were granted the right to stay in Britain. Following the end of hostilities in Europe, Polish troops were gradually brought from the operational zones in Italy and Germany to Britain where, they were dispersed to areas of employment through the Resettlement Corps. Some families and dependants had left with Polish units when they departed the Soviet Union, and had been held in camps in Africa and the Middle East. They also moved gradually to the British Isles, where they had the right to remain or emigrate to any part of the British Commonwealth.

The British government would have wanted its wartime allies to leave Britain, because post-war economic problems and the demobilisation of British soldiers created preconditions for social conflicts. Nevertheless, only a small percentage of Poles opted to return to Poland. News from Poland had forewarned them of possible political difficulties. At the same time, Polish commanders and political leaders in the West, preferred to encourage the ex-combatants to wait for the anticipated war with the Soviet Union. As a result of this they hoped the Yalta decisions would be reversed.

Thus, the community in Poland and that in Western Europe, finally separated from Poland. Poles in the areas devastated by German occupation and war struggled to build state structures, the economy, and to survive in extreme circumstances. They faced very different problems from their compatriots stranded outside their homeland. The latter faced alienation, loss of status and anxiety about relatives and friends in occupied Poland. Henceforth, they would have no influence on what happened in Poland.

# 5   Post-war Poland, 1945–70

The Polish state which emerged at the end of the Second World War, bore little resemblance to the state that had come into being in 1919. The borders had been shifted dramatically to the West. In July 1945, the wartime allies met at a conference in Potsdam. During this meeting, Poland's future was discussed extensively. This resulted in the recognition of Poland's western border on the Odra (Oder) and Nysa (Neisse) rivers. During earlier wartime conferences, the Allies had accepted the incorporation of the cities of Lwów and Wilno into the Soviet Union. Both had strong historic links to Polish culture. Polish access to the coast was consolidated by the incorporation of parts of Eastern and Western Prussia. This meant that the ancient Hanseatic city of Gdańsk, became Polish. In the West, the previously German cities of Szczecin (Stetin), Kołobrzeg (Kolberg) and Wrocław (Breslau) were within Polish borders.[1]

The population of the new state had likewise dramatically changed. The previously varied Jewish communities had always been an integral part of Polish life. The few survivors were now in the horns of a dilemma. In the first post-war years, they would have to face the question of whether to remain in Poland, or to strike out for Palestine. Most notably, from having been a multicultural, multireligious state, Poland became a national state. The citizens of the new state were nearly exclusively Polish nationals of Catholic faith. At the same time, the community was depleted by Nazi genocide, Soviet displacement and arrests, emigration and fighting.

The border of Poland after the Second World War,
indicating territories lost to the Soviet Union and gains
at Germany's expense

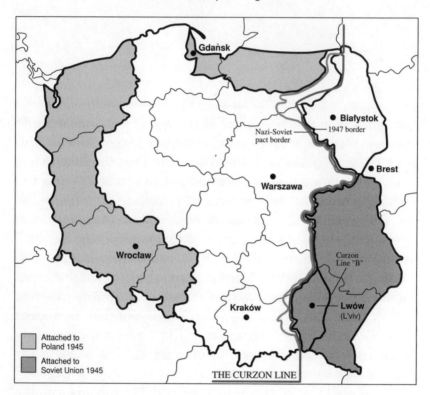

This fighting had engulfed Polish territories in 1939 and 1945. The first post-war census revealed that the population of post-war Poland had been reduced by a quarter, in relation to the pre-war figure. The most productive, educated and active members of the community were lost. Both the Nazi and Soviet authorities had targeted national leaders and the educated elites, including the Catholic hierarchy. The post-war period was a time of great population shifts and migrations. Until the late 1950s, the Polish Red Cross continued its efforts to reunite families scattered during the war.

The Polish economy was devastated. This was due to wartime activities, German exploitation and destruction following German withdrawal, fighting and, finally Soviet exploitation. The German occupation authorities had confiscated all Jewish property, Polish private property and Polish state enterprises. These had all been resources which were useful to their war effort. Ownership of those workshops and enterprises that survived was difficult to establish in such circumstances. In many cases, it was impossible to reverse changes which had taken place over the past six years. In industrial plants, workers had been active in preventing the Germans from destroying machinery and goods as they were withdrawing. Where production could be restarted, it was frequently done by workers who had defended their place of employment and secured it. Their desire to save Polish property reflected a wish to protect it. Morevoer, it was a sign of the growth of worker radicalism. Young workers articulated the wish to have a say in management decision, and a greater degree of control over production.

In the months and, arguably, even during the first years after the war, the authority of the government was unclear. At times, it only extended to the boundaries of the main cities. What remained were scattered remnants of the underground resistance. These varied in character. On the one extreme, some maintained discipline and their loyalty to the London government. Whereas others degenerated into being no more than armed bands, loyal to various leaders. In places, these groupings and armed bands remained very strong. This was because they commanded the loyalty of the population. The incoming government had no power base in Poland and could only count on limited support. From the outset, it was seen as a puppet Soviet organisation. Its members represented rump sections of larger national parties. There was no disguising the fact that communists were generally distrusted. Only the presence of the Red Army, maintained the TRJN in power. Mikołajczyk was included in the TRJN. However, it was still perceived as a Soviet puppet organisation. For the government, the real test was how it would establish its authority throughout the country, combat lawlessness and pillaging and whether it would be able to restart production. The communist-controlled government only had a general idea of how it would establish control. Thus, throughout Poland, the issue was not only that of lack of resources and manpower. Critically, it was of who actually controlled the regions. The TRJN quickly learnt that, while it was able to establish itself in Warsaw, beyond the capital it faced hostility. Agents of the TRJN travelled to the countryside to supervise the implementation of land reform or to inspect factories. They were frequently ambushed and murdered. Historians disagree on whether this situation amounted to a civil war. However, there was no doubt that attacks on the government and its agents were frequently politically motivated. This state of affairs continued throughout Poland until 1948. This was when the government and the newly built up security service and army, finally established their authority. In reality, the community's desire for stability and peace was as much a factor in the establishment of the rule of law as were the government's efforts to combat what was described as 'banditism'.

From the outset, the government was only too aware of its weakness. The presence of the Red Army and the NKVD gave some protection. However, it was hoped to build a new army, based on the Polish units which had fought with the Red Army. While the war against Germany continued, compulsory military service was introduced. Nevertheless, in view of the shortage of reliable Polish officers, Soviet officers were appointed to command Polish units. Additionally, political officers were to supervise the education of the conscripts to try and inculcate the army with new ideas. Special military tribunals tried those deemed to be hostile to the government. In reality, this meant anyone who had been a member of the AK, the BCh or the NSZ units. They were liable to be investigated, imprisoned and, in some cases, executed.

The election took place in 1947. In the period before this time, parties which supported the TRJN were allowed to function legally. Critically, this excluded the nationalist movement. But it enabled the PPS and the PSL to function as legal parties in the immediate post-war period. Both were initially hampered by the many of the pre-war leaders. They were unwilling to return to Poland and refused to participate in the establishment of parties which were, from the outset, going to cooperate with the communists. Nevertheless, by mid-1945, both parties emerged as key players in Polish politics. Within factories, enterprises and mines, trade unions were legal. Although the communists tried to reduce the workers traditional support for the PPS through aggressive tactics and dubious electoral methods. In principle, workers could still join non-communist workplace organisations. In the countryside, the PSL was buoyed by Mikołajczyk's presence in the TRJN. It emerged as the largest non-communist party, preparing to play the role of the legal opposition.

The authority of the Catholic Church was much enhanced during the war. The Primate had departed from Poland in 1939. This raised doubts about his personal judgement. Though the church was not tainted by association with the occupation because of Nazi hostility to the Catholic Church. Part of their strategy was to destroy the spiritual, intellectual and moral leadership of the Polish nation. Hundreds of parish priests and six bishops had been imprisoned, tortured and killed in Nazi concentration camps. Nearly a fifth of the clergy had perished during the war. The bond which existed between Polish national ideas and the Catholic Church was reaffirmed by the common suffering of the time. The end of the war, nevertheless, created new circumstances. Most dramatically, the role of the Catholic Church within Poland was enhanced by the border changes and the extermination of the Jewish communities. In post-war Poland, nearly all citizens belonged to the Catholic faith. The TRJN, initially pursued a conciliatory policy towards the church. This involved sanctioning the return of property which had been earlier confiscated by the Germans. The Catholic University in Lublin was reopened and Catholic daily and weekly newspapers appeared. Nevertheless, conflict was inevitable. The church sought to consolidate its spiritual and economic position. In the meantime, the TRJN pursued a policy of secularisation. This meant the separation of the state and church. These policies brought the two into direct conflict and, ultimately, led to the breakdown of dialogue. This was even before the implementation of draconian, Stalinist policies against the church in 1949. Thus, the period of cooperation was very brief. The church then moved to assume the role of the opposition. Within the PPR strong, anticlericalist sentiments were mitigated by the realisation that it would be imprudent to pursue confrontation with an organisation of such authority in Polish society. Attempts were made to form a Christian party, which would cooperate with the communists. These attempts came to nothing.[2]

The war led to the rise in nationalist sentiments. With that came a desire to rebuild the state on nationalist lines. Borders were extended to the West. This meant that, in 1945, over 2 million German nationals were living within Poland's borders. This number would have been higher had there not been a mass flight of Germans, in the wake of the Red Army's push West. Nor does this figure include German prisoners of war employed by the Poles. From the outset, it was clear that neither the communist-dominated government, nor the Poles, would tolerate the possibility of any German nationals remaining within Polish borders. The German community was made to leave Polish territories by the end of 1947[3]. First through intimidation and, finally, through a policy of forced resettlement. Poles flooded into ex-German areas incorporated into Polish borders. Some were in search of land and farms. Others went to steal property left behind. After the war, previously German territories included in Poland were euphemistically called the Recovered Territories. This had the implication that the recovery of these territories was neither compensation for eastern regions lost to the Soviet Union, nor a claim on defeated Germany. Instead, state propaganda throughout the communist period, put stress on the historic links between Poland and these territories. The government had planned for an orderly settlement of the Poles who had been forced out of areas incorporated into the Soviet Union. In reality, the Recovered Territories were like the Wild West of the USA. They had squatters taking over farms and forcing the authorities to recognise their claims.

German prisoners of war formed a separate category. The Polish government made use of these men in the coal-mining industry. Here, there was a shortage of labour in the first post-war years. Approximately 41,000 German POWs were held in Poland. Their continuing detention contravened the Geneva Convention on the treatment of POWs. However, the Polish government justified their employment by stating that the value of their labour would be set against the reparations, which Poland expected to receive from Germany.

During the interwar period, approximately 5 million Ukrainian nationals lived within the borders of the Polish state. Relations between the Polish state and the Ukrainian community, deteriorated during the 1920s and 1930s. A general disregard for Ukrainian national aspirations was combined with brutal repression. This was primarily aimed at securing the borderlands and fostered strong anti-Polish sentiments within the Ukrainian communities. During Russian occupation, the Soviet authorities favoured the Ukrainians. The Poles, on the other hand, were forcefully removed into the interior. In the summer of 1941, the German army occupied these areas. Their policies on the Ukrainian question were more complex. On the one hand, Ukrainian military units were raised to fight on the German side. But neither autonomy nor independence was granted. In 1943, the Ukraińska Armia Powstańcza (Ukrainian Insurrectionist Army – UPA) was formed to fight for Ukrainian independence. UPA carried out brutal attacks on Polish villages and in particular on military settlements. These became legendary. The Germans had used Ukrainian units for policing duties, as concentration camp guards and to round up the Jewish populations. At the end of the war, there was therefore a clear desire, in Poland, to punish the Ukrainians. An agreement was concluded between the Soviet Union and the Lublin authority. By this agreement, Ukrainian families would be forcefully moved to areas under Soviet control, while Polish nationals would be moved to Poland. The Ukrainian community fought back. After the end of the fighting in Germany, Polish troops were deployed to these regions and forcefully removed Ukrainians to the Soviet Union. In the summer of 1946, the Soviet Union refused to accept any more Ukrainian nationals and the Polish government decided to disperse the remaining 200,000 throughout the

Recovered Territories. The operation was codenamed 'Wisła'. All Ukrainian nationals, who were still living within Polish borders, were forcefully removed to Western Poland and settled in scattered communities. They had no right to return to areas where they had previously lived.[4] Henceforth, the existence of a Ukrainian community in Poland was denied.

In accordance with agreements made in Yalta, Poland was guaranteed free elections. As hostilities ended, all the legalised parties focused on what they hoped, would be an opportunity to establish a genuinely free Polish government. In the meantime, the TRJN proceeded cautiously. It has been suggested that, they actually attempted to disguise their hold on power.[5] Edward Osóbka-Morawski was the leader of a radical section of the PPS. He became the first post-war Prime Minister. Władysław Gomułka was the General Secretary of the PPR and representative of the communist organisation. This had been built up in occupied Poland. He became the Deputy Prime Minister and Mikołajczyk became the other Deputy Prime Minister. Key portfolios were in the hands of either communists or those who had strong links with the communists. Critically, the communists controlled national security, internal security and all economic matters. They declared their commitment to the creation of broadly based progressive blocs. The communists, nevertheless, made absolutely sure that they were in control of the most important developments. Thus, within trade unions, they sought to have communists elected to executive positions. They also did this within the national councils. These acted as local self-government organisations. The general attitude towards the communists and their endeavours was distrustful and workers in most cases remained loyal to their pre-war, trade unions.

The PPR were only too well aware that they were not trusted. They therefore wanted to postpone elections. The communists expected that stabilisation of the security situation in Poland and the first signs of economic recovery, would lead the Poles to support parties which made up the TRJN. This would include the communists. Land reform and the repatriation of the Poles from the Soviet Union were all very emotive and popular issues. They could increase support for the government. Thus, the PPR's tactic, in the first place, was to postpone general elections. In the second place, they tried to persuade the PPS and the PSL, to combine with the PPR in forming a broadly based electoral bloc.

The elections took place on 19 January 1947. At this time, the PPR increasingly conducted an aggressive campaign. All attempts to persuade Mikołajczyk to agree that all parties should go to the elections on a joint slate failed. After this, the PPR proceeded to intimidate and destroy his party. Local PSL organisations were attacked and prominent leaders were arrested and charged with a variety of offences. The peasant community became the object of an intense pre-electoral propaganda aimed at persuading them to vote for the PPR.[6]

PPR tactics towards the PPS were different. The PSL believed that it had a real chance of winning a majority of votes and forming a government on its own. Unlike them, many of the PPS leaders had a strong commitment to left wing unity. Some believed that it was time to reverse the divisions, which had appeared within the socialist movement after the Russian Revolution. The interwar period was a time when the left wing movement did not speak with one voice. This was due to doctrinaire conflicts between the communist and the socialist movements. The growth of the radical right and fascist and Nazi successes were, in part, attributed to left wing disunity. This reasoning led many socialists and communists in Europe to seek some form of accommodation, if not outright organisational unity. In Poland, the PPS managed to rebuild its organisational structure and re-establish its control of trade unions. Despite this, a shared desire for progressive economic reforms, brought the two parties to the negotiating table. However, the degree and precise nature of cooperation was not resolved. The PPR increasingly called for organisational unity. The PPS saw this as no more than a takeover which many socialists rejected. They believed in collaboration and consultation with the communists.[7]

The Soviet Union, nevertheless, continued to determine policies in Poland. To Stalin, relations with the wartime allies were a priority. In 1946, the first signs of difficulties appeared. Initially, Stalin did not want to authorise action in Poland. This would cause Britain and the USA to doubt his earlier commitment on the Polish question. In May he attended a meeting with Polish communists and socialists. At this meeting, he did not give them the green light to destroy the

PSL. Instead, he urged them to work with Mikołajczyk. The communists were trying to weaken the PSL. As part of their tactics, they called for a referendum in which the community was asked three leading questions on whether they supported the incorporation of the Recovered Territories into Poland: whether they approved of land reform and nationalisation of industry and whether they approved of the abolition of the Senate. A 'yes' said three times was to be a vote in support of the TRJN and communist tactics. The results of the referendum were a disappointment to the PPR and their allies, even though the results which were released, suggested a majority in favour of the 3 X Yes call. However, it was generally suspected that the official results were falsified.

During the following months, Stalin's policies towards Poland underwent a change. His next decision was to agree with the PPR that the PSL had to be destroyed and Poland was to be incorporated more closely into the Soviet sphere of influence. The PPR went onto the offensive. In September 1946, PPR and PPS agreed on an electoral strategy. They formed a Democratic Bloc with two other small parties, the Stronnictwo Demokratyczne (Democratic Alliance – SD) and the pro-communist Stronnictwo Ludowe (Peasant Alliance – SL). In the run up to the elections, all means were used to decrease the anticipated PSL victory. Mikołajczyk's supporters were barred from voting on grounds that they had cooperated with the Nazis. PSL offices were attacked and its members were intimidated. Electoral committees were scrutinised to ensure that they were controlled either by communists or those sympathetic to them. 17 January 1947 was the day of the general elections. Intimidation was rife. When the results were announced, it appeared that the Democratic Bloc had won with a resounding 80.1 per cent of votes cast. No one believed these to be the true results. Mikołajczyk protested. He suggested that if the security situation had been different, the PSL could have obtained the expected 60 per cent of the votes. The British and US ambassadors both knew of widespread irregularities, and confirmed that the elections had not been genuinely free. Stalin had made an earlier commitment to Churchill that elections in Poland would be free. When this turned out not to be the case, both Western powers confined themselves to lodging official protests. In any case, little could have been done to alter the course of events in Poland or in Eastern Europe.[8]

The Sejm met on 4 February and the Democratic Bloc's victory was confirmed. Bolesław Bierut became President. He was from the PPR and had spent the war period in the Soviet Union. Józef Cyrankiewicz became the Prime Minister. He was from the PPS and a strong supporter of uniting the PPS and PPR to form one party. During the following months, the regime moved to complete the destruction of the PSL. In September, several of its leaders were put on trial on trumped up charges of having collaborated with the underground opposition. The party's premises were taken over, while PSL members and supporters were purged from government and local authority employment. On 20 October, Mikołajczyk, along with three other members of the party leadership, fled from Poland into exile.[9]

The destruction of what could have become a legitimate opposition was the final act in the process of consolidation of Soviet control over Poland. This coincided with the onset of the Cold War and the collapse of Western collaboration with the Soviet Union, over the future of Germany. The Marshall Aid declaration was made in June 1947. It indicated to the Soviet leadership that the USA intended to use economic recovery as a means of containing the spread of Soviet influence. After the initial announcement, the Soviet leadership took some time to fully absorb the implications of the American announcement. Ultimately, the Soviet response was to consolidate its hold on areas of strategic importance to Soviet security. In this, Poland was foremost.

Until the elections, there was a hope that the Poles would be left to make the decision as to whether Poland would exercise genuine independence or would become closely associated with the Soviet Union. Many held this belief, including well-informed politicians within the government. At the end of hostilities in Europe, Poland was within the Soviet sphere of influence. However, most believed that the country's future path of development would be determined once key decisions concerning Germany had been agreed. This would therefore be after the elections. Mikołajczyk and many non-communist leaders in Eastern Europe had hoped that the

industrialised West would assist Poland in its programme of reconstruction and future industrialisation. The PSL put a lot of stress
on the way in which Mikołajczyk had returned to Poland. His return had been the result of tripartite agreements. In this way, he
guaranteed, for Poland, the right to determine its own political and
economic development. These agreements, according to the PSL,
indicated that the fate of Poland was of critical importance to the
Western democracies. This was not only because of the debt of gratitude which they owed to Poland for having fought against Nazi
Germany. It was also because the Soviet Union had given an undertaking that Poland would be free.

The destruction of the PSL and the consolidation of Soviet control of Poland was completed within a year of the elections. In this
time, the PPS was united with, or, as many would argue, absorbed
by the PPR into a renamed Polska Zjednoczona Partia Robotnicza
(United Polish Workers' Party – PZPR). Civil society, in the form
of associations, local self-help groups, producers' cooperatives and
cultural clubs, all lost their independence. They were taken over by
umbrella organisations controlled by the state. Trade unions were
prevented from acting as genuine organisations representing the interests of the workers. They were also purged of those deemed to be
politically unreliable.

The end of the war put the question of economic development
firmly in the forefront of all international and national debates.
A need for reconstruction also opened the debate on the means of
controlling economic development. Debates were also conducted as
to the extent to which free market forces could be trusted to achieve
economic takeoff and guarantee economic stability. Inflation had
followed the First World War and the Great Depression. This had
started in the late 1920s. Memories of this inflation led to the conclusion that there would be a need for reassessment of the state's
role in the process of economic growth. At the same time, failure
to achieve stability during the interwar period, meant that these
debates were not confined to economic circles, but were conducted
within all political parties and organisations.

In Poland, discussion of economic issues added urgency because of the dismal state of the economy after the end of hostilities. The situation at the end of the war was complex. German

occupation had transformed many branches of the pre-war economy. This was not only through confiscation and appropriations. It was also through exploitation for military purposes. Initially, German policy went in the direction of reducing the productive capacity of the occupied territories. However, after the attack on the Soviet Union, this policy was partly reversed. After allied bombing of German territories, it seemed logical to disperse war industries. Thus, mining and steel production were maintained and even increased in the Silesian regions. Small enterprises and workshops were closed and investment and reallocation of machinery went in the direction of increasing large-scale productive capacity. The result was a reduction in the production of consumer goods and an increase in the production of goods needed for the war effort. Likewise, employment patterns changed during the war. Poles were used as forced labour and underutilised capacity was brought into more efficient operation. Fuller exploitation of the occupied regions, resulted in the doubling of the number of people employed in industry. In 1938, it was estimated that only 808,000 Poles worked in manufacturing. In 1945, this number had increased to 1.5 million.

Polish agriculture had been exploited to its maximum during the period of German occupation. Compulsory supply quotas were imposed on the village community and this, in turn, forced the peasants to increase production. In order to increase output, the occupation administration introduced better live-stock into the villages. These were frequently pillaged from other occupied areas. They also encouraged cultivation of crops needed in industry. These were namely flax, hemp, linen, rapeseed and sugar beet. Improvement in the transport system, both road and rail, aimed at greater military efficiency. This also benefited the economy of the occupied Polish territories.

War activities in 1945 were exceptionally brutal in Polish areas. They destroyed the existing infrastructure and production. When withdrawing, Germans dismantled and moved production back to the Third Reich. What they could not take with them, they blew up. Incoming Soviet troops had no direct interest in maintaining production in Polish regions. This led to disputes between the Soviet military administrators, who often took the view that German property should be used as part of the reparation bill to be settled in the future. Poles, even representatives of the TRJN, who sought to restart production in Poland. Soviet agents were unwilling to make a distinction between genuinely German property, and Polish property which had been confiscated by the Germans. Dismantling and transporting plants and machinery from Polish areas to the Soviet Union, triggered the opposition of the emerging local Polish administrations. They viewed this as pillaging. The TRJN was unable to halt what was seen as the despoiling of Polish industrial capacity by the Soviet authorities. They could only lose authority in the country it claimed to administer. As a result of these difficulties and continuing military activities, Polish GNP in 1945 was only 38 per cent of pre-war levels.

Dislocation was caused by changes of frontiers. This further delayed recovery. The eastern areas lost to the Soviet Union had contained oilfields, salt, potassium, quartz and coal. But Poland gained areas of high-quality agriculture and the mines and steel plants in Upper and Lower Silesia. In Europe, it was generally assumed that coal, as a main source of energy, would be in short supply. Poland stood poised to benefit from the energy shortage. This was because the coal mines incorporated into Polish borders after the war had been relatively untouched by bombing and war activities.

Discussions and proposals concerning agrarian problems had been put forward during the course of the war by parties connected with the government in exile and even the PPR. These bore striking similarities. Those prepared in London, recognised the need for progressive land reform. This included distributing land among the peasants, from estates owned by the state and organisations which were not involved in agriculture, and from property confiscated from traitors and collaborators. It was also assumed that farms of more than 50 hectares would be broken up. The PSL had a major say in preparing this programme and stressed the need to create viable farms. By this, they meant those consisting of between 6 and 25 hectares of land. But land reform was contentious because of the question of compensation to those who would lose their estates. Underpinning all debates was the dilemma as to whether land reform would lead to an increase in production. Land reform was necessary for political reasons. However, the fear was, that it would increase the number of small and clearly inefficient farms. It was generally assumed that to produce a marketable surplus, farms would have to consist of over 7 hectares of land. Though that would still depend on land quality and usage. Thus, a lot of stress was put on industry providing employment for the surplus village population and on high-quality agriculture which would produce goods and an exportable surplus. This programme was similar to the one put forward by parties in occupied Poland. PPR made no reference to collectivisation. Like other left wing parties, it merely referred to the necessity of land reform without compensation.[10]

Nor were there major differences in the various parties' programmes on industry and commerce. There were suggestions that the state should take over natural resources and nationalise key industries, such as mining, machine making, and armament industries. These had been common currency during the interwar period. Industrialisation and economic advancement, with strong state direction, were goals with which the Polish people generally agreed. This was because state involvement was equated with maximum use of resources for the nation's benefit and with modernisation and further industrialisation. The alternative was dependence on foreign capital. This was seen as benefiting non-Poles. Nevertheless, the first aim was to restart production and recovery. In that, the government was heavily dependent on factory committees. These emerged spontaneously in many enterprises and led to workers' co-operation with management boards.[11]

The PKWN manifesto of July 1944, announced that all goods and property confiscated by the Germans, would be returned to their rightful owners. That included property belonging to peasants, workers, workshop owners, the middle class and churches and ecclesiastical organisations. Only property which had belonged to Germans and Polish state property taken over by the occupation administration was to be nationalised. No mention was made of factories, plants and banks.

To the Lublin authorities, land reform was the single most important legislative decision. This was because the majority of the population was still connected directly and indirectly with the village. Another important reason was the need to stabilise food production. The land decree, announced in September 1944, stated that land would be taken from traitors, Germans and landowners who had farms larger than 50 hectares. After 1946, agricultural land in the Recovered Territories was distributed. This led to a conflict between the local officials and government economists and agronomists. The local officials wanted to increase the popularity of the TRJN by distributing the land. The government economists and agronomists urged that the well run and mechanised ex-German farms, be retained in order to raise agricultural productivity. As it turned out, the results of the land reform were disappointing. The peasant community had benefited from land reform decrees introduced by the TRJN. Despite this, during the referendum and the general elections, they did not vote for the Democratic Bloc parties. Instead, they remained loyal to the PSL. Already in early 1945, conflicts had arisen between the rump Peasant Alliance, which had collaborated with the TRJN, and the PPR. The peasant parties viewed land distribution as something which should be implemented by the peasant parties, themselves, at the local level. The PPR distrusted the idea of peasant spontaneity. Instead, they favoured a strong, state role, in the process of transformation. In any case, the PPR made no official reference to collectivisation. For them, land reform was primarily a means of securing the peasant vote.[12] In 1946, relations between the PPR and the PSL deteriorated. As this happened, the communists favoured redistributing land to small and landless peasants, even if this reduced agricultural productivity. The PSL called for strengthening middle-sized peasants and supported peasants' cooperatives. The PPR portrayed this as a sign that the party was siding with the large landowners.[13]

Land reform did not resolve the problem of village backwardness. In spite of the redistribution of land, over 61 per cent of land ended up in farms. These were described as dwarf or small. They were, in effect, up to around 2 hectares of land. This indicated that problems of food production had not been resolved and that overpopulation and underemployment, would still bedevil attempts to modernise agriculture in the future. In 1949, the problem had to be addressed anew. Although by this time, the communists did not have to take into account the PSL. This had, in the meantime, been destroyed.

Initially, the provisional government made no references to nationalisation of production. Nevertheless, German policies during the war, effectively created natural preconditions for the state to assume responsibility for enterprises. The state, in principle, took over all abandoned property and that which had been administered by the Germans. Re-privatisation was made difficult by confusion over previous ownership. Frequently, previous owners were dead or their fate was unknown. Thus, the real conflict over ownership of means of production was not played out between the state and the previous owners, but between the state and factory committees. Such committees had, in the meantime, assumed physical control of factories, mines and enterprises and were organising the resumption of production. Hilary Minc, a communist who had spent the war in the Soviet Union. Under his leadership, the Ministry of Industry and Trade curtailed the radical aspirations of the workers. They had wanted to retain control over managerial and production decisions. Instead, the state adjudicated on all matters concerning ownership.[14]

In January 1946, through a decree of nationalisation of key branches of industry, state control over economic matters was established. Nevertheless, disputes with factory committees continued. Minc aimed to confine their role to that of representing workers' interests within the workplace. In that, the PPR faced opposition from the PPS. Their economists advocated that factory committees should retain a say in production matters. These varied from outright control by worker managerial committees, to factory committee representatives on the managerial boards. These were short-lived debates and the PPR succeeded in reducing and, ultimately destroying, the power of the factory committees.[15]

The state, similarly imposed its policies on workers in private small-scale production, workshops and retail outlets. Workers' co-operatives had had a long tradition in Poland. They continued to develop during the period of reconstruction. It was, nevertheless obvious, that the Communists intended to retain control of production and to force a rapid pace of recovery. In this, the heavy and extractive industries were a priority. The Three Year Reconstruction Plan was announced in 1947. It encapsulated the PPR's plan for Poland's economic transformation. Poland was to become an industrial state. Furthermore, it was to be one in which economic changes would be accompanied by radical social and political changes. The pace of transformation was dramatically stepped up in 1947. This was when the PSL's advocacy of a slow, agrarian-based modernisation programme was defeated. In 1947–48, the PPR attacked and progressively destroyed all other parties, even those with which it had previously cooperated. When this happened, all debates on the future economic model came to an end. Economists connected with the PPS, who had put forward a number of innovative economic theories, were singled out for attack. When the party was absorbed into the PPR, these men were publicly pilloried and forced to make an admission that they had been wrong in advocating a slow industrial development and for having overstated the role of workers' control in that process.[16]

In September 1947, the founding meeting of the Communist Information Bureau (Cominform) took place in the mountain resort of Szklarska Poręba, in Poland. It is usually cited as the starting point of the Cold War. In Poland, the elections and the reassessment of the role of the communists had occurred earlier in the year. This ushered in the period when the Stalinist model was imposed on Polish society. At the same time, Poland was more closely tied into the Soviet bloc, through the signing of bilateral trade agreements. Decisions made at Szklarska Poręba led the communists to assume a leading role in state organisations. Party activists took over managerial positions and key administrative posts. The relationship between the PPR and the state dramatically changed. Poland effectively become a single-party state. Not only this, but the communists also took over the state. They did this to the extent that it became, not merely the ruling party, but the party which ruled Poland by means of direct involvement in all state decisions. The PSL was destroyed and the PPS disappeared, absorbed into the PZPR. But if the PZPR was to assume a leadership role, the party apparatus, as the instrument of policy enforcement, also had to be sharpened and disciplined.

The dispute between Yugoslavia and the Soviet Union emerged during 1948. The need to recast the party so it could become an obedient agent of Soviet polices in Poland led to purges within the PZPR. Initially, the leadership of the PPR, consisted of comrades with diverse wartime experiences. Some, like Bierut, had spent the war in the Soviet Union. Others, like Gomułka, had survived in occupied Poland. As a result, they had very different ideas as to how the communist system would evolve in Poland. Nor did Stalin expect the PPR to speak with one voice. It was, in fact, Stalin, who demanded that the Moscow-based Polish communists, include Gomułka in the PKWN. In 1947, the first signs of the Cold War appeared. This occurred along with a shift in Stalin's assessment of the role of the communists in Poland. Due to these factors, ideological diversity was suppressed. The Soviets demanded that the communist parties in all East European states should establish a single-party rule. After this, and the founding of the Comintern, communists who had proposed a degree of independence from the Soviet Union, came under attack. Gomułka was attacked for having advocated a Polish road to socialism, not dissimilar to Tito's polices in Yugoslavia. He had also opposed collectivisation. This, he felt, would go contrary to the Polish peasants' aspirations. In 1948, he was relieved of the post of Deputy Prime Minster. Critically, the party condemned him for 'nationalist deviation'. This resulted in him being dismissed from the post of party secretary. In its battle against 'deviationists' the PZPR investigators cast their nets widely. Many of the party rank and file, who were arrested during the purges, had been members of the pre-war KPP. Most of the surviving veterans of the Spanish Civil War, ended up in prisons. The leadership of the party was taken over by those who had spent the war in Moscow and knew better than to question Stalin's policies. This group included, Bierut and Minc, Jakub Berman, a Stalinist ideologist. General Marian Spychalski was the Minister of Defence. He had acted as Chief of Staff of the communist Armia Ludowa underground units during the war. He was arrested and his position was taken over by Konstanty Rokossovsky, a Soviet general of Polish background.[17]

The arrests affected all parties which had earlier collaborated with the TRJN. There is strong evidence to suggest that the purges of the communists and their allies were coordinated from Moscow. Accusations were formulated against suspected Polish Communists and socialists. In doing this, links were drawn with Hungarian and Czechoslovak Communists, who were under arrest at the same time. Thus, in addition to being vilified for having allegedly conspired with Tito, they were accused of having been in touch with Laszlo Rajk, a Hungarian communist and Minister for Foreign Affairs. He had been arrested during the purges and executed after a show trial. Polish victims of the purges were also accused of having been influenced by the Noel brothers. These were two US citizens, associated with a relief agency based in Austria. Their names figured on accusations levelled against Rajk and the Czech victims of the purges, notably Slánský. The result was not only the destruction of any internal debate within the PZPR, but, in the long term, the end of a left wing political discourse in Poland. The lively and varied debate on the role of the state and of workers in the post-war state of 1945–47, ended with the imposition of Stalinist ideological correctness in 1948.

The Stalinist period affected all aspects of life. In December 1948 a Six Year Plan was accepted as the basis of future economic development. This assumed a rapid pace of industrialisation, with particular emphasis on metal and chemical production. It was put into effect in 1950. The Korean War created a demand for munitions and this was added to the plan's objectives. In the long term, it was assumed that the initial rapid pace of development, would allow for a future improvement in the standard of living. In reality, consumer and light industries were woefully neglected. Shortages of everyday goods became the norm. The Six Year Plan was not merely an attempt to overcome backwardness and create preconditions for a rapid industrial takeoff. Inevitably, its political objective was supposed to transform Polish society by altering the balance between the agrarian sector, which dominated Polish life hitherto, and urban/industrial life. With Soviet credit and demand for Polish goods, stress was put on big projects. The Nowa Huta steelworks, near Kraków, was a good example of this. These modern, mechanised enterprises were to employ what were to be new workers, committed to the building of a communist future. The chemical and machine industries, in turn, would facilitate the transformation of the backward, stagnant agrarian sector, by making available chemical fertilizers and agricultural machinery. The plan was also to guarantee that Poland would be in a position to defend its borders. The Soviet model of economic development was imposed on Poland, irrespective of its economic feasibility. In 1954, as part of the first debates following Stalin's death, the Central Committee of the PZPR admitted that the standard of living of Polish workers had collapsed since 1947 and that there was a need to review the plan in order to increase production of consumer goods. The anxiety about workers taking industrial action, made this reassessment a necessary exercise.[18]

A decision to collectivise agriculture was made in 1948, after the attack on the so-called nationalist groups in the party. Mindful of the peasants' anxiety about the loss of the recently acquired land, the process was publicly described as bringing peasants into cooperatives. This presented collectivisation as a voluntary process, in which the peasants would be persuaded of the wisdom of coming together and farming jointly. This would thus enable them to purchase and use modern machinery and farming methods. In October 1949, local party groups were instructed to accelerate the process. From 1950, collectivisation of farming became a priority. Coercion and persuasion were used to get the peasants to sign up to collectives. Those who refused were persecuted with increased taxation and threats. Individual farmers found it difficult to obtain seeds, fertilisers and agricultural implements.[19] Nevertheless, in 1955, it was finally agreed to halt the process. Only 9.2 per cent of cultivated land had been collectivised. At the same time, state farms were established. They held approximately 12.4 per cent of cultivated land. In both cooperative and state farms, output was lower than in private farms. The impact of these policies on the village was considerable. Food production stayed inadequate and Polish agriculture remained backward and underinvested. This state of affairs continued, even after 1956, when the decision was made to dissolve the cooperative farms. At the same time, increased opportunities in industry led to a flight of young people from villages to the new industrial complexes. These guaranteed them housing, educational opportunities and a higher standard of living.

Mutual distrust and hostility, characterised all East-West exchanges. This, along with the onset of the Cold War, had a profound impact on Europe. Polish territories were treated as a security zone and Soviet troops were stationed close to the border with Germany. Soviet control over Poland was reinforced by a policy of increasing all forms of dependence on the Soviet Union. West European states limited all contacts with Poland, accepting its place within the Soviet bloc. Poland, like other states in the Soviet sphere of influence, was henceforth "contaminated by Soviet ideology". Economic, social and cultural contacts between Poland and the West were limited. Poland was thus bound to the Soviet Union, with no efforts being made by the West, to reverse this state of affairs.

Poland was drawn more closely into the Soviet economic sphere, both through direct economic and financial agreements, but also through the Council of Mutual Economic Assistance (COMECON). This was an organisation established by the Soviet Union in direct response to Marshall Aid in January 1949. Its aim was to encourage members to specialise in particular branches of industry. Through that, it was to decrease duplication and wasteful overlaps. During the Stalinist period, trade was conducted in such ways that it was invariably more advantageous to Soviet economic development. In the impoverished and war-ravaged Poland, it was widely known that vital raw materials such as coal and sulphur were being sent to the Soviet Union. This caused widespread resentment.

From 1949, Soviet control over Poland extended to all aspects of life. It had purged its leadership of those who advocated a measured approach to economic development and collectivisation. The PZPR, led by Bierut, took a hard line in relation to all those likely to disagree. In these circumstances, the Catholic Church came under scrutiny. In 1949, a Mixed Commission, consisting of representatives of the church and high-ranking ministers, was established to address a number of contentious issues.[20] The Vatican supported the West German opposition to the loss of pre-war territories. This confronted the Polish Episcopate with a number of dilemmas. As long as the Vatican viewed the Recovered Territories as German and not Polish, they came under the jurisdiction of German bishops and only they had the right to appoint parish priests. It was obvious that Poles would not attend churches in which German priests officiated. Thus an uneasy compromise was found whereby the German bishops accepted the temporary appointment of Polish priests. In the context of the extreme political confrontation created by the Cold War, this situation left the Polish Episcopate open to accusations of collusion with hostile powers.

In November 1948, a new bishop, Stefan Wyszyński, was nominated to become archbishop of Gniezno and Warsaw. He succeeded the deceased Cardinal Hlond. His nomination coincided with the rise in tension between the communist state and the church. Wyszyński was not allowed to make the obligatory trip to Rome, to receive the confirmation of his nomination to the archbishopric. Initially, the communists wanted to see a Catholic party in the Sejm. This was a plan that the Episcopate refused to support. Nevertheless, even in these difficult circumstances the dialogue between the two authorities continued. From 1949 onwards, relations deteriorated. Nuns, priests and monks were arrested and accused of having collaborated with the Nazis. Show trials and provocations were staged in order to put the church in a bad light.[21] The final straw came in September 1953 when Primate Wyszyński was arrested and put under house arrest. This situation did not change until 1956. Attacks on the Catholic Church were not merely a reflection of a very real conflict between two powerful ideologies. The historic association between Polish identity and the Catholic religion was obvious. Any attempt to impose a primary loyalty to the state, would entail an attack on that historic association.

During the Stalinist years, Soviet policies towards Poland went beyond subordination of the state to Soviet interests. An integral element of that policy had been attacks on Polish traditions, cultural and social, replacing them with Russian and Soviet symbols. All aspects of life were affected by these policies, from changes to the Polish army uniforms, to the use in schools of Soviet textbooks. These had been translated from Russian and had the compulsory poem to Stalin on the first page.

Stalin's death on 5 March 1953 did not in itself change the situation. The regime relaxed its hold on society, slowly and unwillingly. To the PZPR leadership, this was a time of confusion. They were used to receiving clear and precise instructions on the policies that they were expected to follow. They did not know how to respond to the Moscow communist leadership's preoccupation with domestic matters. Polish communists were unsure of the implications of their own positions in the battle for succession which was taking place in the Kremlin. This caused problems, when Moscow's control over domestic Polish affairs had been all pervading. The initial response was to try and continue as they had done before. Hence the arrests of those suspected of contacts with the West; purges of 'nationalist deviationists' and 'Titoists' and increased attacks on the

Catholic hierarchy. No slowing down of the pace of industrial development was authorised. Even though it was already known that targets outlined in the Six Year Plan, would not be achieved and that the collectivisation drive had failed to deliver increased food supplies.

The first signs of a thaw appeared in March 1954. During II Party Congress, PZPR leadership, closely observed by Nikita Khrushchev, sanctioned the changes. Without making any references to Stalin's incorrect policies, the Soviet leadership wanted to see the separation of the state and party functions. Bierut, henceforth, was to hold the party leadership. Józef Cyrankiewicz, previously leader of the PPS, became Prime Minister. This change did not herald a break with the recent Stalinist past, as Cyrankiewicz had acted as Prime Minister between 1947 and 1952 and Deputy Prime Minister from 1952. No attempt was made to change the top cadre. This continued to be dominated by the triumvirate of Bierut, Minc and Berman. Changes, nevertheless continued within society, the lower echelons of the party and the influential cultural milieu. These changes, however tentative, continued and gradually gained momentum.[22]

Next in line for review was the security apparatus dominated by a much feared and hated Stanisław Radkiewicz. The Ministry of Public Security had, during the Stalinist years, enjoyed extensive powers. The general perception was that Radkiewicz had communicated directly with the Soviet leaders and took his instructions from them. Purges of the PZPR and, in particular, the continuing imprisonment of Gomułka, caused resentment, even within the party. Once the ministry was abolished and its functions were dispersed, the process of reviewing of past sentences could start. Slowly and without public acknowledgement, people were released from prisons. Thousands of Poles, who had been accused of no other crime than that they had belonged to the AK or BCh units during the war, were freed. In 1955, PZPR made an open admission that mistakes had been made in the past. As a result of this statement, party activists tried earlier were granted amnesties. Gomułka was released from prison, though that fact was not made public.

The party leadership's preference, would have been for the changes in Moscow and their implications for Poland, to remain an internal party matter. This proved impossible. In the first place, by releasing prisoners, their treatment and the accusations levelled against them, became the subject of debate. No newspapers addressed the subject openly. However, it was common knowledge that something was going to change and that previous policies were being abandoned. The veil of secrecy had been torn aside in September 1954. Radio Free Europe was a CIA-funded US broadcasting station based in Munich. It ran a series of interviews with Józef Światło who was a top security agent. In December 1953, Światło had defected to the West. Information revealed by him and beamed over Poland during the coming year discredited not merely the government in the public's eyes, but challenged the whole notion that the PZPR was a ruling party. Światło had been the deputy head of Department X. This was a section of the Ministry of Public Security. It had been assigned the role of invigilation of party leaders. Thus, it was revealed that, far from being a ruling party, the PZPR was under the strict surveillance of an internal body, accountable only to the Minister of Public Security. Radio Free Europe continued to be the source of information that most Poles believed to be true. From its broadcasts, people found out that party and government leaders enjoyed a better lifestyle than that which any other Poles could have achieved by honest means. The government's claim to be ruling on behalf of the toiling masses was exposed. This raised doubts about its own position and about the integrity of its leadership. In the streets, debates and discussions, as well as open criticism of the state of affairs, could not be controlled or stemmed any longer.[23]

The PZPR leadership was still reluctant to be either open or forthright in addressing reforms. Changes taking place in Moscow made it impossible for them to stall. These forced the Stalinist leadership to also review their policies in Poland. In February 1956, Khrushchev made a clean break with the Stalinist past. He made a defining speech to a closed forum at the XX Party Congress in the Soviet Union. In it, he accused Stalin of having deviated from the true path of socialism. The speech was to mark a break with the past and allowed the new leaders to distance themselves from the mistakes made earlier. In one stroke, the position of the 'Little Stalins', who had maintained their grip on power in Eastern Europe, was rendered impossible. Fortunately for the Poles, Bierut, while attending the congress, succumbed to illness and died in Moscow. This cleared the way for reforms in Poland.[24]

By then, de-Stalinisation was no longer only a matter for the party leadership. The open Soviet admission of past mistakes, raised hopes for the re-opening of a debate on how Poland was to be ruled and on the extent of Polish independence that the Soviet Union would tolerate. The momentum for further change, would henceforth come from factories, trade unions and the public at large. The intellectual and university community took a leading role both in opening up and publicising debates on recent events and injustices committed by the regime. *Nowa Kultura* (New Culture) was a weekly journal of the Association of Polish Writers. It was one of the first to question past policies to the creative and artistic community. It also voiced concerns about the imprisonment of AK members and distortions in recent history. The journal *Po Prostu* (Simply) published articles in which many contentious issues were aired. The theoretical journal of the PZPR, *Nowe Drogi* (New Ways), likewise entered into the debate. Discussion clubs and debating associations followed. They were increasingly emboldened by the fact that repression and censorship seemed not to be as restrictive as before. The *Krzywe Koło* (Crooked Circle) club was the most prominent of those.[25]

The text of Khrushchev's speech was quickly made available in Poland. In the first place, those who went to Moscow and had been involved in dealing with Bierut's affairs had official copies. Rumours circulated, that illicitly made copies were available on the Warsaw flea market. Finally, the secretariat of the party decided to distribute the text among party activists. At that point, the content of the speech became an open secret. The central committee of the PZPR, divided into open factions. The decision to find a successor to Bierut was made without major disagreements. In reality, since 1954, two factions had emerged in anticipation of an internal battle for the leadership and for, or against, reforms demanded by the Soviet leadership. The Puławska group reflected the reformist wing. These were mainly the young technocrats. While the Natolin one, held on to the Stalinist dogmas. On 17 April, an announcement was made, dissolving the Cominform. Khrushchev started courting Tito in a bid for reconciliation. From Moscow, came news that the Soviet

Union intended to change the basis on which relations had been conducted, with the so-called Peoples' Democracies. It was not clear what that would mean in Poland. At the same time, Poles worried about the military implications of the Soviet Union's new willingness to open talks on Germany and to pursue negotiations on the reunification of Austria. On 14 May 1955, a treaty of friendship was signed, between the Soviet Union and the People's Democracies of Eastern Europe. One of its clauses committed the signatories to support each other militarily. This became known as the Warsaw Pact. To the Poles, it offered assurances of security against Germany. But it was difficult to overlook the conclusion that the Soviet leadership had only decided to create a counterbalance to NATO, when the Soviet initiatives, aimed at reuniting Germany, failed and the German Federal Republic was invited to join NATO.

With changes in Moscow progressing at a rapid pace, the anti-Stalinists in Poland gained an upper hand. Crimes committed during the Stalinist period were discussed in the Sejm at an open session. On 27 April, an amnesty for all political prisoners was declared. Radkiewicz was relieved of his duties. His closest collaborators were arrested and tried for crimes committed during the Stalinist period.[26]

On 28 June 1956, the workers took to the streets. The strikes in Poznań mark a point when the pace of developments eluded the party's control. Workers from the metal and machine factories had earlier tried to resolve disputes concerning new pay rates and taxation. Their representatives, as well as the local security services, knew that the reasons for workers' disaffection were mainly economic. Standards of living had been stagnating and real wages were lower than they had been a year before. The management's unhelpful responses led to anger. On the morning of 28 June, workers spilled out of the workshops and took to the streets. First slogans shouted by the demonstrators still reflected their anger at being cheated of their pay. However, as the workers marched towards the city centre, political slogans were added to pay demands. The striking workers proceeded to attack the headquarters of the secret service and heavily armed troops arrived to fight against them. In the fighting, over 70 workers were killed, though this figure was never made official. Poznań was a signal for other workers to take action. In factories and enterprises across Poland, workers staged meetings. They declared their support for reforms and demanded that the government listen to their grievances.[27]

Most people regarded the current party and government leadership, as having compromised their positions. It was therefore considered that these leaders were unable to lead the reforms. Gomułka's release from prison had become public knowledge. He was increasingly seen as an alternative to the inept Edward Ochab, who had replaced Bierut. The party leadership finally accepted the inevitable and Gomułka became First Party Secretary. Minc's policy of rapid industrialisation was seen as having caused difficulties in the consumer markets. He was criticised by the Central Committee and resigned. At this point, the Soviet political and military leadership, including Khrushchev, decided to fly to Warsaw. They arrived on the morning of 19 October. After a stormy confrontation between the Soviet leader and Gomułka, the Poles won the right to conduct their own reforms, without Soviet interference. There was an additional element of the compromise between the two sides. This was an assurance that Soviet troops stationed in Poland, would return to their bases and that Marshal Rokossovsky would be recalled. The Poles clearly felt slighted that the Soviet side was ignoring Poland's concern over the fate of Germany. The Poles therefore insisted on being consulted on the German talks.

Gomułka aimed to restructure the party leadership and complete the de-Stalinisation process. He still had to deal with the sections of the working class and the intellectuals that had been inspired and mobilised by the prospect of political freedom. This appeared to affect all of Poland. Various groups, representing workers and intellectuals, put forward proposals for reforms. These reforms would have continued Poland's development on a revolutionary path. No group suggested that the economy should be freed from state control and they made no references to denationalisation. Interestingly, workers in the large steelworks around Warsaw, declared their desire to take over management decisions and establish workers' control over production. Only by means of such reforms did they believe that their economic and their political rights could be protected. They, and other striking workers in large enterprises, spoke of reforms, which would have reduced the influence of beaurocrats in factories. By the same token, they would have decreased the power of the state over the workers – the producers of wealth. With a great degree of clarity, the Association of Polish Writers articulated these ideas and further calls for reforms.

It was not a coincidence that the intellectuals felt it their duty to support the workers and to take a position in the events which were unfolding in Poland. There had been a long historic tradition of intellectuals acting as spokesmen for the disenfranchised. This gave them a ready model. In any case, writers who had been able to publish during the preceding years were invariably left wing and, in varying degrees, supported the government of the time. This they did. Although many disagreed with Stalinist policies. In discussing the form and extent of future reforms, both the workers and intellectuals looked to Yugoslavia for ready models. They believed that developments taking place there, reflected more closely what they hoped would be implemented in Poland. This was namely legislation, which would confirm the role of the workers in the new state, by giving them a larger say in economic matters.[28] Tito was the first leader from the communist bloc to congratulate Gomułka on becoming party secretary. Tito advised him to find a Polish road to socialism and not confine himself to choosing either the Soviet or Yugoslav economic and political models.

The heady atmosphere of the summer of 1956, generated both debates and discussions on new modes of production and on the relationship between the state and citizens. This came to an end once Gomułka was assured of the Poles support. It was fortunate for him that he was also able to secure the church's support for reforms. Wyszyński was released from house arrest on 28 October. At the beginning of 1957, Gomułka and Cyrankiewicz held a meeting with Wyszyński. At this meeting, the Catholic Episcopate committed itself to supporting the government during the forthcoming elections. This was in return for a number of concessions. These included the restoration of religious teaching in schools. The new PZPR leadership, and the church shared the wish to avoid fratricidal conflicts and a Soviet invasion.

From this point onward, relations between the state and the church continued. They were uneasy. Nevertheless, they were on the basis of an understanding that both were committed to scaling down internal conflicts. On a public level, relations between the two continued to be strained. The regime had made an earlier commitment to maintain the teaching of religion in schools. Despite this, the regime soon started attacking the church, reducing its activities in the public sphere. In due course, the church lost the right to run nurseries, primary schools and teach religion in state schools.[29] In spite of constantly harassing Catholic institutions, the communists accepted that a head-on attack could be dangerous. In 1965, Polish bishops addressed a proclamation to German bishops. In it, they declared that the two states shared a common Christian heritage. In view of the forthcoming 1000-year anniversary of Poland becoming Christian they 'forgave and asked for forgiveness'. The regime interpreted this as an initiative on foreign policy. This caused a storm as it was believed that the church had no right to stray into these issues. The celebrations of the millennium of Poland's baptism, passed in an atmosphere of hostility and with the government determined to undermine the anniversary.[30]

Nevertheless, behind the scenes, the two maintained a dialogue through the earlier established commission. They continued to be divided by their differing vision of what a Polish state should be. To the Catholic Church and most of its parishioners. Poland could only be a theocratic state, regulated by principles of the Catholic faith, acting in its self-appointed role of defender of the interests of the nation. To the regime, the way forward was the separation of church from the state. The regime was able to provide people with opportunities for personal advancement and economic stability. In return for not attacking the regime, outright, the church accepted certain defined privileges. The Catholic University in Lublin continued to function. A Catholic daily and weekly newspaper appeared regularly and the parish churches, though constrained, were allowed to function. In that respect, the Polish compromise between the communist regime and the Catholic Church was unique in the Soviet bloc.

In the two years after 1956, Gomułka consolidated his position. In the first place, he had to deal with party leaders and the security service. This had been part of the Stalinist system in Poland. Some were expelled, others lost their positions of influence. The notorious Urząd Bezpieczeństwa (Security Bureau – UB) was disbanded and a system of controls was put in place. They were supposed to make sure that the security apparatus never again became powerful enough to act against the party leadership. Polish society, as a whole, benefited from the process. People were released from prisons. An amnesty and then a process of rehabilitation fully recognised the injustices of past sentences. It became possible to discuss the war and immediate post-war period, with a degree of frankness unheard of during the Stalinist years. The role of the AK and the BCh was now analysed as part of the recent historical past without implicating people.

Gomułka's reputation was based on the popular perception that, although a communist, he was committed to the Polish road to socialism and opposed to collectivisation. In 1956, the radical intellectual groups and the workers called for his reinstatement and gave him their unconditional support in the critical October days. Nevertheless, Gomułka's relations with these sections of society were never easy. In the first place, he quickly moved to limit reforms which many sections of society expected would be a natural consequence of the change in party leadership. The anti-Stalinists in the party leadership, treated the elections which took place in January 1957, as a means of confirming their authority. After the elections came a clampdown on the radical elements, who expected the government to introduce workers' control in the factories. Then the regime took action against intellectuals and journalists, who had believed that the October reforms were a starting point of further radical reforms. The regime closed a number of journals closely associated with the heady days of 1956. Workers' demands to having a larger say in enterprise management were blocked. This was done by reducing the role of the workers' councils to support managerial decisions. No attempt was made to change the PZPR's structural or ideological claim to rule. This claim had been established after 1947. Elections were held. Nevertheless, the electoral lists were prepared by an electoral college, in such a way that no independent parties or individuals entered the Sejm without, prior agreement. Thus, two Catholic groups existed within the Sejm, although their powers were always limited. During the years 1956–57, the role of the state was a subject which was closely connected to debates of political reforms. There existed left wing circles and major factories where workers had formed factory councils. Here, it was understood that the workers' political rights would not be guaranteed as long as matters relating to economic development and production were left in the hands of state beaurocrats. Some militant workers called for greater state accountability and respect for human and citizen rights. They automatically also demanded that workers have control over the means of production. Gomułka was not prepared to accept these demands. By the time of the elections, the factory committees were stripped of the right to interfere in managerial decisions. Inevitably, the workers' right to strike was counteracted by the state's claim to represent the working class. The period of debates of alternative economic and political models was brought to an end.

One of the key issues which Gomułka's team had to address was the Five Year Plan. This was to follow the completed Six Year Plan. His predecessors had already outlined new objectives. However, there was general agreement that consumer and light industries had been neglected and that this had had a serious impact on the workers' morale and standard of living. Debates on the reprioritising of industrial targets resulted from the decision to maintain the pace of development in heavy industry. It was also due to the encouragement of production of consumer goods. The State Planning Commission was established after 1956. It stressed the need for heavy, chemical and electrical industries. Thus, by the spring of 1957, Gomułka accepted that production of consumer goods could stand in the way of those priorities. During the following years, the consequence of this reasoning was a continuing lack of investment in the production of goods needed for daily life. In effect, private enterprise was allowed to step into the breach, with the state allowing for the emergence of small-scale workshop production and retail outlets. At the same time, producer cooperatives assumed a larger role in supplying services. During the later 1950s, standards of living rose slowly and inconsistently. This caused frustration and disappointment. Economic exchanges with countries of the COMECON and West European economies increased during this period. It had been hoped that Poland would be able to increase its export to Western Europe. In reality, the opposite happened and Poland's balance of trade during the 1960s was negative. Nevertheless, internal shortages meant that the Gomułka regime was unable to rectify this.

In agriculture, collectivisation was abandoned. Poland was unique in Eastern Europe in allowing the continuation of individual farms. In principle, the issue of collectivisation was occasionally discussed by the Central Committee, in particular when other communist regimes castigated Poland for maintaining capitalist modes of production. In reality, peasants were confident that the state was not likely to force collectivisation. Instead, emphasis was put on modernisation and increased use of machinery. For that purpose, farmers were encouraged to join machine circles and pool resources and production. By these means, agricultural output was increased throughout the 1960s.

Stalin's death and the subsequent changes which took place in the Soviet leadership had an impact on Poland's freedom to determine some aspects of its foreign policy. Khrushchev's initial anxiety was that Gomułka would not manage to maintain control over the pace of reforms. This proved unfounded. In due course, relations between Poland and the Soviet Union appeared to be characterised by a greater degree of independence. In reality, Poland remained a reliable ally of the Soviet Union. Events in Hungary, signalled to the PZPR, the limits of what the Soviet Union would tolerate. The Poles knew that invasion was an option which, if necessary, would be considered. Western passivity during the Hungarian crisis, likewise indicated that the East European states could not count on support in confrontation with the Soviet Union. Gomułka disapproved of the Soviet invasion of Hungary and made small gestures of support for the Hungarians. Though these were never enough to actually challenge Soviet actions. He also expressed disagreement with the trial and execution of the Hungarian Prime Minister Imre Nagy.

Polish foreign policy during this period was pragmatic and cautious. Though it is still not possible to fully explain some of the more interesting initiatives. The Federal Republic of Germany refused to recognise the Oder-Neisse border. This remained a matter of concern to the Poles, and not just the communists. The spectre of a third world war hung heavily over Poland, so recently a victim of German aggression and occupation. This single fact tended to moderate the desire to shake off Soviet tutelage. Gomułka thus pursued a judicious foreign policy. On the one hand, he never gave the Soviet Union any reason to weaken its support for Poland. Whist doing this, he still tried to raise Poland's profile in the United Nations and other international organisations.

A number of initiatives concerning the creation of denuclearised zones in Europe were associated with Poland. It is still not possible to ascertain to what extent these were Polish ideas. Another theory is that the Soviet Union indicated to the Poles that they should present these ideas as their own. In this way, world statesmen would have been more likely to give these ideas serious consideration. In any case, on 2 October 1957, Adam Rapacki, the Polish Minister for Foreign Affairs, put to the XII Session of the United Nations, a plan for the creation of a nuclear-free zone in Central Europe. The Rapacki Plan, as it came to be known, met with a degree of approval and was discussed, together with other, similar proposals during the following sessions of the United Nations. Nevertheless, it never had a realistic chance of success. This was because the context of the Cold War prevented the USA and the Soviet Union, from genuinely accepting demilitarisation as a way out of the political stalemate.[31]

During the second half of the 1960s, the regime faced challenges to its authority. Economic stagnation and shortages caused increased irritation in wider sections of the community. East Germany and Czechoslovakia appeared to be enjoying a higher standard of living and access to consumer goods. This underlined the fact that economic planning was failing to deliver what people increasingly expected to see in shops. This was namely regular supplies of clothes, kitchen equipment, furniture and electrical goods. Children born during the post-war baby boom were coming to a point where they might, in the near future, become independent. But their prospects of securing a flat, however small, were very distant. The older generation, particularly those who had experienced post-war shortages, were no longer willing to accept that twenty years after the end of the war shortages were still the norm. There was an expectation of some reward for years of sacrifices. This expectation was growing and when people were fobbed off with trite propaganda statements, their sense of alienation from the state increased. The most basic level on which non-communists were prepared to accept the regime was that of economic well-being. This was being eroded. With that erosion, appeared signs of irritation.

The intellectual and creative community, which had supported Gomułka in 1956, felt cheated and marginalised. The next generation of intellectuals, nurtured in the post-war egalitarian ethos, expected the regime to abide by its own stated principles. Thus, within universities, students and young academics led the debate on the regime's visible ideological shortcomings. Jacek Kuroń and Karol Modzelewski published first a manifesto and then an *Open Letter*. In these, they criticised the regime for its lack of democratic accountability and commitment to economic reforms. Among the older Marxist intellectuals, many likewise, came to doubt the regime's willingness to do anything other than maintain a grip on power. Amongst those, Leszek Kołakowski, Włodzimierz Brus and Zygmund Bauman were the best known in Poland and in the West.[32]

At the same time, the party leadership was in turmoil for entirely different reasons. The PPR always accommodated groups which had their own diverse perceptions of the way communism was to be established in Poland. Their debates were always conducted with a degree of caution. When they erupted into the open, this was usually due to the Soviet leadership supporting a given faction. This happened in 1947 and again in 1956. During the 1960s, a nationalist group led by wartime communist partisan leader, Mieczysław Moczar, came to prominence. The conflict dated back to the war and the first years of the communist regime. Moczar felt that communists who had spent the war years in the Soviet Union had played down the role of the communists in Poland. He also displayed classic signs of anti-Semitism. He believed that Polish Jewish communists had formed a separate group within the PZPR and that they had a distinct agenda. This was one that was opposed to Polish nationalism. In 1964, he became Minister of Interior. This allowed him and his supporters to take the conflict beyond the narrow confines of PZPR debates. From that point onwards, the activities of the wartime communist partisans were enlarged upon in books and films. The aim was to play down the role of communists in the Soviet Union. At the same time, he reached out to the ex-combatants, whose achievements had not been acknowledged until then. Most obviously, this included the AK and those who had fought in the West.[33]

The Israeli-Arab war of 1967 and the ensuing diplomatic breach between the Soviet bloc and Israel, gave Moczar's group an opportunity to launch an attack on Jews in the party, the army and in Polish society. He defined Jews as Zionists and accused them of loyalty to the state of Israel. He claimed that this loyalty overrode their commitment to Poland. In this way, Moczar, in one stroke, identified all Jews as potential traitors. Gomułka had no track record of anti-Semitism. However, he appears not to have done anything to protect Polish Jews, who were publicly denounced and vilified during meetings held in workplaces. Newspapers carried hostile comments on the role of Jews in post-war Poland and radio programmes repeated accusations of sympathies with Zionism and Israel. Many Jews were expelled from their employment. The result was, that a high proportion of the Jews who had stayed in Poland after 1948, felt compelled to emigrate. As they were leaving, the Poles made one final gesture, intended to humiliate them. On leaving Poland, they were stripped of Polish nationality. They thus became stateless.

Student protests occurred at the University of Warsaw in March 1968. These gave Moczar an opportunity to suggest that Jews were also active within the universities, as leaders of the dissident groups. Student demonstrations were, in fact, precipitated by heavy-handed censorship and attempts to stifle debates taking place in the universities. Moczar led an attack on Jewish and dissident academics and students. He accused them of disloyalty to the Polish state. The party purged the universities of dissidents and arrested students and high school pupils involved in demonstrations. During fighting which broke out first at the Warsaw University and later in other universities, troops were sent in to quell the demonstrations with extreme brutality. The regime nevertheless pretended that these were actions taken by the workers, justly outraged by the students' lack of commitment to their studies and disrespect for the workers' state. During the following year, educational reforms made it easier for children of workers and peasants, to gain places at universities. Male students were drafted into the army for lengthy military training courses. Academic staff who associated with this wave of protest against the regime were dismissed. There were attempts made by the intellectual community to discuss the difficulties of the communist regime. These were blocked.

Within the party leadership, complex battles were fought out, far from the public eyes. Gomułka tried to bring the bloodletting to an end. In reality he did, or could do, nothing to protect Jews, 13,000 of whom were forced to leave Poland. On 19 March 1968, he made a speech to chosen party activists, which was broadcast on radio and TV. He attempted to conduct a debate on the difference between Jews, who were loyal Poles and those who were Zionists. However, he was interrupted by party members. They demanded that he go further. Anti-Semitism united both party and non-party members to the extent that the Party Secretary could not prevent the inevitable consequences. His weakness was thus publicly exposed and might have given the anti-Semitic drive added momentum. The bloodletting now affected the party leadership. Rapacki, came under attack for his Jewish origin. He thus resigned his post as Minister for Foreign Affairs. Marian Spychalski was relieved of his duties. He was the Minister of Defence who had been imprisoned during the Stalinist period and rehabilitated in 1956.[34]

Gomułka lingered on for two more years, his position increasingly compromised. Critically, economic failures lay at the root of the social disaffection. These fuelled both anti-Semitism and dissident activities. They were not resolved.

# 6  From Gierek to Solidarity

The post-1956 regime had no desire to isolate Poland from Western Europe, as the previous regime had. Academics were occasionally allowed to travel to conferences in the West and in the USA and foreign guests were increasingly made welcome in Poland. The result was, that some of the educated young and intellectuals became aware of the political polemics raging in the West. The Paris events of 1968 were analysed with great interest, as were reforms in Czechoslovakia. Poles no longer felt that they were isolated in these matters. More freely than hitherto, students spoke of individual rights, of social justice and of progress. The Catholic Church, although under attack from the regime could count on public support in all circumstances. In the late 1960s young Catholics became aware of the worker-priest movement in Latin America and the Netherlands. This was a new concept of a church, which associated with revolutionary circles. As puzzling as these models were to Poles, they were keen to find out more. It was not a coincidence that dissidents frequently came from privileged backgrounds. Their parents had been directly connected with the post-war regime, or else had benefited from the communists' search for support among the intellectual and creative milieu.[1]

The response of the regime to tentative signs of political dissent was disproportionate in relation to its extent. After 1968, in particular, Gomułka strengthened the invigilation of the universities and students and increased sentences for those who publicly criticised the regime's shortcomings. Kuroń and Modzelewski were once more arrested, as was Adam Michnik. He was a dissident activist, associated with the 1968 demonstrations at the University of Warsaw. Nevertheless, illegal publications appeared with increased regularity, suggesting some degree of organisation. At this stage, the main thrust of the criticism was the gap between the regime's stated principles and its actions rather than a clearly formulated programme for the establishment of a political and economic system, modelled on Western Europe.

What Gomułka failed to note was that within the working class, the slow pace of improvement in the standard of living was causing disaffection. The workers were no longer content with small achievements and were deeply frustrated with increasing shortages of consumer goods and basic foodstuffs. They were ready to take action. Gomułka did not understand these aspirations and his modest lifestyle impressed no one. In reality, people became frustrated with queuing and effective rationing of goods, which they knew were now freely available in the West. The state had made progress in building new housing. However, the new flats were very small, shabby and with windowless kitchens. The demographic pressure of the post-war generations, called for decisive and new economic responses. These were things that the regime was not prepared to consider.

The situation came to a head on 13 December 1970. Price increases on food had been introduced, just as families prepared for Christmas. These increases varied, but on average amounted to 15 per cent. Food bills made up to half of a Polish family's household spending. Therefore, the increases would have had a big impact on the people's anticipated family budget. Most economists agreed that there was a need for changes in the pricing structures. The method and timing was nevertheless badly thought out. The increases came just as announcements were made about changes in workers' pay. These were meant to stabilise the economy, by introducing an element of market forces. The workers' response was to take to the streets. On 14 December, strikes affected the main coastal cities and ports. The Central Committee of the PZPR, made the fateful decision to authorise the sending of troops to quell the strikes. Critically, soldiers were given live ammunition. On 15 December, in a confrontation between striking workers and troops in Gdańsk, 44 people were killed and many more injured. The police and the secret service extended their action, seeking to identify and punish those involved. Rather than seeing the workers' strikes as a sign of despair and anger, the party chose to portray them as orchestrated by 'criminal elements'.[2]

During the critical few days which followed, the party's leadership was unsure as to the significance of the action taken by the workers. More importantly, they were unsure of what to do next. One issue became clear, namely that Gomułka had to go. It would appear that the Soviet Ambassador to Warsaw, conveyed to the members of the Central Committee, a clear warning that Brezhnev wanted to see Gomułka replaced. The Polish party leaders were assured that no invasion was planned. Western reaction to the Soviet invasion of Czechoslovakia had been so serious as to preclude a similar decision in Poland's case. The Poles were left in no doubt that they had to remove Gomułka, as he was no longer considered capable of dealing with the escalating crisis. It has been suggested that the Soviet leadership had also identified a successor and, discreetly suggested to PZPR leadership, who that was to be. This explains why, when the name Edward Gierek was put forward, his nomination was accepted without any objections. Gomułka was incapacitated by either a cardiac problem, or had simply collapsed with overwork and did not put up a fight. On 20 December, Gierek gave his first radio speech. The price increases were withdrawn and assurances were given that wages would be raised. The new party secretary's position was consolidated on 31 December. On this day, he made the bold decision to face the strikers in Gdańsk. Having listened to their grievances, he assured them that he would do his best to deal with the economic problems. In response to Gierek's outright question of whether they would help him, the workers assured him that they would. This widely publicised moment, possibly entirely spontaneous, symbolised the new hope and conviction, that the regime recognised the validity of the workers' grievances.[3]

Gierek was not an unknown man. He had held the post of party secretary of the Katowice mining district since 1954. His stepfather and mother had emigrated to France in the 1920s and his working experience had been entirely in French and Belgian mines. It was there that he had joined the communist Party and was active in the communist-dominated miners' trade union movement. Throughout the war, Gierek worked in Belgium. After the war, he campaigned for Polish miners to return to Poland to participate in the building of socialism. The campaign resulted in the repatriation of nearly 10,000 Poles. These were mainly highly skilled miners and their families, who were settled in the previously German mining district of Upper Silesia. Gierek was unusual among the leading Polish communists for having extensive trade union and party experience and direct knowledge of work in the mines. Other leaders had either spent extensive periods of their adult life in Polish prisons or in Moscow. However, Gierek's political activities were confined to the West.[4] During his earlier political career, he had not been to Moscow. He had thus missed out on party schooling. Unlike most of the PZPR leadership and ideologues, he had a strong empathy with working men. During his time in Katowice, he had earned the reputation of being a loyal champion of the interests of workers and miners in the district. There, Gierek had lifted the status of miners and improved the quality of their daily life. In the years to come, he was to explain that, when he first took control of the party in the mining district, most underground work was still being done by German prisoners of war. Later, it was done by men defined as politically unreliable. These who had been compulsorily drafted to work in the mines. Gierek changed this by stressing that mining was a skilled job. He fought for higher wages and for the regime to recognise its dependence on coal. As the regional party boss, his influence went well beyond that of party affairs. He noted that mines were allowed to retain a proportion of profits by putting them into social funds. These were little used and built up into enormous surpluses. Gierek insisted on freeing these resources and channelled them into the building of model housing estates, recreational and rest facilities. Katowice was known as an area where otherwise scarce goods were available.[5] Gomułka's, careful economic policies had resulted in stagnation. Gierek was determined to replicate his earlier successes in Katowice, on a national level. Few in the party leadership were better placed to provide what Poles wanted during the 1970s, namely better quality goods, well supplied shops and an assurance of a higher standard of living.

Gierek was determined to lead Poland out of the shadow of the Soviet Union. In this aim, Gierek initially benefited from Gomułka's recent foreign policy successes. Gomułka had distrusted Aleksander Dubček, the Czechoslovak Communist Party secretary. Gomułka had therefore opposed the reforms taking place in Czechoslovakia during 1968. In the summer of 1968, he had also authorised the use of Polish troops as part of the Warsaw Pact invasion of Czechoslovakia. The Soviet Union decided that relations between the Soviet Union and the Federal Republic of Germany could only be improved, provided Germany accepted Poland's western borders. In this way, Poland was rewarded for its loyalty. In 1970, Willy Brandt, Chancellor of the Federal Republic of Germany, came to Poland and signed a treaty. This normalised relations with Poland and recognised the post-war border.[6]

Gierek went well beyond what any previous party boss had done. He was described as a communist without phobias about the West. In this way, he responded positively to French attempts to build alliances with East European states. At the same time, he tried to maintain good relations with West Germany and to extend contacts with the USA. Gierek made visits to the West. In addition, he made sure Western politicians came to Poland. In 1972, President Richard Nixon visited Warsaw. Efforts were made to improve contacts and economic relations with Britain, Italy and Switzerland. Gierek was equally mindful of the need to retain good relations with Moscow.

The impressive list of foreign policy initiatives has to be understood in the context of Poland's rapidly changing economic policy. Gierek had a vision of Poland becoming a modern state. He understood this to be one which would enjoy the benefits of rapid growth and of economic contacts with the advanced Western economies. Polish economic and political independence was something the Soviet leadership encouraged. With each visit to Western capitals, Gierek sought to build economic contacts. He did this in order to secure funds and agree on licences. These would allow for production of Western goods in Poland. Know-how, as well as machinery, was purchased from the West. This became a model for further development.

To this end, Gierek broke with the previous policy of strict economic control of agriculture. For the first time, farmers were freed from the duty to supply the market with clearly defined quotas of produce, at prices set by the government. Introducing free market forces into agriculture was supposed to encourage the farmers to improve production. Progressively, state control over farmers' activities was abolished. For the first time since the war, farmers were genuinely free to grow what they wanted and in quantities determined by the market and their own inclinations. At the same time, farmers were given extensive credits and loans. The more enterprising among them established greenhouses and plastic tunnels, in which vegetables could be grown intensively and out of season. Others merely expanded their houses and then took out more loans. The result was not always what the Gierek regime had hoped for. The production of food for the markets decreased. This was due to several successive droughts; lack of state control over food production and the pricing of agricultural goods. At the same time, the state was obliged to increase import of cattle feed.

The changing appearance of Polish streets and shops, seemingly testified to Poland's transformation and modernisation on the basis of closer financial and trading links with Western Europe. Berliet buses, Fiat cars and numerous consumer goods, produced in Poland under licence agreements, suggested that Poland was part of the Western economy. New and bold investments indicated a great degree of optimism. This presupposed that Poland would be able to pay off loans by selling goods produced in Poland, to the West. Western banks, flush with money, encouraged Poland to take out further loans. During the first years of the 1970s, incomes rose, as did the general standard of living. The dingy and drab days of the Gomułka era were ridiculed, while Poles persuaded themselves that they would henceforth be part of the Western consumer world.[7]

Gierek's attitude towards the issue of party membership was distinctly different from that of his predecessor. Gomułka had sought to increase working class party membership. In reality, membership of the party had long become a career move for many young and ambitious people, whether on the factory floor or in the management. Young people had vied for admission to universities. These had been vastly oversubscribed. Therefore, membership of the youth wing of the communist party had been a prudent insurance policy. Gierek broke with that policy. The economy was dependent on the trained, skilled and technically literate workers, as well as on the university-educated young professionals. This had required a reassessment of the previous policy of distrusting those whose professional positions, origins and aspirations did not define them as working class. Gierek had no such preconceptions. He permitted wage differentiations. These rewarded the technocrats for their skills, without requiring them to make the pretence of political loyalty. This led to the emergence of confident managerial strata in state enterprises. The notable difference between these people and their equivalent in the West was that the state did not test their managerial and technical skills in terms of the enterprise performance or profit. What was required of them was to work within their expertise. In return, the state provided them with a satisfactory standard of living.[8]

In the middle 1970s, the rocky foundations of Poland's economic miracle, became only too obvious. But the situation was not necessarily one which the Poles could have anticipated. By 1975, the debt repayment had started rising. In 1975, servicing the foreign debt swallowed 25 per cent of export earnings. In 1976, foreign debts were absorbing 36 per cent of export earnings. Poland was not only falling behind with repayments. The situation in the West had dramatically changed. The Arab-Israeli War started in 1973. The oil-producing states decided to use oil sales as a diplomatic weapon. These factors led to a financial crisis in the West. Inflation in the West rose and short-term loans dried up. Poland, from having been a very good investment proposition, became a debt problem. Short-term loans were recalled. Increases in food prices were inevitable, but the Gierek regime knew only too well what might be the consequences of such decisions. The relationship between the state and the people was based on the unspoken understanding that progress and well-being would be guaranteed in return for political stability. This tenuous equilibrium was sometimes described as consumer socialism. It was destroyed by the threat to what the Poles had come to enjoy. This was namely a modicum of comfort and access to consumer goods, whose production was unable to keep up with growing wage income. In the summer of 1976, the Sejm approved a package of food price increases. Nothing could disguise the fact that these increases, like the previous ones, were arbitrarily imposed, without proper consultation and without different forms of pay and reward being considered. Strikes broke out immediately. The largest of these took place in the Ursus tractor factory in Warsaw and the Walter ammunition factory in Radom. Though other industrial towns were also affected by street action. Gierek was forced to announce that the new pricing schemes would not be implemented.[9]

The regime's reaction was to hold back on economic decisions, which could create a politically volatile situation. At the same time, organisers and participants were severely punished in strikes. During the following months, workers from the two main strike centres were detained, tried and sentenced. They nevertheless found support among the intellectuals, with whom they hitherto had had little contact. During the first half of the 1970s, writers, intellectuals and progressive thinkers, grouped around the universities and Sejm deputies connected with Catholic circles. They openly criticised the state and its policies. Some were liberals and some were Marxists. Others merely considered themselves to be democrats. They were linked in their increased willingness to openly criticise the regime. They criticised it for its lack of respect for human rights, for visible signs of corruption and venality, as well as its alienation from those it claimed to represent. In 1976, intellectuals offered to support workers on trial for having participated in the June strikes. Such support was initially confined to aiding workers with advice and in practical ways. The first group of intellectuals who participated in this initiative, gave the association the name of Komitet Obrony Robotników (Workers' Defence Committee – KOR). Thus, for the first time under communism, dissident intellectual groups and workers came together.[10]

The West appeared to take a genuine interest in developments taking place within the countries of the Soviet bloc. This emboldened the dissident intellectuals into defying the regime. The communist regimes of Eastern Europe had entered into close economic, cultural and political contacts with the West. This had effectively tied their hands. Public opinion in Western Europe had an impact on government policies. In some cases, it also impacted on the extent of economic contacts with the communist states. Relations between the Soviet Union and the West were normalised. One consequence of this was that human rights became a factor in relations between the two. Poland was a co-signatory of the Helsinki Accords in 1975. It thus had guaranteed to respect the rights of its citizens. This meant that the dissident organisations were able, not only to make reference to specific government undertakings. Furthermore, and more damagingly, they were able to inform human rights organisations in the West, of the communist governments' breaches of these principles. Human rights issues had a larger impact than hitherto, on the degree to which Western European states were willing to forge and maintain links with Poland. For Polish dissidents, this meant they could be confident that their harassment by the regime, would not go unnoticed. It could also have a negative impact on the eastern governments' willingness to grant Poland further moratoria on the repayments of debts. For the first time, dissident groups came into the open. They distributed leaflets, published books and became active beyond the narrow confines of their own milieu. In this way, the names of many dissidents became well known. Radio Free Europe helped to disseminate their ideas and to familiarise the Polish public of their aims and activities. The names Moczulski, Kuroń, Michnik and Mazowiecki, all became known in the West, as much as they were already known in Poland.

The party was likewise affected by the debates taking place in Polish society. During this period, attempts were made to challenge the leadership. In particular, efforts were made to introduce some accountability and to develop genuine methods of consultation. The young technocrats and skilled workers, in those days, were likely to have joined the party purely to further their employment prospects. They felt stifled by the party hierarchy. There was a practice of instructions being passed down from the top to the bottom, without any methods for feeding information or decisions from the grass roots to the leadership. Nevertheless, attempts were made to introduce a degree of accountability and to open the dialogue within the closed party ranks. These attempts were not successful. This was in spite of loyal PZPR members warning that the party was becoming remote and out of touch with daily realities.

After 1976, police action against dissidents became more widespread. The Catholic Church openly defended the persecuted, but also built bridges with the dissidents. The Episcopate had associated great hopes with the change which took place in the regime's leadership in 1970. Wyszyński and most bishops, thought that Gierek would not be as dogmatic as his predecessor had been. He had experience of the way Western European governments appeared to work amicably with the various churches. It was therefore thought that he would be more willing to negotiate with the Episcopate. The Central Committee, likewise, assumed that relations with the Vatican and the Episcopate could be normalised and areas of conflict could be reduced. In fact, both operated on very different assumptions.

During the communist period, the authority of the Catholic Church, far from being diminished, had increased. To those opposed to Soviet domination and the communist regime it had imposed on Poland, the church had come to epitomise the essence of Polish religious and cultural identity. The situation was very different from that in Western Europe. There, with the exception of Franco's Spain and Portugal under Salazar, the state had successfully reduced the churches' influence and interference in state matters. Occasional conflicts still took place. But there was no doubt about the state's role. At best, the churches fought to maintain control over their property, schools and charitable facilities. In this respect, the Polish situation was distinct. The Poles fought to maintain the Catholic Church's influence in all aspects of life, spiritual and secular. This was no less than a battle to retain the Polish national identity, if not a battle for the survival of the nation. The Episcopate, in its long-term fight against secularisation, clearly benefited from this prevailing view. They knew that the Poles would always support the church and its policies. This was especially because of the nature of the regime in power. To Gierek and his team, the struggle to reduce the church's authority was an ongoing objective. Unlike the Gomułka regime, the party leaders of the 1970s sought to achieve this less by confrontation. The made more use of contacts, negotiations, talks and diplomacy. Ultimately, the communist regime, like the Catholic Church, shared the same objective of seeking to maintain social order. Even if they did this for different reasons.

Questions relating to the ownership of eccelesiastical properties in the Recovered Territories and state objections to the building of new churches were issues which dominated state-church contacts in the early 1970s. The first was resolved amicably in the first years

of the Gierek period. This was done by granting the church ownership of most of the previously, German, ecclesiastical property.
The second matter was much more confrontational. This was due
to the regime's policy of prohibiting churches to be built in new
working class estates and towns. During the early 1970s, it became
obvious that this policy was not diminishing people's interest in
religious activities. Nevertheless, even when the regime did allow
the building of new churches, the Episcopate was still unhappy
about the continuation of restrictions. Only half of the official requests resulted in positive decisions. There was an anxiety that a
more sympathetic attitude to the Episcopate's requests, would lead
it to assert itself further. The regime's refusal to be more generous
was motivated by this anxiety. Catholic clergy, throughout Poland,
flouted regulations, often illegally changing the use of buildings
and adapting them for use as church premises. In the eastern borderland, the church was unwilling to set aside its historic conflicts
with the Orthodox and Uniate Churches. In many instances, it
took over premises vacated by the Ukrainian population, which
had been expelled during the post-war period. In these illegal actions, the church was surprisingly dismissive of the claims of other
Christians.[11]

At the same time, the Gierek regime re-established contacts with
the Vatican. These had been virtually broken off after 1968. The unresolved issue of the Concordat, offered an excuse for meetings and
talks. In reality, the regime had a strong ulterior motive for opening
talks with the Vatican. It was hoped that the Pope would put pressure on the Polish Episcopate, to abandon its policy of confrontation
with the communist regime. The ultimate aim was for the Episcopate to cease attacking the communists, and to support its social
policies. Wyszyński was not prepared to do this. He believed that
this would amount to the church legitimising an illegal regime. In
any case, the Polish Episcopate was wary of the regime establishing
better relations with the Vatican. They were fearful that Rome might
take a softer line on some of the issues which the Episcopate considered to be of crucial importance to its role in communist-ruled
Poland. The Vatican was, nevertheless, not willing to become involved in conflicts between the Polish state and church. Because of

this, Gierek's policy towards the Vatican was inconclusive.[12] Generally, the previous policy of attacking, vilifying and confronting the Catholic Church was discontinued. However, in the 1970s, attempts to diminish the importance of religion in Polish society were continued by different means. The regime started using its extended contacts with the West, to encourage larger debates on anticlerical and left wing progressive themes. All these efforts yielded limited returns. To the majority of Poles, being an observant Catholic was a reaffirmation of their national identity against the communist regime. Few cared to consider any negative aspects of church intervention in daily life, or even in the world.

During the second half of the 1970s, Wyszyński authorised the church to take a more active role in criticising the regime's economic policies. By 1976, the church was open in its condemnation of the consequences of government policies. It took the side of striking workers. The fate of arrested workers, protesters and dissidents, became a subject to which the clergy returned to frequently, in their sermons. In the meantime, the Episcopate took up their cause in its periodic meetings with the regime's representatives. The church was the only institution which enjoyed a degree of autonomy. It therefore made its premises available for dissidents, so they could hold meetings and seek sanctuary against arrest.

On 16 October 1978, an ideological bombshell hit Poland. Cardinal Karol Wojtyła, archbishop of Kraków, was elected Pope. He took the name John Paul II. Once the ruling party leaders had come to terms with the enormity of what had happened, they sent their heartfelt congratulations to the Vatican. However, there was no escaping that the balance of power had shifted against the regime. The regime was increasingly isolated and unpopular. The religious authority, on the other hand, would never be required to prove itself by assuming responsibility for temporal matters. The cards were henceforth stacked in favour of those with spiritual power and against those who claimed temporal right to rule. For most Poles, the election of a Pole to head the Catholic Church was confirmation of the validity of the Promethian conviction. This said that, through suffering, the Polish nation would be reborn. As was the custom, the new Pope made a pilgrimage to his homeland. From 2

to 10 June 1979, Poland celebrated the Pope's visit to Poland and
the PZPR had no choice but to act as the hosts.[13]

By the summer of 1980, the economic situation in Poland
had created preconditions for political instability on an unprece-
dented scale. Strikes broke out in factories and enterprises. In most
cases, the workers wanted wage increases. In reality, the situation
could no longer be assuaged by more money in pay packets. By
then, the regime's authority had been destroyed. Its ineffective-
ness had been exposed, while at the same time the opposition
had gone beyond addressing minor and/or local grievances. Shortages had always been endemic in Poland. These had been exacer-
bated by the government's attempts to pay off some of Poland's
international debts. These, by then, had spiralled out of control.
In 1984, Poland owed $26.8 billion, In 1985, the figure had in-
creased to $29.3 billion. In 1986, it was $33.5 billion. By 1987
Poland's foreign currency debt was $41.4 billion. Poland was not
even able to pay the interest on its debts. Debt repayments exceeded
Poland's debt[14] Re-establishing equilibrium required an increase in
exports and a reduction in imports. Consumer goods, in particular those of daily use and food were increasingly difficult to find
in the shops. They were either channelled through the commer-
cial shops, where higher prices were charged, or went to the black
market.

The regime's ability to manage its critics, seems to have decreased at the same time. By 1979, opposition groups were well
known. Their leaflets, regular publications and programmes were
produced and disseminated widely. Dissident movements acquired
clearer profiles. Some were anti-Soviet, others nationalist. This was
the case with the Young Poland movement on the coast. At the
same time, workers' strike committees and self-defence groups proliferated. These usually called for the workers to be allowed to form
trade unions. The official trade unions were ineffectual. They only
existed to promote party and state policies. Trade union officers
were supposedly elected. In reality, the leadership made nomi-
nations without consulting with the union members. In the circumstances, the workers wanted to establish their own genuinely
free organisations which represented their interests. The situation was similar to that in 1956, when workers had established

factory councils. These had proceeded to make radical demands for workers' participation in management decisions. Throughout the summer, disturbances and strikes took place in many major state enterprises. These lacked coordination and in, all cases, the management sought to diffuse them through direct negotiations and partial concessions to workers' demands.[15]

On 14 August, a strike broke out in the Lenin Shipyard in Gdańsk. Initially, this was similar to those which had flared up in Poland throughout the summer months. Disturbances started when workers found out that Anna Walentynowicz was dismissed by the management. She had been known for being a leading force in the campaign for free trade unions. What had started as a protest against the management's arbitrary and vindictive decision, quickly became a strike. Lech Wałęsa, a welder who had been earlier sacked from the shipyard, entered the shipyard to join the strikers. A negotiating committee was formed, with which the management reluctantly opened talks. By then, other enterprises along the coast had joined in the strike. The workers' grievances were precise. As a key demand, they wanted the right to form their own trade unions. Other points on the list of grievances were no less important. Although they were clearly less politically charged. The list of demands included the reinstatement of sacked workers and a call for the erection of a monument dedicated to workers killed in 1970. Workers occupied the workplace, thus paralysing production and making it impossible for the management to sideline them. This was an interesting aspect of the strike. With the Central Committees' reluctant approval, the Gdańsk shipyard managers sat down to the negotiating table with representatives of the strike committee. By 16 August, an agreement of sorts had been reached. The management agreed to increase wages and to reinstate sacked workers. Although it was unclear whether the issue of free trade unions had been resolved. The strike committee reluctantly undertook to end the occupation of the shipyard. It was at this point, that the course of events changed. As the workers were informed of the compromise, women amongst them refused to accept it and called on the strikers not to support the deal. This led to a moment of reflection and the strikers decided to resume their action. They had the support of thousands of workers along the coast on strike. The matter had gone beyond being a workplace grievance. It had become a fight for the right to establish free trade unions. From this point, the workers realised that, until the managers agreed to this key demand, they would still have the power, and no doubt also the will, to go back on any compromises agreed.

The next stage of the confrontation, took the form of an outright contest between the organised workers and the regime. Workers' representatives from the Gdańsk shipyard were joined by those from other coastal work enterprises. They formed an Inter-Enterprise Strike Committee. In Gdańsk and Szczecin, the strike committees coordinated their actions with each other and with other small enterprises. The strike committees took the name 'Solidarity'. In all cases, the strikers called for free trade unions. The regime's response was to do what it had always done in the circumstances, namely, to mobilise. Known activists were arrested and the party tried to go on the offensive. Neither of these actions succeeded in intimidating the workers. The party was demoralised, and many of its workplace activists were in agreement with the striking workers. Gierek hastily returned from his holiday in the Crimea. An address to the workers to end the confrontation by Prime Minister Edward Babiuch was followed by one made by Gierek. Both were broadcast on television, but failed to stem the momentum of the events. Strikes spread through the country and paralysed the economy and daily life. The regime had no alternative but to open talks with the strike committees, of which the Gdańsk committee was the most important.

By then, the strikers and the various dissident movements had seen, in the events unfolding on the coast, the opportunity for which they had been waiting. They assumed the initiative. The police attempted to limit communications between major towns, by cutting off telephone links putting up roadblocks. But the regime had lost the propaganda war. Dissidents in Warsaw contacted Western journalists directly and offered them leaflets, information and updates on the developments in Gdańsk. Representatives of the Western media, swarmed into Poland to observe the unique situation of workers challenging the communists' right to rule. The activities of disaffected groups and dissidents had, in the past, provided the Western media with an opportunity to attack the communist regimes. However, in this case, events in Polish coastal enterprises, promised a much more interesting political conflict. The free trade unions were undisputedly mass, working class organisations. Western journalists of all political persuasions, representing a variety of news agencies, arrived in Poland. They headed for Gdańsk. On arrival, they were faced with the spectacle of the locked shipyard gates, festooned with religious and patriotic images, as well as the red and white Polish flag. In the forecourt, a mass was being celebrated by Father Jankowski, in whose parish the shipyard lay. The strike committee increased the regime's discomfort, by demanding the right to free trade unions. These were in accordance with the Conventions of the International Labour Organisation, to which Poland belonged.[16]

The workers' relations with the dissident intellectuals, established a new pattern. In the past, the two social groups had rarely cooperated. Only after the strikes of the early 1970s were tentative relations established between the two. On 22 August, Tadeusz Mazowiecki, Bronisław Geremek, along with other members of KOR, succeeded in evading road blocks. They made their way to the Gdańsk shipyard, where the strikers welcomed them. Their reputations preceded them and they were invited to form a panel of experts. Nevertheless, the workers maintained absolute control over decisions relating to the composition of the strike committee and the negotiations. The intellectuals knew better than to overstep the boundaries in the relationship that was still tentative.[17] The government was unable to break the strike. The fact that Gierek appeared to be incapable of dealing with the situation, caused an internal crisis. In the lead-up to the talks with the strikers, Stanisław Kania took over. A purge of provincial officials and party leaders was instigated. A reshuffle of the Politburo followed. On 6 September, Gierek was forced to resign in favour of Kania, who secured the support of the Soviet leaders.[18]

In the last days of August, Gdańsk, and in particular the shipyard, became the centre of the historic conflict between the communist regime and the organised workers. It was there, that the government representatives were forced to go, to negotiate the end of the strike. In reality all Poles knew that the real issue was to force the regime to concede political reforms, on the basis of the 21-point agenda presented by the strikers. On 31 August the two negotiating teams reached an agreement. The workers' victory led to a fundamental revision of the regime's relations with its citizens. The right to form free trade unions, the right to strike and guarantees of freedom of expression clearly stood out as distinctly political, compared to the latter points of the agreement. These referred to improvements in working conditions and social provisions. The ideology of the regime was to rule on behalf of the working people. This ideology had been destroyed. The concessions made in Gdańsk, changed the political landscape. The three political demands challenged that claim. Moreover, it put in motion reforms and changes, which allowed for the people to determine the course of further developments. The Gdańsk agreement did not destroy the PZPR's monopoly on power. But it defined the limits of the regime's authority. Henceforth, it could not rule without the full and active cooperation of the workers. At the same time, government negotiators were forced to agree to a number of economic reforms. These mainly related to supply and pricing. They had to concede demands for the dismantling of special facilities and provisions enjoyed by party, security and police functionaries. In retrospect, it can be seen that the demands put forward by the strikers, indicated concern for equality, justice and transparency. At this stage there was no assumption that a genuinely pluralist political system, would emerge as a consequence of the concessions made by the government. Nor was it assumed by the workers, that state control of the economy was, in itself, the source of the economic problems. What they attacked was inefficiency, corruption, waste and bad practices. Free market forces and the restructuring of the economy in favour of the private sector were not policies put forward by the workers. On the contrary; they demanded better provisions for workers, improved maternity leave and a good state health system. They did not realise that they might be initiating a course of events which would destroy the paternalistic, albeit corrupt state system. They clearly only assumed the survival of the existing political system.

During the weeks following the signing of the Gdańsk agreement, strikes continued in other parts of Poland. Gradually, but decisively, industrial relations in all enterprises were transformed New free trade unions emerged everywhere. By then, Solidarność, the name taken by the coastal strikers, was generally used to describe these new unions. It was also used to describe the process of political mobilisation. This had taken place during the summer of 1980. The intellectual advisors cautioned the strikers against complacency. The government was suspected of wanting to claw back the concessions granted. Enterprise managers were prone to bypassing the trade unions. The strength of the working class lay in its ability to organise and to speak with one voice. On 17 September, over 30 of the major strike committees, met to agree on the structure of the free trade unions. These described themselves as the Independent Self-Governing Trade Unions. This was in contrast to the state-approved trade union. They were fearful that the government might try to divide and then sideline them. This was what had been done in the case of the factory committees in 1956. The new trade unions therefore decided to form a national body with a federated structure. This allowed local trade unions a greater degree of flexibility, while avoiding internal divisions. These occurred when trade unions were established on an industrial basis. Wałęsa was the unchallenged leader of the Gdańsk talks. He headed the Solidarity Trade Union movement.

In the months to come, the problems confronting the workers multiplied. The mass mobilisation of workers had occurred due to economic stagnation, a shortage of food and a failure in the production and delivery of basic goods. Solidarity like the government, knew that these problems would continue. Nevertheless, leaders of Solidarity were unwilling to be drawn into government decision making. Even though they agreed with its desire to stabilise the situation in Poland. But, even with indirect power, came the responsibility to find a solution. This required the Solidary trade unions to define the extent to which they would become partners in the government's search for a way out of the present situation. The government, on the other hand, knew that for any reforms to succeed, it needed Solidarity's approval. Thus, the scene was set, not only for a test of authority between the two, but also for internal conflicts within Solidarity.

An interesting element of the Polish story was the absence of Soviet military intervention. Hungary, in 1956 and Czechoslovakia in 1968, both testified to the Soviet Union's determination and ability to control the pace of changes within its sphere of influence. Events

in Poland were observed with glee in the West, but within the Warsaw Pact, each member state was anxious about the impact that
Solidarity would have on its own internal stability. The Czechoslovak and East German leaders, in particular, wanted to limit the
'contagion' spreading to their countries. They had one advantage
which militated against their citizens following the Polish example. This was namely economic growth and stability. Gustáv Husák
and Erich Honecker were the respective leaders of the Czechoslovak
and East German communist parties. They restricted the movement
of Poles into both countries. But they did not call for joint action
against Poland by Warsaw Pact forces. Within the Soviet political
and military leadership, anxiety was expressed about events unfolding in Poland and their wider implications. Plans for the invasion
of Poland were drawn up. However, the option was not considered beyond the planning level. The reasons for the apparent Soviet restraint were many. The international situation limited the
Soviet Union's freedom of action. In comparison with 1968, the
Soviet Union's relations with the world key players had changed.
The disastrous diplomatic and military consequences of involvement in Afghanistan, acted as a warning against too hasty action in
Poland. The Soviet Union could not afford to get bogged down in
another conflict. The Soviet Union depended economically on the
West. However, the West was reluctant to assume responsibility for
Poland's growing foreign debt. This reinforced doubts about taking
action, which could have serious long-term consequences.

   The Soviet Union was not the only world power anxious about
the likelihood of civil strife enveloping Poland. In the USA, Secretary of State Zbigniew Brzezinski had parents who had migrated
from Poland to the United States, when he was a child. He therefore
had an interest in developments in his country of origins. In any
case, the Carter administration did not propose to take pre-emptive
military action against the Soviet Union. Instead, it was made clear
to the Soviet leaders that any intervention in Poland would have
an impact on the way the USA viewed its economic links with the
Soviet Union and the communist bloc countries. In that, the USA
was generally in advance of what the Western democracies were
signalling.[19] France and Germany, and to some extent, also Britain,
wanted the problem to go away. The demands of Polish workers

were recognised as valid. However, no encouragement was given to them to believe that Western governments would directly support them. The matter was an internal Polish problem. In any case, Western governments had to consider the impact of recent events in Poland, on the country's ability to service its debts. Prime Minister Margaret Thatcher, gave vocal support to Polish trade unionists. This caused some bemusement in the United Kingdom, where her government was in the process of reducing trade union input into policymaking. In reality, statements of support were gestures intended for internal consumption. Little was actually done to offer the Polish government a way out of the economic crisis. It was left to West European trade unions to offer practical and financial aid to Polish workers. They did this throughout the period leading to the fall of communism in Eastern Europe.

The period from August 1980 until the winter of 1981 was a time of mounting crisis. The economic situation continued to deteriorate and shortages became endemic. The establishment of free trade unions didn't resolve anything. Confusion reigned within enterprises. On the one hand, managers were uncertain about how to incorporate Solidarity into management decision making. On the other hand, trade union activists tried to carve out a decisive role for the trade union. In the circumstances, it was not possible to draw a clear distinction between economic and political demands. The economic crisis had progressed too far to be resolved by the simple remedy of higher wages and better working conditions. By March 1981, it was apparent that Solidarity was, to all intents and purposes, becoming an opposition party. It still refused to accept responsibility for putting forward solutions to the problems created by the regime it criticised. The government, the security forces and industrial managers had failed in their stated aim of stabilising the situation. Moreover, they remained paralysed with uncertainty as to how to respond to the new realities. Negotiations between the two sides repeatedly broke down, were resumed and again broke down. Solidarity's response was to call for national strikes. Nevertheless, these were standoffs, which led to no new solutions.[20] In March, the security service brutally attacked a Solidarity meeting in the town of Bydgoszcz. The outrage provoked anger and the government was forced to hold an enquiry. The incident focused the attention of the Solidarity movement, on its own deep, internal divisions. This highlighted the critical question of what was to be the free trade union's role in Poland. Was it to lead a renewal, resulting in a political transformation, where workers would be involved in management decisions? Or was it to remain a trade union and resolutely refuse to be drawn into matters of state, merely defending the interests of the workers in places of employment? A key dissident ideologue of the period, Jacek Kuroń, tried to steer Solidarity in the direction of the first. Many within the trade union and the Catholic advisers distrusted him. His main opponent was a Solidarity firebrand, Jan Rulewski. He recognised that Solidarity was more than just a trade union. He also cautioned against them becoming involved in managerial decisions. It was his conviction that political reforms had to take place before economic changes could be implemented.[21]

In spite of its inspirational role and the challenge to the communist regime, Solidarity's theoretical legacy was scant. What impressed West European thinkers was the evident political maturity and spontaneity of the working class. Here was an example of the workers, unprompted by political leaders from outside their community, formulating new ideas and showing organisational skill. Likewise, their political awareness was impressive. In the context of the still ongoing Cold War, the workers were able to paralyse and bring to its knees a communist regime. This impressed conservatives and anti-communists. By the same token, left wing critics of the communist regime, identified with the Polish workers. Their claim to rule rested on the belief that they were doing so on behalf of the workers. If that regime was attacked by the workers, then the falsity of the communist ideology was revealed. In Western Europe 'Solidarity with Solidarity' campaigns proliferated. This, at times, created strange alliances. In reality, the Solidarity movement emerged in such specific circumstances, that it could offer no model or theory, which could be applied elsewhere. The two driving forces in the Solidarity's emergence were the inefficiency of the Polish centralised economic system and the distinctiveness of Polish nationalism. Thus, Solidarity activists were very clear and vocal in what they opposed and what offended their sense of natural justice. Corruption, low wages, bad work practices, all needed eradicating.

Free trade unions were the only guarantee of the workers' voice being heard. Solidarity, however, was not able to offer suggestions as to how to remedy the very economic problems, which lay at the root of the workers' disaffection.

Western journalists found it intriguing how pious Polish workers appeared to be. However, few chose to dwell on the full implications of the nationalism, which underpinned Solidarity's apparent clear sense of identity. In reality, Polish workers who fought for free trade unions did so because they identified only with other Polish workers. They had no aspirations either to encourage or speak on behalf of other workers, not even those in other Communist countries. There was an absence of any sense of internationalism. The Solidarity movement received support from international trade unions and workers' organisations. However, this was a very Polish organisation. It incorporated many of the prejudices of Polish nationalism, namely anti-Semitism and xenophobia. In its eventual social programme, the Solidarity movement was unashamedly backward-looking. Women strikers had been very important in the formative days of August 1980. Afterwards, they were quickly sidelined and none were allowed to assume a position of responsibility. In their attitude towards women's problems, the male trade unionists were paternalistic. They also made it clear that a woman's place was at home, looking after children and cooking. They fought for improved maternity leave and better provisions for mothers. However, they did not put forward any wider social demands relating specifically to women employees. Visiting Western trade unionists frequently noted that the Polish trade unionists were clear in their demands for political rights. However, Polish trade unionists expressed racist and nationalist sentiments and struck male chauvinistic poses. Some visitors found these offensive.

Even before the imposition of martial law Solidarity was transformed. The leadership did not succeed in putting forward alternatives to the government's policies, of which they were so critical. By August 1981, with the economic situation continuing to deteriorate, Solidarity was at a crossroads. Strikes were used to attack the government for its apparent mismanagement of the economy. However, this did nothing to change the situation. At the same time, they refused to discuss price increases. This blocked the way for reforms. Nor was the government prepared to change its tactics. The Deputy Prime Minister, Mieczysław Rakowski, had led the government team in its talks with the Solidarity leaders in August. He had made it clear that the aim was not to draw trade unions into consultation, but to obtain their support for policies which the government wanted to implement.[22]

The August talks clearly underlined the limits of cooperation. This was a point that was further confirmed during the Solidarity Congress. This took place in September and continued until October. Cooperation with the government in its aim to stabilise the economic situation was, undisputedly, the most pressing topic. Though in addressing this issue, other equally contentious and difficult issues were addressed. The Solidarity leaders were not able to formulate an alternative economic programme. This reduced the movement to only two options: either cooperating with the government's policies, or opposing it. Self-management and the workers' right to choose directors were widely discussed. But these were not accepted as a final policy. Wałęsa was able to steer the trade union away from a direct confrontation with the government.

During this period, the Episcopate became more active than hitherto, in brokering agreements between the Solidarity movement and the regime. In September 1980, Primate Wyszyński met a Solidarity delegation. Henceforth, constant contact was maintained between the two, undoubtedly facilitated by Wałęsa's piety and the church's desire to avoid a revolution in Poland. The Catholic Church was not a passive observer of events unfolding in Poland. On the contrary, it had its own agenda. The church was suspicious of the influence of left wing intellectuals on workers' organisations. At the root of the Episcopate's involvement in politics lay a fear that political upheavals might usher in new forces. This could lead to a challenge to the church's spiritual monopoly. This explains the Episcopate's willingness to maintain contact with the regime. At the same time, it cautioned Solidarity against challenging the authority of the state and causing civil strife. On a local level, parish priests and bishops sided with the strikers and trade unionists. But the Episcopate played a long game and maintained all contacts with the regime.[23] On 28 May 1981 Cardinal Wyszyński died. From Rome, came news of an attempt to assassinate the Pope. In July, Józef Glemp was appointed as Primate of All Poland. The Pope's health continued to be a source of anxiety and, as a result, the Vatican's role in Polish internal affairs was reduced. Glemp nevertheless, continued Wyszyński's concilia-tory role, Though it was only too clear that he did not have his predecessor's authority. Nor did he share his vision of the church's direct involvement in politics. In November, at Glemp's initiative, Jaruzelski and Wałęsa met to discuss the establishment of a Front of National Conciliation. The Solidarity movement continued its pol-icy of criticising the regime. But they did address the critical ques-tion of its own role in the situation. By then, Jaruzelski had already decided to impose martial law. The army was thus preparing itself for the new role. The church could do nothing to bridge that gap.[24]

The October Congress of the PZPR had defined the limits to which the government was prepared to go in accommodating Sol-idarity. These limits were shown to be inflexible. The party leader-ship feared that Solidarity wanted to see the collapse of the national economy, in order to justify an outright conflict with the govern-ment. The party leaders showed an unwillingness to understand the trade union's dilemmas. Solidarity's reluctance to support the government was seen as evidence of hostility and a determination to destroy socialism. The workers' call for joint management deci-sions in enterprises was likewise seen as an attack on the state, from which the management derived its authority. During the congress, Prime Minister and Defence Minister General Wojciech Jaruzelski, replaced Kania as First Party Secretary. While the party's author-ity was in decline, the army was seen stepping into the vacuum. The militarisation of the state apparatus proceeded. Jaruzelski as-sumed responsibility for Poland. At this particularly difficult time, this was surprising. Although he was a member of the Politburo of the PZPR, he was seen as a military man. He had neither spent time in the Moscow party schools, nor in the communist resistance movement. On the contrary, he appeared to be a victim of Soviet policy. During the war, he had been deported with his family, to the Russian interior. There, his parents died. His professional career was entirely linked with the military establishment. Although from the late 1960s, his profile within the PZPR leadership became more prominent. In 1981, it was difficult to anticipate what his policies would be. He was variously described as a liberal and a conservative.

Nevertheless, in his capacity as Minister of Defence, he had been responsible for the decision to send troops to quell workers' strikes in the coastal industrial town in 1970 and 1976.

On 13 December 1981, a State of War was declared. Civil authority was transferred to the army and civil laws were suspended. As Poles woke up in the morning of 13 December, they found that the new authority was firmly in place. The Military Council of National Salvation, headed by General Jaruzelski, now ruled Poland. The new authority was imposed with military efficiency. It aimed at the destruction of all autonomous civic organisations which had emerged during the past year. Radio and television stopped transmission and telephone lines were cut. Military men and special units of the police patrolled streets. This allowed the military regime to swoop on Solidarity offices. These were closed, and all leading members of Solidarity were arrested. Those who were deemed to have been involved in, or contributed to, the collapse of the communist regime's authority were also arrested. Thousands of Solidarity activists were among those arrested and interned in special camps. Wałęsa was kept in isolation. Jaruzelski aimed to destroy, not only all forms of civil mobilisation, but also the grass roots and local communist party structures. These, in recent years, had lapsed into indiscipline. From within the lower echelons of the party membership had come calls for more consultation and accountability. The emergence of the Solidarity movement had caused a crisis. Despite this, the party leadership had resolutely resisted such reforms. They had therefore further undermined the credibility of the already demoralised party cells. A purge of the regional party structures, restored the balance of authority. Edward Gierek was also interned during this period. The militarisation of Polish life was complete. In key industries, workers and managers were subordinated to military law. Military men took over decision making. Censorship and the imposition of curfew completed the process.[25] In the circumstances, the Catholic Church became the only organisation which the Jaruzelski regime dared not attack. Church and ecclesiastical property offered asylum to those threatened with arrest. They became the only places where meetings and lectures could take place.

The imposition of martial law destroyed the organisational structure of the Solidarity movement and similar civil organisations. But

the authority of the communist party was also irrevocably undermined. The key feature of this period was the replacement of trusted
party hacks, in positions of authority, with military officials. The
army, hitherto kept out of politics, replaced the now increasingly
weak PZPR. Although, like all organisations within the communist
regime, the army was nominally subject to party discipline. It had always enjoyed a degree of political autonomy under the supervision
of its own political officers. Jaruzelski's actions destroyed the myth
of a politically neutral army, standing guard over national interests.
The army had shown that it had political objectives. Moreover, it
had also had the discipline and determination, to assume the role
of guardian of the socialist order in Poland.

The workers' initial response was to fight back. Those who had
evaded internment, tried to organise a new, underground Solidarity movement, that could call on the support of the community.
Workers went on strike and people demonstrated in the streets. In
response, troops were sent in to disperse the strikers. The most brutal action took place in the 'Wujek' coal mine, where nine miners
were killed. The Solidarity movement was decimated by arrests. The
activists disseminated pamphlets and even established a radio station. Through these actions, Solidarity remained more than just a
memory to Poles. Nevertheless the Jaruzelski regime succeeded at
paralysing most forms of opposition. Only by spring was a structure
of underground illegal organisations built up. Even then, it always
existed precariously. Underground Solidarity was only able to coordinate and organise one-off events, such as demonstrations and
protests. It was impossible to rebuild the trade union organisation.
The focus was on rallying the community behind actions that would
keep the memory of Solidarity alive. Solidarity was committed to negotiations. However, it was impossible to define a programme. The
two main dissident organisations, the KOR and the Konfederacja
Polski Niepodległej (Confederation of Independent Poland – KPN),
were weakened by arrests. A number of prominent activists were interned, tried and sentenced for having earlier advocated opposition
to the regime. In October, the regime introduced legislation. This
effectively defined Solidarity as an illegal organisation.[26]

In these circumstances, the church tried to mediate. Primate
Glemp and Pope John Paul II, called on the government to show

restraint and avoid bloodshed. Both, nevertheless, held back from putting forward clear proposals. In any case, the Jaruzelski regime seemed determined to set the clock back to the period before August 1980. Secularisation policies were once more implemented. These had no regard for the changed perception of the role of the church. From the brief legal existence of the Solidarity movement, the church had increased its standing and political confidence.

Martial law was suspended on 19 December 1982. Only in July 1983 was it finally ended. Wałęsa was released from internment in December 1982. Some internees, or to be more precise, political prisoners, were released during 1982. Only in September 1986 did the regime state that the last of those deemed to have committed crimes against the state, had been released. These were only gestures. No attempt was made to restore the freedoms won in August 1980. This situation, nevertheless created a problem for the government. Political concessions would not be countenanced and brute repression could only work in the short term. Therefore, some accommodation had to be found on the basis of shared objectives. The gap between the regime and the population was immense. Only a common desire for economic stability could lead to tentative cooperation.

A decision was made to declare State of War. This could not have been done without Soviet approval. Indeed, the Soviet leadership expected the PZPR to stabilise the situation. Nevertheless, the difference between the Polish and earlier Czechoslovak case was that Jaruzelski had been told that he could not expect Soviet military support. But it had been made clear to him that he was to put a stop to strikes and challenges to the authority of the communist regime and its Soviet ally. Jaruzelski was also warned that, if he were to fail in that task, Brezhnev would back a rival Polish leader, one who could complete the task expected of him. The Soviet leadership was prepared to help the Poles stabilise the economic situation and restore production. This had been severely affected by the withdrawal of West European loans and assistance. Thus, imports of raw materials from the Soviet Union to Poland were increased, as were supplies of food. Economic contacts with countries of the Soviet bloc were increased and credits extended.[27]

Nevertheless, the economic situation in Poland, continued to be dire. There was little evidence of improvement during the first year of martial law. The Polish economy continued to present a be-wildering picture of stagnation, bottlenecks, mismanagement and corruption. The black economy had seemingly replaced the official economy. Strict rations were imposed on all vital foodstuffs. This was the only way to provide the population with basic goods. West-ern relief and charitable organisations sent food, clothes, medicines and sanitary products to Poland. In 1983, signs of change for the bet-ter were noted. These suggested that the economic situation might have stabilised.

Jaruzelski continued to retain a strong grip on the pace of lib-eralisation. Dialogue with the community had been terminated. Therefore, the only authority which could represent the interests of the population was the Catholic Church. Nevertheless, the regime was unwilling to note the need for dialogue between the regime and representatives of the population. Jaruzelski intended to reverse the growth of the Catholic influence in public life and particularly in education. Thus the church found it difficult to speak on behalf of the Solidarity movement. One of the biggest areas of conflict during this period, turned out to be a quarrel between the regime and the Episcopate. This concerned the Pope's planned visit to Poland. This was to participate in the celebrations for the 600th anniversary of the icon of the Black Madonna in Poland. The regime feared that the Pope's visit would lead to mass demonstrations. The church supported Solidarity and the Pope disapproved of the imposition of the State of War. This led the regime to postpone the visit until 1983. The visit took place in June with a strict proviso that the Pope would not meet Wałęsa. Nor was he allowed to go to the coastal towns of Gdańsk and Szczecin. John Paul still defied the regime by expressing support for the Solidarity movement and making fre-quent references to the injustice of internment and state repression. Nevertheless, he failed to persuade Jaruzelski, to open a dialogue with the underground opposition.

Jaruzelski appears to have wanted to pursue a slow, though iden-tifiable, liberal policy. Censorship was relaxed. To start with, imper-ceptibly, then more openly. This allowed for a broader discussion of economic reforms. Behind closed doors, the party leadership was locked in a confrontation between the hardliners and the liberals. Jaruzelski increasingly took the side of the liberals. In particular, he looked at the way economic reforms had been introduced in Hungary. In this internal party conflict, Moscow supported the hardliners, though nothing was done to aid them actively.

On 19 October 1984, a Catholic priest, Jerzy Popiełuszko, was murdered. He had been an outspoken critic of the regime's abuse of human rights. There are indications that Jaruzelski seized on this outrage to reduce the power of the security services and hardliners. Unusually, the trial of policemen accused of having killed the young priest, took place in an open court. The trial was reported widely in the media. The result was that the Ministry of Interior was purged and Czesław Kiszczak, a trusted friend of Jaruzelski, was appointed to head it. Thus, by 1986, Jaruzelski had replaced many of the party leaders with his military associates. This gave him a larger degree of control over the party and state apparatus. Party membership collapsed. No attempts were made to return to the earlier discussions on the relationship between the grass roots and the leadership. The regime was only too well aware that it had to uphold the pretence of the party ruling on behalf of the people. In the situation where the party and state were irrevocably alienated from the people, the pretence became more glaring than before. This was in particular because of the population's visible desire to establish its own representative organisations. In the 1960s and 1970s, membership to the party and its various associated organisations had offered a career path. In the 1980s, young professionals shunned the party. The leadership of the PZPR grew, while the rank and file decreased in numbers. Worse was to follow. In 1947, parties had been forcefully absorbed into the communist party. They now reasserted themselves. Socialists and peasant party activists both openly challenged the PZPR. Within the community, a variety of new ideas were openly discussed. On one extreme of the political spectrum was the nationalist right. This party was usually associated with ex-combatant associations. It now became active and staged displays of strength. On the other extreme, youthful anarchists put forward alternative ideas. These varied from outright dissociation from politics, to attacking the state. All disseminated pamphlets and illegal publications. In reality, it was increasingly difficult to state confidently which publications were legal and which were banned. The government was unable to control political debates. The only way

the party and the regime could redeem themselves in the eyes of
the Polish community was to provide economic well-being. For that
to happen, there was a need to return to the negotiating table with
Western banks. They would have to persuade the USA to abandon
economic sanctions imposed after the imposition of the State of
War and to maintain Soviet economic support.

By 1986, the Jaruzelski regime accepted that it needed to resume
a dialogue with broader representatives of the population. But the
government believed this would have to be done on the regime's
terms. In reality, the situation was changing fast. In the Soviet Union
Mikhail Gorbachev became the First Party Secretary. This precluded
the use of force in Poland. Attitudes towards the Catholic Church
were very important in Polish internal politics. In this respect, Gorbachev stole the march on the Polish communists, by making a
visit to the Vatican in 1986. In January 1987, Pope John II agreed to
see Jaruzelski. In June, the Pope visited Poland. The church's intervention aided the thaw. There was a shift, from resolving Poland's
economic policies through state reforms, to consulting with sections of the underground opposition. This required the government
to establish an appropriate forum. To that purpose, Jaruzelski created the Consultative Council. Through this, he planned to open
talks with chosen representatives of the opposition. The leadership
of the underground Solidarity and many dissident intellectuals did
not believe that the communist regime would collapse. They only
hoped that Jaruzelski would be persuaded to liberalise public discussion and allow for a certain percentage of seats to the Sejm to
be filled through free elections. The key proponent of this idea was
Michnik. He had the support of prominent dissident intellectuals,
such as Jan Lityński and Jacek Kuroń. When Jaruzelski's initiative
fell short of their expectations, Wałęsa responded by announcing
the formation of an Interim Council. This was to do the same
as the government's Consultative Council, but with a broader social dialogue. This included underground and, still illegal, political
organisations.

There was still a demand for the re-legalisation of Solidarity. This
continued to be an obstacle to the opening of talks between the two
sides. On 31 August 1988, Wałęsa met Kiszczak, to agree to preconditions for the opening of a dialogue. These were henceforth referred

to as the Round Table Talks. These first contacts were facilitated by the church, which provided venues and acted as a mediator. During these meetings the main points of the future dialogue were outlined. Wałęsa agreed to support the government's package of economic reforms. In return, he demanded that Solidarity be legalised and the government commit to restoring political pluralism in Poland.

Jaruzelski's team had chosen to open talks with Wałęsa. However, he had no mandate to speak on behalf of either the Solidarity movement or the dissident groupings. Within Solidarity there were radical elements. These people saw the opening of talks as a compromise and disagreed with Wałęsa. They usurped the authority of the Solidarity movement. Among these were many of the Solidarity leaders of the 1980–81 period. These included Andrzej Gwiazda and Jan Rulewski. Wałęsa, nevertheless continued to be seen by most Poles as the spokesman of the Solidarity movement. His authority and standing within the opposition was undisputed. He was the most easily recognisable symbol of the Solidarity movement and the recipient of the 1983 Nobel Prize for Peace. Critically, he was also the person on whom the Episcopate had based its programme for reopening talks with the regime. On 27 January 1989, both sides agreed to agenda, composition and objectives of the talks. These opened on 6 February. Both sides sat to the table, still unsure as to the possible outcome of the talks. Neither realised that by the time the final agreement would be signed, the clock would be set back to before 1947. The single-party dictatorship would be abolished.[28]

# 7    Post-communist Poland

The Round Table Talks steered Poland on the road to transformation. They went from being a communist, single-party regime, to a democratic state. Changes occurred in the wake of transformation. The results were neither planned, nor anticipated. Nevertheless, once the communist hold on power was broken, all aspects of life in Poland were inevitably affected.

The talks opened on 6 February 1989. They ended with the signing of the final agreement on 5 April. Even before the official inaugural meeting, the outline of the agenda had been agreed. Both sides had a strong sense of the direction in which they would try to move the talks. Only during the opening and closing session did all the delegates and their advisors actually meet at the specially built round table. The real negotiations were conducted in smaller groups. Of the official delegates to the talks, 14 were from the ruling party, 6 from the government-supported trade unions, 20 were opposition delegates, 14 represented independent organisations and 2 were Catholic bishops. Once the various advisors were added to the final tally, the total came to 452. Wałęsa led the opposition team, supported by Zbigniew Bujak and Władysław Frasyniuk from Solidarity. Bronisław Geremek, Tadeusz Mazowiecki, Jacek Kuroń and Adam Michnik, acted as Wałęsa's advisors. Czesław Kiszczak and Stanisław Ciosek led the government side. Aleksander Kwaśniewski was a young member of the PZPR. He had already made his mark on the course of the negotiations. Missing from the table were representatives of the radical sections of Solidarity. These included some of the prominent leaders of the underground Solidarity, who had maintained the memory of the free trade union, during the period of the State of War. Those who opposed talks with the communists were sidelined. The church had advised Wałęsa not to seek cooperation with them. Wałęsa chose his own team. The result was that the opposition team was united and spoke with one voice. The government side increasingly became fractured. In particular because the government-supported trade unions distanced themselves from the government delegation and came to represent an independent force.[1]

The key item on the agenda was that of political reforms. Both sides understood that, until they had reached an understanding on this issue, they would not be able to proceed with other matters. After extensive talks, it was agreed that general elections would take place and a new government would be formed. The communists were guaranteed 65 per cent of the seats in the Sejm. 35 per cent would be decided on the basis of free elections. A Senate was to be formed and all seats to that body were to be allocated as a result of free elections. Subsequently, it was agreed to establish the post of President. Both sides tacitly agreed that Jaruzelski would be allowed to assume that responsibility. This completed the package of political reforms. The President's prerogatives were to be wide, including the right to impose a state of emergency. Economic matters were discussed in a special forum. However, neither the government nor the opposition brought new ideas to the negotiations. The economic crisis continued to affect the country. It provoked strikes and protests. The government appeared to have run out of steam and had no new initiatives as to how to cope with the problems overwhelming it. The opposition, on the other hand, had no inclination to assume responsibility. Nor did they have anything new to propose. Index-linking of wages was discussed. So were suggestions for workers' participation in industrial management. In reality, both sides shied away from discussing economic affairs. Privatisation was not a phrase that was used at the Round Table Talks.[2]

The government emerged from the talks, convinced that it would be able to secure at least 50 per cent of seats in the Senate and thus guarantee the continuation of communist control over the legislature. They accepted that the opposition would have an increased role. However, there was no assumption that the agreements just signed, spelled the end of communist control over Poland. On the other side of the political spectrum stood the dissident groups. These had opposed any deal with the communists. They varied from the nationalist KPN, to radical youth organisations. They attacked the Solidarity negotiating team, accusing them of complicity in maintaining the communist system. This, they believed, could and should have been destroyed outright. The re-legalisation of Solidarity, appeared to them to be merely a concession. One which the communists were willing to make in order to stay in power.

The Catholic Church had played an important role in the talks. Both sides wanted the bishops at the negotiating table. To the government, this was an assurance that this powerful organisation would be party to any agreement made. It would thus act as guarantor of decisions made. But the Episcopate had its own agenda. Its involvement in the talks was not a disinterested act of mediation. The church knew, from recent developments, that Poland stood poised on the threshold of dramatic changes. It was critically important for the church to secure for itself a role within the new vision. There was anxiety about the influence of the radical sections of the Solidarity and youth movements. These the church sought to sideline. In addition to this, there was a fear of further secularisation. In its quest to maintain its spiritual influence in Poland, the Catholic Church appreciated the importance of keeping a finger on the political pulse of the nation.[3]

The elections to the Sejm and Senate were scheduled to take place on 4 June. The announcement was made in April. The period between this and the date of the elections was a time of mass mobilisation. The communist rulers were still confident that they would command the loyalty of sizeable sections of the society. The opposition was increasingly differentiated and were on a steep learning curve. As it turned out, it was this element of the developments, which gave the Solidarity activists and the anti-government forces, their advantage. Citizens' committees appeared to organise the electoral campaign of the opposition. These transformed themselves into electoral colleges. They selected candidates and managed electoral campaigns. In some cases, already existing Solidarity structures formed the basis of the electoral colleges. In others, they came into being on the initiative of local people, activists or parish priests. In all cases, Solidarity tried to retain control over the appointments of candidates. This brought to the fore the unresolved issue of how the anti-government forces were to collaborate. On the one hand, intellectuals and former advisors thought in terms of a broad liberal-democratic front, united in one organisation. Others already envisaged that the opposition would divide into distinct tendencies. These would more clearly define their political affinities. For the duration of the pre-election campaign, the first model prevailed. Some groups decided not to collaborate with the citizens' committees, but to field independent candidates. Moczulski, the leader of KPN, and some Solidarity activists opposed what they saw as the Round Table compromise. They decided not to throw in their lot with Wałęsa's grouping.[4]

During this period, the atmosphere was conducive to the opening up of blank spots in recent Polish history. Certain issues were now discussed openly in Polish daily newspapers and the media. These subjects included the Katyń forest graves; Soviet appropriation of Poland's pre-war territories and imprisonment of AK fighters and their removal to the Soviet Union after the war. One of the results of the Round Table agreement was the emergence of independent newspapers. The best known was *Gazeta Wyborcza*. The editor of this newspaper was the highly respected Adam Michnik. State television and radio were obliged to grant the opposition access to publicise their electoral material. The heady atmosphere of freedom was in no way dampened down by Moscow. On the contrary, the Soviet leaders, conspicuously, kept silent on events unfolding in Poland. They thus signalled that they viewed the forthcoming elections as Poland's internal matter.[5]

As a result of the Round Table agreement, the government had the right to appoint deputies to 65 per cent of the seats in the Sejm. 35 per cent of the seats in the Sejm and all the seats in the Senate were to be freely contested. The opposition campaign, handled itself expertly and with a high degree of community participation. It aimed to mobilise the voters; to inform them of the programmes and to explain the procedures. All were therefore surprised on the day of the first round of voting, when only 72 per cent of those eligible to vote, turned out to cast their votes. The result was a stunning victory for the anti-government forces. Of the 61 seats to the Sejm, which were to be freely contested, 60 went to the Solidarity candidates. Votes to the Senate, likewise, revealed an outright victory for the anti-government opposition. When asked about their views on the subject, the Soviet spokesmen, in line with earlier policy, declared that this was a Polish matter. Thus, the challenge to the post-war communist system came not only from Poland's citizens, but was made possible because the Soviet Union decided Poland was no longer in its security zone. Soviet intervention in Polish internal affairs was no longer considered an option in Moscow.

It had been decided that the new government would not be appointed until the final decision was made about the presidency. Therefore, the composition of the government was not agreed immediately after the June elections. As it turned out, the presidency was a foregone conclusion. It is widely suspected that during the Round Table Talks Wałęsa's team had agreed that Jaruzelski was to become Poland's President. There were those within the Solidarity movement who would have wanted to revisit this agreement after the recent electoral victory. However, neither Wałęsa, nor those close to him, considered this to be prudent. The opposition's electoral success offered an entirely new possibility, namely of a Solidarity candidate becoming Prime Minister. Talks and discussions took place. These concened the appointment of Jaruzelski to the presidency. In the course of these talks, the Solidarity movement splintered. Some Solidarity deputies voted for Jaruzelski. Wałęsa did not put himself forward. It was widely suspected that he hoped to stand for President in the next elections. Many activists were not used to political compromises. Their only political experience had been of relentless struggle against communism. These activists found it difficult to accept Wałęsa's apparent realism. Earlier fissures widened, as Wałęsa conducted the negotiations. Until then, he had drawn into his confidence, some of the KOR intellectuals from whom he derived most of his strategic ideas. This irritated many of the old Solidarity activists and the young. They shared the view that there should be no compromise with the communists.

At the same time, the intellectuals were disunited as to how Solidarity should seek to form a government. Michnik and Geremek advocated building an alliance with the reformist sections of the PZPR. Mazowiecki, on the other hand, warned against undue haste in reaching for power. His view was that cooperation could lead to the opposition becoming tainted, through its association with the hated regime. He warned that, by becoming a member of the coalition government, Solidarity would be held responsible for the unresolved economic problems. As Mazowiecki sagely pointed out, the economic policy pursued by the government had had disastrous consequences. Solidarity, along with most of the opposition groupings, had not put forward an alternative.

The alternative to working with the government in finding solutions to the existing economic problems was to seek alliances with the non-communist ruling parties. These were the Zjednoczone Stronnictwo Ludowe (Peasant United Peasant Alliance – ZSL) and the Stronnictwo Demokratyczne (Democratic Alliance – SD). Both were small rump parties. In 1945, they had thrown in their lot with the communists. They had never been genuinely independent and had no influence on policymaking. During 1980, both parties saw an opportunity to emerge from behind the communist party. General Czesław Kiszczak was the Minister of Interior in the outgoing government. He made several attempts to form a government. This meant that the small rump parties were more willing to collaborate with Wałęsa. Wałęsa focused on these parties in his search for allies to form a government. Contacts were made by the ZSL and SD, namely through the two lesser known opposition activists, the Kaczyński brothers. Wałęsa actions alienated Geremek and Kuroń. Wałęsa put a proposal to the leaders of the two potential allies. His proposal was that Mazowiecki should be the next Prime Minister. This was a compromise choice. It was guaranteed to meet with the coalitionists' approval and with popular support. Mazowiecki was a highly respected Catholic leader, whom the church would also support. Kuroń and Geremek would not have fitted this role, Geremek, because he was Jewish and Kuroń due to his radical past. Wałęsa's arbitrary decision was made with no reference to his Solidarity colleagues. It prevailed. A government was formed. It was headed by Mazowiecki, but with Jaruzelski as President. The President's prerogatives were wide and in many respects undefined. Mazowiecki, in the meantime, had no experience of power. More worryingly, his power base in the Solidarity movement was fast fragmenting. What appeared, during the Round Table Talks, as a long-term plan for broadening the base of governance, rapidly changed. Unexpectedly, the opposition had formed the first government. Worryingly, it had no clear programme that would guide it through the first governmental decisions.

In the Mazowiecki government, the PZPR remained in control of the main ministries. These were notably interior and defence. Solidarity, nevertheless, was the largest grouping. It retained the Ministry of Finance. Thus, Leszek Balcerowicz was assigned the main task of the Mazowiecki government. This was namely the stabilisation of the economy. Growing inflation and budgetary deficits on their own account, limited the options to freeing the economy of all constraints. In that, Mazowiecki and Balcerowicz followed closely the neo-liberal monetarist policies advocated by their Western economic advisors and Harvard economists. Nor was it a coincidence that the 'shock therapy', introduced by Balcerowicz was in line with the Washington Consensus policies of the International Monetary Fund and the World Bank. These were about to be discredited in the emerging market crisis of the 1990s. The consequences of the rapid transformation were dramatic. From January 1990, all state controls on prices of commodities and food were removed. Wage increases were frozen. In order to balance the budget, state investments were reduced, while taxes were increased. Domestic credit was limited and interest rates were increased. It was assumed that free market mechanisms would lead to the reduction of inflation. Initially, Mazowiecki made no reference to privatisation. Though in its final form Balcerowicz anticipated an inevitable change in the structure of ownership of means of production. The first reforms were steered through the Sejm and Senate in December 1989. In June 1990, the first privatisation proposals were put to the Sejm. In the spring of the following year, the government faced the political consequences of the economic policies.

This plan came to be known as the Balcerowicz Plan. The implementation of it led to protests and strikes on an enormous scale. This, undeniably caused the tempo of transformation to slow down. Though even at the height of the countrywide protests, the government was determined to proceed, regardless of the social and economic consequences. Balcerowicz's policies met with wide approval in the West. As a result, financial support was forthcoming for Poland. The Soviet Union was becoming increasingly preoccupied with internal stability. Balcerowicz was therefore aware that Poland could no longer count on any assistance from them. The COMECON market had to all practical purposes, collapsed. All of the other previously Soviet satellite states were undergoing a process of rapid liberalisation. Balcerowicz was thus fighting to establish, for Poland, an independent position in the international markets. Mazowiecki and his government, in the same way, sought to defend Poland's interest in the Soviet–German rapprochement. This, ultimately, led to the reunification of Germany.

Initially, Mazowiecki's government conducted a cautious foreign policy. The Poles sought to assure Gorbachov that they would not seek to withdraw from the Warsaw Pact. There was an initiative for a change of relations between the satellite states and the Soviet Union. This initiative came from other countries. Poland was not in the forefront of demands for the renegotiation of relations. In November 1989, Chancellor Helmut Kohl visited Poland. The results of what initially looked like a momentous visit were limited. The attention of the West German leader was on reunification. This, he outlined in a ten-point plan soon after returning from Poland. The Polish leaders noted that Kohl made no commitment to respecting Poland's post-war border. This was an issue which was bound to come up if Germany was reunited. The Soviet Union had been the guarantor of Poland's post-war western border. But at the end of 1989, Poland was not an issue on which the Soviet policymakers could be detained. Much weightier problems faced them in the conflicts between Armenia and Azerbaijan. In principle, Gorbachov's attitude towards Poland continued to be helpful. Nevertheless, the Soviet Union was willing to make an open admission of responsibility for the Katyń massacres. This went hand in hand with increased unwillingness to support Poland economically. Soviet troops continued to be based on Polish soil. As long as the issue of the western border was not resolved, the Poles accepted that this was necessary. All in all, in the face of the scaling down of the Cold War, Poland stood to lose the support of a powerful Soviet ally and faced the prospect of dealing with Germany on its own.

Mazowiecki's government had to lobby hard to be included in the '2 + 4' talks on the reunification of Germany. On 3rd October 1990, a single German state came into being. As a result of these talks, Poland obtained a guarantee of the inviolability of its border with Germany.

The unification of Germany and the end of the Soviet Union led to a changing international configuration. This required rapid diplomacy. The Polish government had little experience of foreign policy. It had to address the key question of Poland's place in the new world order. Since the Second World War, Poland had not been free to formulate its own foreign policy. In any case, the fear of German revanchism dominated Poland's relations with the West. This made the Soviet Union Poland's key ally. In the circumstances, membership of the Warsaw Pact was of critical importance to Poland. Now Polish politicians had to consider the question of Poland's security without the Soviet Union. This inevitably brought them back to the question of Germany's objectives. The US was reluctant to reopen the question of Germany's borders. Therefore, as long as united Germany remained a member of NATO, Polish politicians felt Polish interests would be guaranteed. In the meantime, Polish foreign policy in the East was aimed at covering all options. Attempts were made to maintain good relations with Moscow. At the same time, they were mindful of the rapid disintegration of the structure of the Soviet Union. Negotiations started with the republics which bordered Poland, namely Ukraine and Byelorussia. In reality, until the situation stabilised, the Poles clung to the security which the Warsaw Pact had offered. But already plans were being formulated for Poland's entry into NATO in the long term. In its relations with Western Europe, the Mazowiecki government merely accelerated progress which had been taking place in recent years. Poland had already established financial and economic relations with West European partners. The issue of debts bound Poland to West European institutions. In 1990, Mazowiecki visited Belgium. There, he informed Jacques Delors that Poland looked forward to being included in the European Union (EU).

Domestically, the Round Table Talks were followed by the emergence of genuine political pluralism. The PZPR continued, increasingly devoid of authority and rationale. In the meantime, other

parties emerged, both new and not so new. The membership of
the PZPR became less interested in supporting the party. What previously had been an important avenue for professional advancement was now merely a discredited political party. During the XI
Congress of the PZPR in January 1990, two options were discussed.
Some believed that a new party should emerge, though not entirely cut off from its past. The majority favoured this option. A
minority-supported alternative was for a new party to be formed,
based on the social democratic traditions of Western Europe. Both
factions, nevertheless accepted the demise of the communist party
as it had functioned since the war. In due course, it became apparent that any party claiming allegiance to the PZPR past, would
fail to make an impact on the new Polish political scene. The final decision was to form a supposedly new party with the name of
Socjaldemokracja Rzeczpospolitej Polskiej (Social Democracy of the
Polish Republic – SdRP). The party leader, 36-year-old Aleksander
Kwaśniewski, consciously espoused a modern European image for
the party. Kwaśniewski adopted a name that harked back to a pre-
communist past and shedded the old, stuffy and dogmatic image
of the communism past. In this way, he attracted young radicals to
the party. These were people who still believed in a socialist future
for Poland.

The peasant ZSL made transformation easier by presenting itself
as a victim of communist policies. By reclaiming the old name of
the PSL, the peasant party drew on the Witos legend and the more
recent one of Mikołajczyk. During the interwar period, the peasant
movement had remained divided. Thus, despite its impressive numerical growth, it remained divided. During 1945–47, Mikołajczyk
had expected that the PSL would win elections without the need
to enter into a coalition agreement with either the communists or
the socialists. In 1947, the party was destroyed. All that remained
was the rump ZSL. This had no genuine commitment to representing the interests of the peasant community. But it was a political
vehicle for a few peasant leaders, who were willing to collaborate
with the communists. In 1991 Rural Solidarity emerged as a new
force. Up until then, the peasants in Poland had no political organisation, which they could genuinely call their own. In the Stalin

years, forceful collectivisation had been pursued. After this, the peasants were only loosely integrated into the process of political transformation that had affected Poland. During the 1960s and more so during the 1970s, peasants were supported by government funding. This left many of them in debt, but secure in the knowledge that the government would not call in those debts. Attempts were made to introduce modern crop techniques and advanced animal husbandry. However, small-scale farming continued to be the norm in Poland. Thus these attempts left little scope for mechanisation and modernisation. Under communism, Polish agriculture stagnated. Amply cushioned by state subsidies, peasants had few economic incentives to improve their way of life.

With the disintegration of the communist system, state support for agriculture collapsed. This belatedly led to debates on modernisation. In these, the question of consolidation of land and introduction of market forces had an impact. They affected not only rural life, but also the politics of peasant parties. The emergence of market gardening and greenhouse farming had been encouraged during the Gierek period. This had already transformed the production of food. These growers and wealthy farmers would look to the peasant parties for support with mobilisation and protection against the import of food from the West. Small farmers wanted their political representatives to campaign for increased subsidies and guaranteed high prices. These were in addition to assurances that foreigners would not be allowed to buy land in Poland. In May 1990, three peasant organisations came together to form a new party. The new party consisted of the ex-party members of the now defunct ZSL, together with activists from Rural Solidarity and those seeking to reclaim the PSL of the Mikołajczyk period. These people uneasily decided to cooperate. The fall in real incomes in urban areas and growing imports, created a crisis for Polish agriculture.

Mazowiecki's government was unprepared for the ferocity of peasant protests. During the summer of 1989 and again in 1990, the peasants organised mass actions. They blockaded national roads; stopped the movement of trains and demanded that the government pay high prices for food and reduce the credit rate interests paid to the farmers. Mazowiecki was confronted by nationwide and well-organised opposition. He bowed to pressure and put more money into agriculture. Though it was clear that, until the issue of the backwardness of Polish agriculture was addressed, such measures could only be temporary.

In October 1990, 154 political parties legally registered with the courts. What was so striking was the variety of organisations which laid claim to political leadership. Some were of a quixotic character. Among them, the Beekeepers' and the Beerdrinkers' parties stand out. In reality, the Poles were freed from previous constraints. In this context, they were still learning how political representation worked. Most new parties did not come into being as a result of grass roots initiatives. The process of party formation in Poland has been described as elite driven. It has been defined as a process determined by politically minded activists, frequently already occupying prominent roles in the process of transformation. Most of Poland's citizens were unfamiliar with the democratic parliamentary system. Thus, voters tended to view parties as civil associations rather than as electoral structures. They acted as transmitters of their interests and aspirations to the legislative body. Until the first genuinely free elections, political parties, their supporters and activists were not able to function as in Western democracies. Small parties emerged. These investigated and formulated political programmes. However, many of them soon withered away.

The break-up of the leadership of the Solidarity movement was the most important fallout of these processes of differentiation and political maturing. The main conflict occurred between Mazowiecki and his patron Wałęsa. Wałęsa had pushed forward Mazowiecki's candidacy for the premiership. It was no secret that he had done this because the former wanted to be free to stand for the presidency. This did not mean that he wanted to keep out of government decision making. On the contrary, he had hoped that Mazowiecki would act as puppet, obediently accepting Wałęsa's instructions. This did not happen. As Mazowiecki became more confident in his role, his earlier patron appointed his own people as editors of the Solidarity newspaper. He then supported Jarosław Kaczyński, a vocal critic of the government's policies. What followed was a process of polarisation. Wałęsa distanced himself from his previous intellectual advisors and allied himself with those criticising the government

for deliberately slowing down political transformation and privatisation.

The first free political contest between the post-communist
forces, took place in the context of the November 1990 presidential elections. During the electoral campaign, it looked as if the
main contest would be between Wałęsa and Mazowiecki. Possibly
unwisely, Mazowiecki refused to campaign on the basis of promises
for a better future. Instead, he asked that he be judged on the basis of his achievements as Prime Minister. He spoke of a slow and
steady process of reforms, and transformation. He defended the Balcerowicz reforms but promised to increase the housing budget and
spending on agriculture. Critically, Mazowiecki failed to dispel rumours that he was Jewish. In the Polish context, anti-Semitism was
and still is the norm. Thus, in nationalist circles, the accusation that
Mazowiecki might be Jewish was a an extremely damaging accusation. It was fanned by the centre right and by Wałęsa's statements.
In these statements, Wałęsa claimed that he, unlike his opponent,
was a genuine Pole and therefore represented Polish interests. Far
from condemning his opponent for introducing anti-Semitic under-
tones into the campaign, Mazowiecki's team responded by publicising evidence of his baptism. Mazowiecki's campaign was lacklustre.
Wałęsa, on the other hand, used all his authority as the leader of the
Solidarity movement, to present himself as the man of the people.
He attacked his main opponent's intellectualism. This he contrasted
with his own ability to respond to people's needs. He promised to
deal with the remnants of the communist system and implement
economic reforms. It was easy for Wałęsa to attack the Balcerowicz reforms. These had caused mass unemployment and reduced
real incomes, pensions and allowances. Wałęsa promised to push
on with privatisation. He argued that all would benefit through the
distribution of privatisation bonds.

There were other, more colourful candidates in this presidential
election. Nevertheless, Wałęsa and Mazowiecki were seen as the key
protagonists. It was therefore a shock when the results of the first
round of elections were released. Mazowiecki was out. He had only
secured 19.08 per cent of votes. Wałęsa did not secure the necessary
50 per cent majority. In the second round, he faced a man who
had no political base in Poland and no programme. But he had

conducted a slick campaign and appealed to the Poles' desire to improve their dreary daily existence. Stanisław Tymiński was a Polish businessman. He had first emigrated to Canada and then to Peru. He had used personal funds to put together a well-conducted campaign. In his campaigns, he assured Poles that they could emulate his achievements. His political base was the supposed party X. This seemed to have no obvious membership. His economic programme amounted to solutions, the details of which he did not divulge. But they were supposedly locked in his personal computer. In spite of his apparent shortcomings, Tymiński secured 23.1 per cent of the votes. In the second round, 74.25 per cent of those taking part in the elections, supported Wałęsa. The route from worker activist to President was thus completed. It nevertheless remained unclear as to whether Wałęsa had the political and personal skills to act as the leader of the new Polish state.

In accordance with the intermediate version of the 1992 Constitution, which was known as the Small Constitution, the President still retained extensive powers. These included the right to nominate the Prime Minister, Minister of Interior and Minister for Foreign Affairs, as well as the head of the national bank, the Narodowy Bank Polski. On being elected President, Wałęsa was faced with the immense task of putting together a team that would govern until the general elections took place. The broad Solidarity movement had disintegrated and there was a widening differentiation between the various strands of political ideas. These two factors made Wałęsa's task all the more difficult. In any case, political activists realised that if they were associated too closely with the present problems, they might blight their and their parties' electoral chances. Jan Krzysztof Bielecki's government was formed in January 1991. It was the most stable government of that period. Unfortunately, Poland experienced a worsening economic situation, during which Balcerowicz continued to be Minister of Finance. The devaluation of the Polish currency and an anti-recession package, caused a strong reaction from within the Solidarity trade union and from the rural community. The government faced stiff opposition in the Sejm. In addition, they had to contend with Wałęsa's interference. The latter quickly lost popularity. When faced with problems, the previously charismatic trade union leader turned against his advisors. He increasingly surrounded himself with people who were of little help to him in his new role as President. Of those, no doubt, the most unusual was his chauffeur, whose advice Wałęsa sought in preference to that of his government. Wałęsa was fast becoming an embarrassment. During meetings with the press and foreign visitors, he appeared to lack the necessary social graces and his personal behaviour was uncouth and aggressive. He modelled himself on Piłsudski and responded to his critics with claims that he had been solely responsible for the fall of communism. In reality, political maturing had led the trade union element of the hitherto broad Solidarity movement to more defined organisational structures. These were applied in relations with trade union members and within the workplace. Many of the well-known Solidarity activists, moved towards national politics and formed new parties. What had previously been Wałęsa's power base was no longer there.

The first genuinely free general elections took place on 27 October 1991. The campaign was fought with the full use of all modern methods of persuasion. Political parties paid a lot of attention to presentation and made sure that their leaders were well turned out and attractive. Tymiński's success during the presidential campaign had taught party leaders that the electorate could be manipulated. Long-winded and sophisticated explanations were abandoned. Instead, catchy and easy-to-understand slogans were offered on billboards and in TV advertisements. All parties spent considerable amounts of money on publicity. Some employed public relations advisors, in particular from the USA. These were supposed to give a veneer of excitement to the otherwise earnest campaigns.

The electoral campaign leading up to the general elections of 27 October 1991 was fought with real commitment. There was no doubt that very real issues differentiated the parties. It was therefore a shock, when it was revealed, that only 43.2 per cent of those entitled to vote went to the polls. This figure contrasted sharply with the average 70 per cent electoral participation during the first years of the new Polish state during the interwar period. Subsequent research revealed the main factor determining people's attitude towards elections. This was the recent economic transformation. Unskilled workers, the uneducated and those living in small communities had been severely affected by the economic restructuring and unemployment. They were indifferent to the elections. Individuals' economic situation and the loss of economic opportunities had led to political apathy. Belatedly, Poles were finding out how the capitalist system worked. The result was political indifference. Low participation in the elections indicated disappointment with the achievements of the post-Solidarity period. It is debatable as to whether economic liberalisation had ever been the aim of the Solidarity movement. Nevertheless, in the 1990s the paternalistic structures of the previous regime were being dismantled. From guarantees of full employment, to medical and social provisions for pensioners, war veterans and invalids, an underclass emerged. This underclass was economically inactive and outside the scope of politics.

The results of the elections were inconclusive. No electoral grouping secured an outright majority. Thus, the formation of the first truly free government in post-war Poland was delayed by the need to put together a coalition. Nevertheless, the elections led to the emergence of three major political forces. The Unia Demokratyczna (Democratic Union – UD) brought together supporters of the Mazowiecki government. Some of his allies, nevertheless voted for Bielecki's liberal party. This weakened the UDs, which showed in the elections. This grouping secured the votes of those with higher education and people who had benefited from the recent economic changes. The post-communist Sojusz Lewicy Demokratycznej (Democratic Left Alliance – SLD) brought together left wing and radical elements, in particular from among white-collar and skilled workers. The PSL was the third largest political grouping within the Sejm. The village population abandoned the post-Solidarity parties and voted nearly entirely for one of the two peasant parties. In this way, they split their vote. The right wing parties had failed to unite before the elections. Nevertheless, the KPN was able to secure 8 per cent of the votes. They thus confirmed their importance within the new political scene in Poland.

It fell to Wałęsa, in his capacity as President, to form a new government. This proved to be a difficult task. It was made much more difficult by Wałęsa's determination to prevent the SLD and the UD, from forming a coalition. This meant that he went to great lengths to bring together the other parties, mainly the centre, Christian and conservative ones. In the end, a coalition government was put together. But the KPN refused to participate. Jan Olszewski was a well-known dissident from the communist period. He led the KPN and it survived until June 1992. The Olszewski government marked a stage in the development of a post-communist Poland. Those who had previously ruled and had been closely connected with the regime lost power. New politicians now took matters into their hands.

A key policy was dismantling the security apparatus. The army, likewise, was purged and new appointments were made. These reflected the new political reality. Revelations were made of the extent of civil collaboration with the communist security apparatus. These led to a search for those who had been tainted by collaboration with communists. This degenerated into a witch-hunt. Politicians sought to outbid each other by making accusations against all those who had held positions of responsibility during the Communist period. Furthermore, most of the new deputies and all the new ministers had no political experience. They were unused to subordinating themselves to party discipline and supporting the policies of the government which they themselves had formed. It was not uncommon to see a minister publicly attack the government in which he or she held a portfolio. The Small Constitution defined the President's prerogatives and the functioning of the executive and legislative organs. This was vague on a number of matters. Thus, many procedural matters were still unclear. The final version of the constitution was being discussed in a specially appointed forum. But, from the outset, Wałęsa was in conflict with the government and in particular with Olszewski. The President believed that he had the authority to dismiss and appoint the Minister of Defence. The Prime Minister was convinced that he had absolute control over the army. The appointment of Hanna Gronkiewicz-Waltz. Wałęsa's protégé to head the Narodowy Bank Polski, caused further disputes. Politics appeared to be driven by the President's animosities towards the Sejm and particular personalities, rather than by government policy.

The Olszewski-led government fell, amidst accusations that numerous Sejm deputies and government ministers had collaborated with the communist regime. The next coalition faced the same problems. Waldemar Pawlak, the new prime minister, was the leader of the PSL. In accordance with the Small Constitution, he could not appoint the Minister of Interior or the Minister of Foreign Affairs. This immediately created scope for disputes with the President. When he was unable to put together a coalition, Pawlak resigned and Hanna Suchocka, from the UD, formed a new government. The main supporters of the new government were parties which described themselves as liberal and Christian. The new Prime Minister lacked political experience. However, the government she put together showed a higher degree of stability, than any previous one. A number of important reforms were approved by the Sejm, before it fell on 28 May 1993.

Secret service files containing evidence of cooperation with the communist regime continued to be verified. The issue did not go away and bedevilled the next government. An accusation that a given politician had, in the past, worked with the communists or a mere accusation that a file had been created by the security service could destroy a person's political career. Wałęsa was not immune to these accusations and it was rumoured that he had been an informer. Some of his previous allies within the original Solidarity Free Trade Union were willing to believe that the security service had recruited him. This matter repeatedly and inconclusively returned to the Sejm.

A new feature of Polish political life during the 1990s was the emergence of extra-parliamentary politics. Poland made a very successful transition to parliamentary democracy. However, the economic situation created unemployment. Through that, preconditions were established, whereby sections of Polish society had no, or limited interest in supporting the young democracy. Suchocka's government faced first mass waves of industrial strikes to secure higher pay. Strikers frequently voiced anti-government slogans. In reality, the trade unions had no desire to enter directly into politics. Upper Silesia was the centre of several waves of strikes during 1993. Under communism, miners had enjoyed a privileged status. During the 1990s, demand for Polish coal had fallen and the government was no longer interested in supporting unproductive coal mines. Other industries suffered because of Western competition and fall of demand from what was previously the protected East European market. Added to that was anxiety about Western companies buying up Polish enterprises only to close them down. This reduced competition with their own production. Suchocka's government accelerated the privatisation process and oversaw the transformation of the banking and financial sector. Many saw this as a step forward and the first sign that Poland was emerging out of the recession. However, others saw these reforms as a betrayal of their own, and the nation's interests. Some industries had adapted to modern methods. There were also enterprises which foreign investors wanted to buy in order to continue production. These industries and enterprises, offered continuing employment to workers. Other places also did this, though on a smaller scale. Workers employed in coal mining, steel production and unprofitable industries, faced mass unemployment. Whole areas of previously industrialised Poland were blighted by this hitherto unknown phenomenon. A similar process of differentiation started occurring in agriculture. State farms collapsed. Those previously employed in them had nothing to look forward to and no way of starting a new life. More entrepreneurial farmers looked forward to talks on Poland joining the EU; economic assistance in modernisation and land consolidation. The mobilisation of disaffected communities had occurred because they had believed themselves to have been overlooked by the new political leaders. Certain areas were blighted by the collapse of previously thriving industries. Young people from these areas, along with blue collar workers, turned to direct action. In the second half of the 1990s, some sections of rural communities, likewise, took matters into their own hands. They staged protests, roadblocks and disrupted rail freight. They especially did this when they suspected that cheap food was being imported into Poland. Direct action came to be seen as a justified way of putting pressure on the government. In some cases, it was even seen as a way of destroying the social and political consensus. This was a consensus which these groups believed, excluded them. Many Poles were largely nationalist and no longer constrained by political autocracy. They therefore felt free to hate those who appeared to be responsible for their plight.

Little united the emerging radical right wing parties of the post-communist period. However, they all agreed on the defence of the interests of the nation and support for the national economy. Anxiety about the loss of national identity was also emphasised. In their pronouncements, the nationalist leaders attacked the World Bank and the European Union. They claimed that both organisations would, in some way, lead to the nation's dissolution. This would happen through the loss of its economic, cultural and social heritage. These parties and organisations either had strong links with the Catholic Church or appropriated symbols of that faith. This was in their claim to represent the interests of the nation.

During the early stages of political transformation, none of the radical nationalist parties were able to secure seats in the Sejm. This explains their resort to mass protests and preference for direct action. The nationalist and neo-fascist organisations in Poland were not united. This was the key source of their weakness during the 1993 elections. The extreme right wing parties were dominated by leaders who perpetuated the divisions within the right wing, by firmly adhering to the ideas of one particular past ideologue. This was usually Dmowski or Piłsudski. The KPN's leader was Moczulski. He defined himself as a follower of Piłsudski's ideas and would have nothing to do with the Stronnictwo Narodowe (National Alliance – SN). This revered Dmowski. Both parties were active. However, they never recovered from their disastrous showing in the 1993 elections. Internal splits took their toll. During the coming years, the radical nationalist parties were reduced in importance. They occasionally emerged as possible partners in the process of building larger coalitions.

Two new forces emerged during the mid-1990s. What distinguished them from the nationalist right wing parties was that they made no pretence of being heirs to past movements. The Polish Nationalist Party was led by Bolesław Tejkowski. This party was the most virulently anti-Semitic and anti-parliamentarian emerging party. The structure of the organisation was loose and had undergone several transformations. Nevertheless, the party's constant feature was its association with the newly emerging skinhead culture in Poland. It remains the movement of the young and unemployed. The main focus is on violent street action. What is most surprising is that some governments in Warsaw have been willing to tolerate this. Tejkowski's supporters identified Jews as the biological enemies of the Polish nation. They have attacked all those whom they accuse of being Jewish. This includes any organisation, community or person, whose actions are perceived to be damaging to the interests of the Polish people. Unusually, the radical right has been robust in accusing the Catholic Church of having betrayed Poland. They have suggested that many bishops and Pope John Paul II were Jewish. More recently, the radical right and the skinhead groupings have come together to form a broadly based organisation. This has taken the name of Młodzież Wszechpolska (All Poland Youth – MW). This organisation had lent its support to right wing and nationalist parties, particularly in attacking left wing political organisations and youth movements. Sexual diversity, in particular homosexuality, has been added to the list of disorders in the Polish nation, which this neo-fascist organisation is determined to cleanse. Their activities have been tolerated and even encouraged by some centrist and right wing parties.

In January 1992, a new political party brought together disaffected peasants. This was the Samoobrona (Self-help) organisation, established by Andrzej Lepper. It first appeared on the political scene during Olszewski's government. Militant sections of the organisation occupied the Ministry of Agriculture, demanding the cancellation of debts. Lepper had one clear objective. This was to attack the government for its neglect of agriculture and peasant interests. From the outset, his followers set out to make their mark through direct action. During the summer of 1992, they organised road blockades. They aimed to display their power and the impotence of the authorities. Well-publicised marches onto the capital and hunger strikes followed. Briefly, President Wałęsa endorsed Samoobrona's actions. Though this was mainly to embarrass the government. Lepper's approach to politics was, and remains, unhindered by any ideological ballast. According to his early programme, Poland was to follow neither a capitalist nor a socialist path. In effect, it would follow a Polish path. Initially, Samoobrona was viewed as a harmless expression of grass roots mobilisation. However, this has changed in recent years. Lepper stood for presidency in 1995 and secured 1.32 per cent of the votes. During the 2001 elections, Samoobrona won 53 seats in the Sejm. In 2005, they improved on this performance by winning 56 seats in the general elections. The biggest surprise was the organisation's victory in the elections to the European Parliament. Five

deputies from Samoobrona sit in the European Parliament. They
forged an alliance with the European extreme right. The reasons
for this electoral breakthrough, lay in the increasing public disillu-
sionment with the progress of transition. This disadvantaged large
sections of the population, most notably in the villages. There, the
PSL has been perceived to be the party of the middle and wealthy
farmers. They are benefitting from EU subsidies and trading links
with Western Europe. Lepper has skilfully manipulated the party's
image to embrace extra-parliamentary, high-profile escapades, with
a vocal defence of the interests of the small peasants in the Sejm. His
focus on national interest and Christianity as guidelines for Poles
has strong appeal to the uneducated.

In 1993, general elections took place in accordance with new
electoral laws. The aim of these was to eliminate the instability
created by the proliferation of small organisations. To obtain representation in the Sejm, parties had to secure a minimum of 5 per
cent of votes cast. In the case of electoral coalitions, these had to
secure 8 per cent of the votes. Parties competed for seats in electoral
districts and for a share of seats from a national list. In the run-up to
the elections, popular opinion swung behind the post-communist
SLD and the PSL. The break-up of the Solidarity movement, further
increased the probability of their success. Some have since blamed
Wałęsa's internal manipulations for the weakening of Solidarity. He
attempted to form an electoral structure loyal to himself. This was
curiously reminiscent of Piłsudski's efforts during the early 1930s.
Wałęsa chose the name Bezpartyjny Blok Wspierania Reform (Non
Party Bloc in Support of Reforms – BBWR) as the name of his party.
By doing this, Wałęsa made a direct reference to the BBWR of the
inter war period. This was nothing more than a party of the ruling coterie. Wałęsa's presidential party had no programme beyond
supporting its leader. The Solidarity movement and then the post-
Solidarity parties splintered further. Throughout this, the SLD and
the PSL remained steadfast and focused. In a startling reversal of the
results of the 1991 elections, the two parties secured one third of the
votes cast. The results indicated that voters were critical of the actions of the post-Solidarity politicians. The economic consequences
of the period of transformation, had an impact on their choice
of representatives. Interestingly, it was observed that the Polish

voters, at that stage, preferred post-communist parties, to the newly emerging post-Solidarity ones.

The above trend was confirmed with a further seismic change in the Polish political scene. In 1995, Aleksander Kwaśniewski was elected to presidency. The surprising feature of his victory was that the Poles rejected a number of candidates with impeccable anti-communist credentials, in favour of a man who had been directly linked with the communist regime and made no apologies for his past. His victory was partly due to the failure of the right wing parties to agree on a candidate. It was also due to Kwaśniewski's ability to transform the post-communist left into a social democratic party. He made a clear reference to the West European socialist tradition. In this way, he was able to present himself as a man of the future. He supported Poland joining the EU. This had an appeal to those who wanted to see Poland as a Western, developed state, with all the economic advantages this model appeared to offer. Kwaśniewski confirmed his success as a head of the modern European Polish state when he went on to win the next presidential elections. His presence at the helm, no doubt helped Poland through a turbulent period. Throughout this period, political parties again appeared to splinter. This forecasted a difficult time in national politics.

The fall of communism led to the reversal of a previously aggressively pursued policy. This policy attempted to remove the Catholic Church from public life. Indeed, many sections of society, saw this as a time to reassert the importance of Polish national identity. Mazowiecki's government quickly bowed to pressure and restored the teaching of religion in schools. Everyone understood the teaching of religion to be the teaching of the basics of the Catholic faith. The church and its supporters were equally quick to demand that all confiscated property should be restored. A wild process of grabbing of buildings was only halted when it was revealed that the priests generally saw this as permission for the Catholics to claim all ecclesiastical property. This included Protestant and Uniate property. The key debates within the Sejm were on the issue of abortion. The church fought for a ban on abortions in all circumstances. Its opponents tried to limit it to cases where the woman's life was in danger and to pregnancies that were the result of rape or incest.

The latter groups progressively lost out to the Catholic supporters. The Catholic supporters managed to steer through the Sejm legislation. They restricted abortion to an extent that makes it virtually unobtainable in Poland. Parish priests were buoyed by a sense of mission and a determination to mould Poland into a confessional state. They have used the pulpit to condemn doctors who were willing to perform abortions, dispense contraceptive advice and even offer antenatal tests to women.

In politics, the Episcopate tried to ensure that only parties which subscribed fully and absolutely to the Catholic programme and teaching were allowed to use the name of Christian. Thus, most Christian parties have strong links with the nationalist and right wing movements. No progressive Christian movement has emerged in Poland. Involvement in state politics has had its dangers. The church has generally tried to unite diverse right wing parties. The failure of right wing candidates, therefore reflected badly on the church. In turn, these setbacks led to internal disagreements as to whether the church should assume a centre stage role in politics or just offer spiritual advice. The second course of action has always seemed a safer and more prudent option. Though on more than one occasion, parish priests and the leadership have succumbed to the temptation of the first, only to find that the benefits have been unclear. Since the fall of communism, Poland has been a society which not merely tolerates, but expects the church to be present in all aspects of secular life. Thus, the fall of communism led to conspicuous displays of the church's presence in all manner of events. These included the opening of new buildings, railway stations, bridges, schools and army parades. This, in turn, led to a decrease in the tolerance of the rights of other faiths, notably the Orthodox Church in Eastern Poland.

The national elections took place in September 1997. An unusual electoral grouping emerged. This was headed by the Solidarity trade union and included nearly thirty smaller parties and organisations. They took the name of the Akcja Wyborcza Solidarność (Solidarity Electoral Platform – AWS). This party made an appeal to the electorate on the basis of a nationalist programme. Family values and support for Christian principles, formed the basis of its social programme. This implied advocacy of generous state funding. The SLD had ruled in coalition with the PSL. They came second. The peasant movement was in disarray. The AWS coalition government was hampered by several major personality disagreements. The most obvious one when the head of the Solidarity trade union refused to take a seat in the Sejm. He had brought together the AWS. Marian Krzaklewski, the architect of the AWS electoral strategy, was hoping to stand against Kwaśniewski in the 2000 presidential elections. A conflict of interest immediately emerged between the trade union's workplace role and that of the AWS. This put the Solidarity trade union at the head of a ruling coalition. It effectively discredited Krzaklewski. In forming a government, the AWS allied itself with what had been the UD. It was now renamed as Unia Wolności (Union of Freedom – UW). This resulted in the formation of a most unlikely government. It was led by Jerzy Buzek. Though well intentioned, he was unknown. Buzek was a nominee of Krzaklewski's. The new government also included Balcerowicz as the Minister of Finance and Geremek as the Minister of Foreign Affairs. In all cases, the AWS tried to form parallel organisations to limit the power of the UW ministers.

After the formation of the AWS-UW government, many of the issues which had been aired earlier, returned to the Sejm with a vengeance. The government took an ultra-critical view of the recent past and proceeded to implement legislation. This legislation required those holding public office, to declare whether they had collaborated with the security service. To that end, it was agreed to establish the Institute of National Memory. Here, all relevant files were deposited for use, as required, to verify collaboration. Control of the institute became a political issue. Thus, the matter of the communist past was unresolved. Not only this, but it continued to fester and cause further divisions. The aim of the verification legislation, had been to draw a line between the communist past and the evolving new democratic system. The result was the opposite. Accusations and counter-accusations were made against prominent politicians and state employees. These continued to undermine public confidence. The President expressed his disagreement with this apparent witch-hunt. He vetoed attempts to make it a criminal offence to withhold information about collaboration with the communist secret service.

On 2 April 1997, the Sejm approved the new constitution. A referendum showed that 52.7 per cent were in favour. The public had therefore given its verdict on the new consitution. The constitution was the object of prolonged inter-party conflicts. Two very different concepts of a new Polish state existed. The conflicts were a result of a clash between these two concepts. The model of Poland as a theocratic state was opposed by the liberal and socialist parties. They clearly preferred a secular state. The result of numerous compromises has been a constitution. This is peppered throughout, with reaffirmations of the importance of the Christian faith in Polish life. Though in its main outline, this is a document confirming the liberal and democratic character of the Polish republic.

The coalition government survived until 2000. The AWS and the UD were fundamentally incompatible. The AWS structure was unstable. Taking these two factors into account, the survival of the coalition government was a major achievement. Nevertheless, it was no surprise, that the SLD won the next general elections in 2001. The oscillations in the political scene, still reflected the search for a stable economic and political model. This enabled Poles to come to terms with the consequences of liberalisation of the economy and destruction of many of the social provisions. These had been part of the communist system. Despite the unwillingness of the Poles to admit it, the realities of the free market economy, came to many as a surprise. There were many who were aware of the gaps between the communist rhetoric and the realities. In the 1990s, they experienced, for the first time, the advantages and disadvantages of the capitalist system. Many had had some contacts with the West. Despite this, few were prepared for some of the harsher consequences of both democracy and economic freedom. During the initial period of transformation, the extent of unregulated economic activities was startling. On every street corner, traders set up tables and camp beds. From these, a huge variety of goods were sold and services provided. Some scenes reminded visiting foreigners of the first post-war months. Poles seemed to be trying to buy, sell, trade, exchange and provide services, which hitherto had been controlled by the state. In due course, the local authorities regulated much of this. Initially, many thought that retail trade was a guaranteed road to enrichment. However, the first bankruptcies and insolvencies caused many budding entrepreneurs to reflect. Advertisements and political campaigns undoubtedly created an optimistic image. These usually focused on consumption, indicating that flash cars, quality suits and other symbols of success could be easily achieved. The reality was distinctly different. For many workers, Balcerowicz's reforms marked the beginning of the slide into unemployment. Inflation ate into people's savings and reduced the value of their pensions. Only in retrospect did people note that the communist regime had been generous towards war combatants, invalids and pensioners. The post-communist governments no longer guaranteed the continuation of travel and health allowances. Index-linking of pensions and allowances was disputed between trade unions, the state and organised social groups. Pensioners, in particular, became a vocal and influential section of the Polish community. They unfailingly blamed all and sundry, and frequently Jews, for the loss of allowances enjoyed during the communist period. In 1990, 4.9 million Poles were drawing old-age or invalidity pensions. In 1999, this number rose to 9.4 million. On the other side of the demographic coin were the young. They used the communist period less and less as a benchmark against which to evaluate their economic, educational and professional opportunities. In these circumstances, the population reacted with pained surprise when faced with rising unemployment. Nothing had prepared Poles for the downside of the freedom they had fought for so valiantly. In 1993, 2.9 million economically active people were registered as unemployed. In 1999, the unemployment figure stood at 2.3 million. But of those, 32.5 per cent were people in the 14–24 age range.

Political life in the period after 1999 was affected by these changes to a larger extent than could have been anticipated. The initial processes of party formation and emergence of civil society were complex. However, by the beginning of the 1990s, it looked as if the parties were dividing themselves along the obvious axis, from the left to the right. The economic and democratic consequences of the transition period, then led to a next round of party divisions and political upheavals. Thus, in the opening years of the twenty-first century, the key parties once more splintered and re-formed. This generated new combinations. Of those, the emergence of a new centre party, the Platforma Obywatelska (Citizens' Platform – PO), and the centre right Prawo i Sprawidliwość (Law and Justice – PiS) were most noteworthy. The latter benefited from the right wing parties' failure to provide a coherent single political programme. Moreover, they benefited from the support of those who felt that they had been neglected by successive governments of the post-communist period. Old-age pensioners, those on disability pensions and those living in small towns and villages, voted for PiS in the 2005 general elections. The swing to the nationalist right wing parties was compounded by the formation of a coalition government. This included Samoobrona and the Catholic Liga Rodzin Polskich (The League of Polish Families – LRP). PiS' grip on power was reinforced by President Jarosław Kaczyński's choice of his twin brother, Lech Kaczyński, as Prime Minister. The route of the SLD, had been caused by a number of high-profile scandals. Of these, the Rywin affair was most damaging. It implicated the party leadership in accusations of collusion in the business affairs of an ex-KGB agent. Many liberals and left wing politicians felt that the PiS-dominated government was reversing Poland's intellectual and cultural union with Western Europe. The result was that the government was free to implement policies demanded by the nationalists. The Kaczyński brothers were keen to remould state institutions in line with their vision of Poland as a Catholic state. Thus, any earlier legislation which was perceived to have been in conflict with Catholic values was reversed. This was most notably applied to legislation relating to family planning, antenatal care and abortion. Legal rights were attributed to the foetus from the moment of conception. Since then, abortion has been deemed to be a crime against a living person. Andrzej Giertych, from the LRP, was appointed to head the ministry of education. This was seen as a step back in time. In particular because he insisted on the teaching of religion in schools and his stressed patriotic teaching. Sexual and cultural diversity were opposed by the government. Under European Union legislation, they were unable to outrightly repress homosexuls and those advocating tolerance. However, the Kaczyński brothers and leaders of the PiS-led government actively encouraged skinhead and nationalist youth groups to attack those taking part in Gay Pride marches. Brawls and standoffs between the Młodzież Wszechpolska and anarchist youth organisations frequently occurred. They added fuel to the already strained relations between the nationalist right government and their opponents. Once more, the street, rather than the Sejm, was the arena for political exchanges.

The PiS government had renewed its interest in using the communist past to criticise its opponents. As an unexpected consequence, the Catholic Church had been discredited. On coming to power, PiS, together with LRP, renewed calls for the extension of the verification process. This means that those in positions of trust and state employment are obliged to supply certificates, confirming that they did not collaborate with the security services during the communist period. The result of this has been a regular trickle of information from the Institute of National Memory archives. Since the death of John Paul II, the Polish Episcopate has battled to retain its authority. The main difficulties have not been attacks from the left, nor the emergence of anticlericalism within the community. On the contrary, the left has found it prudent to go along with the progressive interference of the church into secular matters, while the population remains as devout as before. The main difficulty for the Episcopate has been the divisions caused by internal conflicts, which previously the Pope resolved. It is increasingly apparent that the Primate has failed to impose his authority on the various factions within the Polish Catholic Church. The most obvious source of trouble has been the Catholic radio station, Radio Maryja. This is led by Father Rydzyk. The station and its controllers represent a backward-looking and extreme anti-intellectual strand of Polish Catholic observance. Many within the Episcopate disagree with the line taken by the radio station. However, they know better than to dissociate themselves openly from sentiments voiced by Rydzyk. These have found a ready echo in the minds of many Poles from the provinces. The government and some of the more censorious priests have, up to now, portrayed collaboration with the security services as a sign of moral weakness. This moral weakness is on the part of those who frequently succumbed to pressure, rather than working with the secret policy voluntarily. Through the winter of 2006/07, leaks confirmed that members of the clergy had spied on their colleagues during the communist period. The esteem in which the Catholic Church had been held in Poland was replaced by initial bewilderment and, in some cases, contempt. The full implication of these and similar revelations has still to emerge.

The fall of communism brought into the open a subject which the previous regime considered too thorny to tackle. This was the fact that national minorities and people of different faiths, live within Poland's borders. The communist regime had used its claim to the defence of Polish national interest as a means of securing support. This policy never worked entirely to their advantage. Attempts were made to present communism as a political system which would guarantee national self-expression. However, these were contradicted by the ruling party's ideological monopoly. In the attempt to use nationalism to enhance the communists' standing, the existence of national minorities within Poland's borders was conveniently avoided. Lip service was paid to the regimes' supposed guarantees of the Polish citizens' right to national and religious self-expression. However, in practice, the situation was very different. The Catholic Church, while persecuted, was strong enough to successfully stave off most attempts to confine its activities to the church. Other faiths were easier to sideline. In the immediate, post-communist period, obviously discriminatory legislation was abolished and a number of religious groups, hitherto banned, were allowed to extend their activities to Poland. Nevertheless, the minority faiths, which had existed in Poland before the war, fared worst, both during and after the fall of communism. The largest group of non-Catholics is made up of the Eastern Rite Christians (561,000), followed by Jehovah Witnesses (123,000), Lutherans (87,000) and Jews (1200). In present-day Poland, unless supported by powerful lobbies and funds from abroad, these denominations face official discrimination and the hostility of the Catholic Church. John Paul II had gone a long way towards reopening a dialogue with other faiths. He also sought reconciliation with the Orthodox Christians and the Jews. It is debatable whether parish priests and nationalist politicians, in their quest to reaffirm Poland's commitment to Catholicism, have any understanding of the Pope's message of tolerance.

Nearly 1 million people, who declare themselves as belonging to different ethnic groups, presently inhabit Poland. The largest of those are the Ukrainian and German communities (each approximately 300,000), Byelorussian (250,000), Roma (30,000) and

Lithuanian and Slovak people. In addition, Poland is experiencing a new phenomenon of foreigners settling in Poland, opening businesses and becoming naturalised. There is a slow influx of West European growers and farmers. These people see an opportunity, in Poland, to purchase farms and become involved in specialist cultivation. As well as this, there is an influx of large Vietnamese trading communities.

In relation to the Jewish community, Poland has experienced the most painful problem of social and political maturing. The Jedwabne revelations have highlighted this phenomenon. Anti-Semitism is fanned by extreme Nationalist sentiments and tolerated by most parties and spiritual leaders. It remains a seemingly respectable sentiment. This has nevertheless led to a number of crises. These have suggested to the Poles that, Western European and US public opinion is revolted by many of the casual anti-Semitic pronouncements. The site of the Nazi concentration camp in Auschwitz was the background for two crises. One involved a group of nuns. They established a convent in close proximity to places associated with Jewish martyrdom. The other crisis occurred when a monk erected a number of high crosses on a gravel pit, where the Nazis had killed Jews. In both cases, Jewish community leaders interceded by pointing out that the erection of Christian symbols, amounted to appropriation of the camp and prevented Jews from praying within their vicinity. To Polish nationalists, the issue was merely a reaffirmation of Poland's Catholic character. Only the Papacy's intervention led to the closing of the nunnery and the removal of the crosses. The next conflict with the Jews came after the publication of a book by an eminent historian, Jan Gross. This was about the killing of Jews in eastern areas earlier occupied by the Soviet Union, in the summer of 1941. Gross revealed that Poles, emboldened by the entry of German units, had massacred the Jewish community around the town of Jedwabne. His accusation against the perpetrators was compounded by his conclusion that the Communists did not want to tackle the crime after the war. The local Catholic priest waded into the debate. He supported those who denied that the crimes had been committed. The Jedwabne scandal divided the Catholic Church. The Pope, Archbishop Glemp and most of the bishops, joined in a mass of expiation. In this way, they hoped, to close the matter. This has been far from the case. Academics are seeking to make a name and secure publications. They are adding their voices and suggesting that the Jews had been the authors of their misfortunes by supporting Communism. There are fears that Poland will be taken over by foreigners and, in particular, by international financial interests. These would be supposedly headed by Jews. These have given impetus to contemporary anti-Semitism. Poland's entry into the EU has done little to dampen these suspicions. Were one to believe in the arguments put forward by Samoobrona, the LRP and Radio Maryja, Germans stand on Poland's border, poised to buy up land, while Jews are already in Poland, using every known legal loophole to reclaim Jewish property and any other property they can lay their hands on. The Polish Constitution and law provide for the prosecution of those making discriminatory and inflammatory remarks. However, it is impossible to think of a single case wherein anyone has been punished for making anti-Semitic comments in public. These attitudes have brought some Polish Members of the European Parliament, close to other fascist and racist groupings, also in the European Parliament.

A challenge was posed by the formation of the Solidarity free trade union, and/or the election of a Polish Pope. Many Poles believe that this was one cause of the collapse of the Soviet Union. It is also believed to be one of the causes of the collapse of communist regimes in Eastern Europe. In reality, what had happened in Poland was, but an element of a much larger picture. The collapse of communism in Poland was largely facilitated by the changing balance of power in Europe. The end of the Brezhnev Doctrine and the effects of the Gorbachev reforms, effectively signalled the end of Soviet intervention in Poland's internal affairs. New dialogues were established with the West and Germany was reunified. These factors changed the basis on which relations between East European states and the capitalist West, had evolved earlier. These realities spelled the end of the COMECON and the Warsaw Pact. Both were abolished in 1991. Poles had hoped that these symbolic acts would be followed by Poland's return to Western Europe. In effect, they hoped for admission to NATO and the EU.

The idea of joining NATO was generally supported by the Poles. They saw in it a guarantee of security against the Soviet Union and support in future talks with the government of a united Germany. However, the issue of joining the EU, raised controversies. Poland's still powerful eastern neighbour was an important factor in determining NATO's willingness to admit Poland. In 1991, the Soviet Union was officially dissolved. It was replaced by the Russian Federation, whose leader Boris Yeltsin, opposed Polish aspirations. President Kwaśniewski was predisposed to maintaining good relations with Russia. The changes in the Soviet Union reminded him and other Polish politicians, of Poland's weakness in European politics. As long as the Russian government objected to Poland's admission to NATO, neither West European, nor US politicians, would defy it. The first step was taken in 1994, when Poland joined the Partnership for Peace. This was an attempt to placate Russia, while opening talks for the admission of Poland, Hungary and the Czech and Slovak Republics to NATO. Negotiations continued. In the meantime, Polish military units were invited to participate in training with NATO units. Funds were made available to allow Poland to modernise and standardise military equipment. In 1995, further progress was made. The US Congress, now dominated by the Republican Party, voted in favour of extending NATO membership. An important factor in the US decision was the change taking place in Russia. An electoral success was achieved by communist and nationalist groupings. This caused concern. With that, it reduced the Congress' willingness to work with the Russian government.

During the pre-accession talks, the NATO powers demanded that the Polish government establish control over military matters. This, in turn, led to a conflict between Wałęsa and the SLD. The so called Small Constitution was otherwise known as the provisional constitution. It gave the President the right to appoint the minister responsible for military matters. The President insisted that it also give him direct control over a number of special units. These had been established during the Communist and immediate Communist period. This led to a clash with the SLD government. By the time Poland joined NATO, the final version of the Constitution had been accepted. This thus removed the President's right to make decisions on the subject. In December 1996, NATO formally announced its intention to enlarge. This was followed by the acceptance of Polish, Hungarian and Czech applications for membership. Full membership was finally granted in 1998.

Poland has turned out to be a loyal, though some would suggest too obedient, member of NATO. Peacekeeping duties in Yugoslavia have more recently been followed up by a military contribution to the occupation of Iraq and the policing of Afghanistan. The Poles supported President Bush's Middle Eastern policies. In doing so, the Poles have infuriated the French President and the German Chancellor. They opposed involvement in Iraq. These controversies have had little impact on internal politics. Most Poles view the involvement of their troops in international action, as a sign that their country is within the hallowed circle of Big Powers. This is where they believe Poland naturally belongs. Another, greater, controversy occurred in 2006. The centre-right government has been allowing US airplanes to land in Poland. These airplanes carried prisoners to Guantanamo Bay. There are rumours that this cooperation has even extended to the establishment of US detention and torture camps. These rumours are being substantiated by the new US President Barak Obama. He has admitted to the fact that the Bush administration did indeed use Polish bases for this purpose. Support for US policies has been opposed by small left wing and anarchist youth movements. The leader of the LRP has been a recent surprise critic of Poland's unquestioning compliance with President Bush's policies. Most of those who are aware of these issues, view support for the USA either with indifference, or as part of new global responsibilities. These are responsibilities which, they would like to believe are Poland's lot.

Poland's integration into the EU was fraught with numerous problems. While Poles wanted to be part of Western Europe, it was unclear exactly what this meant. In 1989, Poland was finally given the opportunity to redress its exclusion from Europe. Few agreed as to what would make Poland belong to Western Europe. In reality, this was frequently no more than a wish to put some distance between Poland and the Soviet Union, and the poverty, backwardness and lack of stable political institutions. These are problems which had characterised Eastern Europe at the beginning of the twentieth century. A search for positive models and images of the West yielded few clear answers. The nationalists were not able to offer any positive suggestions as to why Poland should join the EU. They also feared that Poland would not be treated as an equal partner. Successive governments failed to give Poles clear leads. This is because domestic issues, rather than foreign policy initiatives, dominated political debates. In March 1994, the SLD-PSL government, approved Poland's formal application to join the EU. This turned out to be the easiest part of the process, since all parties were united on this one principle. Extensive disagreements focused on the conditions on which Poland would join. The EU countries had their reasons for anxiety about Poland's admission and set out strict conditions which they expected Poland to comply with.

Talks on Poland's accession to the EU, stalled during the four years of the AWS-UW coalition government. The public perception of Western Europe was closely linked to the painful process of economic transformation and privatisation, which appeared to benefit foreign companies. In the rural areas, the fear of foreigners buying up Polish land outweighed the supposed advantages of EU agricultural subsidies. It became apparent that there was a need for educational programmes, if only to get away from negative stereotypes. The AWS was not capable of doing this, mainly due to its complex composition. This made it impossible to agree on so divisive an issue as conditions for Poland joining the EU. UW was a weak partner and its own pro-European programme was opposed by the AWS. The peasant movement remained deeply divided over the EU. They saw it as a rival to Poland's agricultural sector. The PSL never resolved its dilemmas. Its leaders, in principle, supported the common agricultural policy. This would, in due course, benefit Polish farmers. Small farmers, in most of Poland, were less convinced of the benefits to them of this policy. Doubts persisted and the militant opponents of the EU joined Lepper's Samoobrona direct action against the import of cheap foodstuffs.

In 2001, the AWS lost the general elections. The SLD was able to form a new government. The socialist politicians accelerated negotiations for Polish entry into the EU. Leszek Miller, the Prime Minister, calculated that, with the disintegration of the right wing and post-Solidarity parties, the Catholic Church was the only organisation which could influence the public. A visit to the Vatican was a particularly astute move. John Paul II supported the idea of Polish membership of the EU. The next move was to persuade the Episcopate that it had nothing to fear from Poland joining Western Europe. Polish bishops had earlier pronounced themselves against the EU. They had done this on the grounds that this would lead to increased secularisation and liberalisation of laws on abortion and euthanasia. In a reversal of the previous attitude, Primate Glemp visited Brussels. The result was an official statement read out from pulpits in March 2002. It declared the Episcopate's support for the European Union membership. It was widely suspected that the Social Democratic party-led government had given the bishops an undertaking to drop its avowed policy of liberalising the restrictive abortion law. In return, the Catholic leaders undertook to support Poland's accession to the EU. Henceforth, the SLD abandoned all references to the need to liberalise the abortion laws. In the meantime, the bishops resolutely supported Poland's application to join the EU. Fringe groupings continued to voice their opposition, most obviously those connected with Radio Maryja, Samoobrona and the LRP. Their arguments ranged from claims that Poland's commitment to Christianity would be destroyed, to warnings that foreigners would buy up Polish land. A variation on the first was a call for Poland to join the EU in order to reaffirm Europe's Christian character. The SLD and PSL nevertheless pushed on with negotiations. These were completed at a meeting in Copenhagen in December 2002.

In order for Poland's accession be confirmed, a referendum had to be conducted. This was held in July 2003 and resulted in an overwhelming vote in support of membership. This act, in itself, finally symbolised Poland's return to the community of Western European states.

# CONCLUSION

Poland's recent history has been a record of the struggle for independence and a search for a model of a state. The national revolution took place at the same time as the structures of a liberal republic were debated. The desire for independence and the need to define the boundaries of the national state were accompanied by a search for a just relationship between citizens and the state, which was to represent their interests. Thus, the interest of the nation became a potent theme. At times, it conflicted with the increasingly accepted principles of individual rights. Before the First World War, there were debates on whether Poles would succeed in re-establishing their state. These were influenced by the liberal and democratic model of representation accepted in Western Europe. To Poles, nevertheless, these political trends would create dilemmas of whether the national question should either dominate or be subordinated to the dilemma of democratic representation. In that, the Poles faced the question of whether a state based on democratic principles could serve the interests of the nation. At the root of this debate was the dilemma of whether this model would be strong enough to serve the interests of the nation. At the beginning of the twentieth century, some Polish thinkers questioned the relevance of West European models to the specific Polish circumstances. As a result, modern Polish history has been affected, in equal measure, by these two debates. In these, economic and social progress were advocated as a means of both overcoming backwardness and defending the interests of the nation as a whole.

When the Polish Kingdom vanished from the European map, serfdom was still the dominant form of land ownership in the villages. The landed gentry dominated the economic and political life of areas which had previously belonged to the Polish Kingdom. This, in turn, limited the development of commerce, manufacture and, subsequently, held back the industrial takeoff. Progressive thinkers unsuccessfully tackled these issues. Thus, the discourse on the restoration of the Polish Kingdom was closely linked to the need to reform the economic and political system. Several factors further undermined the gentry's dominant role in Polish life. These included successive national uprisings, emigration and, finally, the policies of the partition powers. This, in turn, had an impact on thinking concerning the restoration of Poland. The landed gentry no longer dominated the struggle for independence. With that, they could not defend the idea of Poland as the republic of the nobility.

On the eve of the First World War, it was widely accepted that if Poland were to emerge as an autonomous, or even an independent, state, its institutions and economy would have to be modelled on new concepts. The interesting question is, from where did Polish national and community leaders derive their ideas? Their discussions were, in the first place, dominated by the desire to gain independence. Was social, economic and political progress always subsumed into that one overriding desire – the restoration of a Polish state? How much were Poles affected by debates taking place in developed West European states, where the liberal model was the norm? Most of the ethnically Polish areas were under Russian control. Thus, how much did Polish leaders assimilate and respond to the controversies within the clandestine groups in the Tsarist Empire? Finally, did the Poles formulate their own, distinctive ideas?

It is always difficult to quantify the extent to which political ideas affected debates on the Polish question. However, it is noteworthy that Poles never felt isolated or sidelined from intellectual and political developments taking place in European capitals and intellectual centres. Polish thinkers were part of the great debates raging, both in Western Europe and in Tsarist Russia. Even before an independent Polish state became a practical possibility, discussions on the political institutions of future Poland were far advanced. In Polish territories, a full spectrum of parties and organisations with distinct ideologies, had emerged. The quest for independence dominated their programmes. However, they usually went well beyond that obvious objective. As documented in the earlier chapters of this book, these parties and organisations knew independent Poland would have to tackle poverty. This would be either through the development of agriculture or industrialisation. The debate on the future relationship between the new state and its citizens was closely linked to plans for economic advancement. This, in turn raised the question of who was to have the right to vote: the propertied classes or those who, through their work, created wealth. At the same time, the ethnic composition of the future state was a matter of concern. Any desire to reconstruct Poland in its pre-partition borders could not be reconciled with plans for an ethnically homogenous Polish state.

Independent Poland emerged, in equal measure, from several factors. These were: Germany's defeat during the First World War; Austria's disintegration; the collapse of the Russian Empire and, finally, the Polish nationals' desire for statehood. The result was that the first administration had one clear objective. This was namely the defence of the Polish nation and its right to independence. The borders of the state were defined as a result of conflicts during the formative early period. Ostensibly, it was the Paris Peace Conference that adjudicated on Poland's western border and its access to the sea. In reality, ethnic conflicts between the Poles and Germans had as much an impact in defining borders in Silesia and the so-called Corridor. The most obvious territorial and ethnic clashes, nevertheless occurred in the east and southeast. The character and objectives of the new Polish administration were defined by the military campaigns on those borderlands.

Hence, during the interwar period, the newly emerged Polish state was insecure in its borders. All its neighbours, in varying degrees and with varying determination, sought to review the postwar frontier settlements. In Poland, national minorities were viewed as potentially hostile and likely to make common cause with their co-nationals across the border. The Jewish communities became objects of prejudice. The establishment of a seemingly modern, liberal, democratic, system did not reduce this. Nationalism was a driving force in the new Polish state's internal politics. Poland's founding fathers had had aspirations that Poland would become a modern European state. Despite these, the country more closely resembled other states in East and Southeast Europe. There, the national revolution subordinated the newly espoused liberal state structure to one, overriding priority. This was the defence of the nation.

At the same time, Polish politicians, community leaders and professionals sought to outline for Poland a development plan. In this, economic reforms postulated continuing state involvement. The modern Polish state was one in which neither peasant nor socialist parties wholeheartedly embraced free market principles. Moreover, there was a strong sense of responsibility for the development of a modern industrial society. This went hand in hand with a desire to retain control over the nation's resources. Politically, as well as economically, Polish territories, more than ever in the past, looked towards the West. They rejected any cooperation with the revolutionary government in the Soviet Union. They were also distrustful of Lithuania and Czechoslovakia. Poland was alienated from these countries by territorial conflicts. In 1934, Poland had, in the first place, looked to France for military and economic support. Only when they had been disappointed in those hopes, had they considered establishing good relations with Nazi Germany. During the Piłsudski period and the period described as the rule of the colonels, several priorities determined internal and foreign policy choices. These were both military and national priorities. Poland's policies in the run-up to the outbreak of the war were characterised by insecurity, but also by adventurism. When Nazi Germany took action to destroy Czechoslovakia, Poland's military rulers sought to increase their popularity. They did this by redressing territorial grievances. In addition, they grabbed Czech territories, to which Poland had no previous claim.

The German attack on Poland in September 1939 and Soviet complicity in the destruction of the Polish state did not end the complex debate. This both preceded and accompanied the period of independence. In spite of assertions to the contrary, underground resistance movements addressed the question of the character of the post-war government. They did this as much as they tried to resist and alleviate occupation. In the course of the war, a need for unity prevented open conflicts between the various groupings. Nevertheless, they all prepared plans to capture power during the critical period when occupation would come to an end. Such plans remained high on the agenda discussed during the latter half of the war. It was generally assumed that the end of hostilities would be followed by a civil war. It was also assumed that the first post-war administration would emerge as a result of military confrontation between revolutionary workers, forces loyal to the government in

London, nationalist forces and the Western powers. Political programmes had been prepared during the course of the war. These
were a means of instigating the debate. But they were also a means
of preparing the ground for the post-war battle for power. Left wing,
centre and nationalist movements addressed various issues. These
included questions of political and economic reforms, future borders and relations with national minorities. There was a need for
economic progress and social justice. These went hand in hand
with the importance of security, good relations with neighbours
and commitment to the post-war European balance of power.

Soviet domination of Polish territories after the Second World
War first constrained and, after 1947, cut short all debates on
Poland's form. Poland's post-war borders were determined by the
simple happening of Poland falling within the Soviet sphere of influence. The Poles had had no say on how these were defined. The
eastern border was decided by the Soviet Union. This refused to
restore territories captured in September 1939, to the Polish. The
border with Germany was determined as a result of the talks between the Soviet Union and Great Britain. In the 1947 elections,
a communist-dominated government was established. After this,
all discussion on internal reforms ended and Poland was finally
included in the Soviet bloc. The Stalinist model was imposed on
Poland. It penetrated into all aspects of life. This model, nevertheless assumed the modernizing role of the state. It did this through
the process of economic transformation. This led to social changes.

To most Poles the Communist period was synonymous with sub-
jugation. Only occasionally were they able to return briefly to open
debates on social justice and political representation. The year 1956
marked a time of mass mobilisation. During this time, ideas on
workers' control over management decisions, went hand in hand
with attacks on the Stalinist state. When Gomułka re-established
the party's authority, the debate was first adjourned and then ended.
Thus, the last attempt to formulate new models of governance, came
to an end. Henceforth, dissident movements would publicise their
criticism of the failings of the communist system. But they had no
way of bringing the debate into the open and, in particular, to have
an input into state policies. In 1980, the Poles once more challenged
the political power of the state. This was not with a desire to replace

it, but only to secure representation within the existing political system. The establishment of the free trade union movement, unexpectedly resulted in the collapse of the authority of the party. With that, the state also collapsed. The state had appropriated for itself the right to determine the course of change. By then, the path to reform led in one direction only. This was namely the establishment of a democratic elected assembly and the introduction of a free market economy.

Poland's accepted criteria for admission to the European Union consolidated the economic and political system. This had evolved in Poland since the fall of communism. The establishment of a free market economy and acceptance of the democratic model of representation were the two most important conditions for Poland being included in the community of the developed European states. Admission to the EU has acted as a guarantee of Poland's continuing political and economic transformation. It has also defined the model, thereby ending the nationalist dream of self-determination.

# NOTES

## INTRODUCTION

1 Przemysław Hauser, 'Polska Odrodzona w Europie' in Wojciech Wrzesiński, (ed.) *Polska a Europa (X-XX wiek)* (Wydawnictwo Uniwersytetu Wrocławskiego, Wrocław, 2004), pp.75–85.

2 Adam Zamoyski, *The Polish Way. A Thousand-Year History of the Poles and Their Culture* (John Murray, London, 1987), pp.286–8.

3 Timothy Snyder, *The Reconstruction of Nations. Poland, Ukraine, Lithuania, Belarus, 1569–1999* (Yale University Press, New Haven, CT, 2003), pp.202–4.

4 Roman Szporluk, 'Polska: Powstanie teorii i praktyki nowoczesnego narodu (1770–1870)' in Andrzej Ajnenkiel et al. (eds.), *Sens Polskiej Historii* (Uniwersytet Warszawski, Warszawa, 1990), pp.94–100.

5 Michael G. Müller, 'Czy rozbiory uniemożliwiły wejście Polski na drogę nowoczesności?' in Andrzej Ajnenkiel et al. *Sens Polskiej Historii*, pp.146–150.

6 Jerzy Lukowski, *Liberty's Folly, The Polish–Lithunanian Commonwealth in the Eighteenth Century, 1697–1795* (Routledge, London, 1991), pp.150–51.

7 Ibid., pp.176–7.

8 Jerzy Lukowski, *The Partition of Poland 1772, 1773, 1795* (Longman, London, 1999), pp.19–20.

9 Krystyna Zienkowska, *Stanisław August Poniatowski* (Zakład Narodowy im. Ossolińskich, Wrocław, 1998), pp.126–29.

10 Adam Zamoyski, *The Last King of Poland* (Weidenfeld & Nicolson, London, 1997), pp.128–131.

11 Jerzy Lukowski, *Liberty's Folly. The Polish–Lithuanian Commonwealth in the Eighteenth Century*, pp.247–51.

12 Andrzej Chwalba, *Historia Polski, 1795–1918* (Wydawnictwo Literackie, Kraków, 2005), pp.151–53.

13 Jerzy Lukowski, *The Partitions of Poland*, pp.166–75.

14 Szymon Askenazy, *Napoleon a Polska* (Wydawnictwo Bellona, Warszawa, 1994), pp.234–5.

15 Marian Biskupski et al. (eds.), *The History of Polish Diplomacy X-XXc* (Sejm Publishing House, Warszawa, 2005), pp.323–33.

16 R.F. Leslie et al., *The History of Poland Since 1863* (Cambridge University Press, Cambridge, 1980), pp.41–6.

17 Lech Trzeciakowski, *The Kulturkampf in Prussian Poland* (East European Monographs, New York, 1990), 141–162.

## CHAPTER 1

1 H.H. Hahn, 'Prymus modernizacyjny i uścisk integracyjny – rola państwa w kształtowaniu mentalności politycznej Polaków w drugiej połowie XIX wieku', in Jerzy Topolski et al. (eds) *Ideologie, Poglądy, Mity w dziejach Polski XIX I XX wieku* (UAM, Poznań, 1991), pp.290–91.

2    Piotr S. Wandycz, *The Price of Freedom. A History of East Central Europe from the Middle Ages to the Present* (Routledge, London, 1992), p.176.
3    Trzeciakowski: *The Kullturkampf in Prussian Poland*, pp.116–17.
4    Ibid.
5    Ibid., p.139.
6    Ibid., pp.160–61.
7    R.F. Leslie et al., *The History of Poland Since 1863* (Cambridge University Press, Cambridge, 1980), p.28.
8    Ibid., pp.19–20.
9    Piotr S. Wandycz, *The Lands of Partitioned Poland, 1795–1918* (University of Washington Press, Seattle, WA, 1974), pp.220–21.
10   Ibid., p.222.
11   Ibid., pp.201–6.
12   Ivan T. Berend, *History Derailed. Central and East Europe in the Long 19th century* (California Press, Berkeley, 2003), pp.151–2.
13   Stefan Wasilewski, *Pięćdziesiąt Lat Zwątpienia, Nadziei i Walki* (Książka Polska, Warszawa, 2002), pp.99–103.
14   Ibid., p.102.
15   Ibid., pp.103–4.
16   Ibid., pp.107–8.
17   Ibid., pp.114–15.
18   Alvin Marcus Fountain II, *Roman Dmowski: Party, Tactics, Ideology 1895–1907* (East European Monographs, Boulder, CO, 1980), pp.41–2.
19   Roman Dmowski, *Myśl Nowoczesnego Polaka*, 7th edition (Koło Młodych Stronnictwa Narodowego, London, 1953), p.56.
20   Ibid., p.91.
21   Roman Wapiński, *Narodowa Demokracja 1893–1939* (Zakład Wydawniczy im. Ossolińskich, Wrocław, 1980), pp.75–80.
22   Ibid., pp.83–4.
23   Lidia i Adam Ciołkoszowie, *Zarys Dziejów Socjalizmu Polskiego*, Vol. I (Gryf Publications Ltd., London, 1966), pp.9–11.
24   Ibid., Vol. II, London, 1972, pp.215–23.
25   Norman M. Naimark, 'The history of the "Proletariat". The Emergence of Marxism in the Kingdom of Poland, 1870–1887', *East European Quarterly (Boulder)*, 1979, pp.63–6.
26   Ibid., pp.81–4.
27   Ibid., pp.84–6.
28   Lucjan Blit, *The Origins of Polish Socialism. The History and Ideas of the First Polish Socialist Party 1878–1886* (Cambridge University Press, Cambridge, 1971), pp.57–8.
29   Ibid., pp.58–67.
30   Jan Kancewicz, *Polska Partia Socjalistyczna w latach 1892–1896* (Państwowe Wydawnictwo Naukowe, Warszawa, 1984), pp.45–7.
31   Andrzej Garlicki, *Józef Piłsudski, 1867–1935* (Scolar Press, London, 1995), p.23.
32   Robert Blobaum, *Feliks Dzierżyński and the SDKPiL; A Study of the Origins of Polish Communism* (East European Monographs, Boulder, CO, 1984), pp.68–71.
33   Kancewicz: *Polska Partia Socjalistyczna*, pp.401–6.
34   Olga A. Narkiewicz, *The Green Flag. Polish Populist Politics 1867–1970* (Croom Helm, London, 1976), pp.23–5.
35   Ibid., pp.44–9.
36   Ibid., p.69.
37   Ibid., pp.114–15.

38 Andrzej Zakrzewski, *Wincenty Witos chłopski polityk i mąż stanu* (Ludowa Spółdzielnia Wydawnicza, Warszawa, 1977), pp.26–7.
39 Narkiewicz: *The Green Flag*, pp.131–43.
40 Janusz Gmitruk, *Ruch Ludowy w Polsce. Zarys dziejów* (Muzeum Historii Polskiego Ruchu Ludowego, Warszawa, 2003), pp.9–10.
41 Garlicki: *Józef Piłsudski, 1867–1935*, pp.40–42.
42 Robert E. Blobaum, *Rewolucja. Russian Poland, 1904–1907* (Cornell University Press, Ithaca, NY, 1995), pp.48–51.
43 Blobaum: *Feliks Dzierżyński and the SDKPiL*, pp.122–6.
44 Blobaum: *Rewolucja. Russian Poland, 1904–1907*, pp.99–100.
45 Andrzej Micewski, *Roman Dmowski* (Wydawnicto 'Verum', Warszawa, 1971), pp.113–15.
46 Krzysztof Kowalec, *Roman Dmowski* (Editions Spotkania, Warszawa, 1996), pp.116–21.
47 Blobaum: *Rewolucja. Russian Poland, 1904–1907*, pp.201–6.
48 Blobaum: *Feliks Dzierżyński and the SDKPiL*, p.176.
49 Garlicki: *Józef Piłsudski, 1867–1935*, pp.60–63.

## CHAPTER 2

1 Paul Latawski (ed.), *The Reconstruction of Poland, 1914–23* (Macmillan in association with the School of Slavonic and East European Studies, University of London, London, 1992), pp.195–6.
2 Micewski: *Roman Dmowski*, pp.220–3.
3 Paul Latawski, 'Roman Dmowski, the Polish Question and the Western Opinion, 1915–18: The case of Britain', in Paul Lawawski (ed.), *The Reconstruction of Poland, 1914–1923* (Macmillan, Houndmills, 1992), p.3.
4 Garlicki: *Józef Piłsudski, 1867–1935*, pp.69–71.
5 Latawski (ed.): *The Reconstruction of Poland, 1914–23*, p.196.
6 Titus Komarnicki, *Rebirth of the Polish Republic. A Study in the Diplomatic History of Europe, 1914–1920* (William Heinemann Ltd., London, 1957), pp.93–7.
7 Garlicki: *Józef Piłsudski, 1867–1935*, pp.84–5.
8 Ibid., pp.46–7.
9 Mieczysław B.Biskupski, *The History of Poland* (Greenwood Press, Westport, CT, 2000), pp.42–4.
10 Louise L. Gerson, *Woodraw Wilson and the Rebirth of Poland 1914–1920* (Archon Books, CT, 1972), pp.48–50.
11 Marian M. Drozdowski, *Ignacy Jan Paderewski. A Political Biography* (Interpress, Kraków, 1981), p.91.
12 Wiktor Sukiennicki, *East Central Europe during World War I: From Foreign Domination to National Independence*, Vol. I (East European Monographs, Boulder, CO, 1984), pp.327–8.
13 Blobaum: *Feliks Dzierżyski and the SDKPiL*, pp.22–2.
14 Sukiennicki: *East Central Europe during World War I*, pp.395–6.
15 Garlicki: *Józef Piłsudski, 1867–1935*, pp.86–7.
16 Jan Zamoyski, *Powrót na mapę. Polski Komitet Narodowy w Paryżu 1914–1919* (Państwowe Wydawnictwo Naukowe, Warszawa, 1991), pp.52–3.
17 Latawski: 'Roman Dmowski, the Polish Question and the Western Opinion, 1915–18', pp.8–11.
18 Zamoyski, *Powrót na mapę*, pp.60–1.
19 Sukiennicki: *East Central Europe during World War I*, Vol. II, p.732.
20 Ibid., pp.208–9.

21 Teodor Ładyka, *Polska Partia Socjalistyczna (frakcja Revolucyjna) w latach 1906–1914* (Książka i Wiedza, Warszawa, 1972), pp.169–74.
22 Jerzy Holzer, *PPS. Szkic Dziejów* (Wiedza Powszechna, Warszawa, 1977), pp.64–7.
23 Ibid., p.91.
24 Zakrzewski: *Wincenty Witos, chłopski polityki i mąż stanu*, pp.68–71.
25 Ibid., pp.75–8.
26 Holzer: *PPS. Szkic Dziejów*, pp.96–8.
27 Garlicki: *Józef Piłsudski, 1867–1935*, pp.88–9.
28 Ibid., pp.89–90.

## CHAPTER 3

1 Zamoyski: *Powrót na mapę. Polski Komitet Narodowy w Paryżu 1914–1919*, pp.70–2.
2 Margaret Macmillan, *Peacemakers. The Paris Conference of 1919 and Its Attempt to End War* (John Murray, London, 2001), pp.221–2.
3 Kay Lundgreen-Nielson, 'Aspects of American policy towards Poland at the Paris Peace Conference and the role of Isaiah Bowman', in Paul Latawski (ed.), *The Reconstruction of Poland, 1914–23*, p.97.
4 J. Pajewski (ed.), *Problem Polsko-Niemiecki w Traktacie Wesalskim* (Instytut Zachodni, Poznań, 1963), pp.247–9.
5 Anna M. Cienciala, 'The Battle for Danzig and the Polish Corridor at the Paris Peace Conference of 1919', in Paul Latawski (ed.), *The Reconstruction of Poland, 1914–23*, pp.81–4.
6 Ann M. Cienciala and Titus Komarnicki, *From Versailles to Locarno, Keys to Polish Foreign Policy, 1919–25* (University Press of Kansas, KS, 1984), pp.46–50.
7 Ibid., pp.88–90.
8 Lundgreen-Neilen: *The Polish Problems at the Paris Peace Conference*, pp.291–4.
9 Cienciała and Komarnicki: *From Versailles to Locarno*, pp.151–70.
10 Garlicki: *Józef Piłsudski 1867–1935*, pp.95–7.
11 Titus Komarnicki, *Rebirth of the Polish Republic. A Study of the Diplomatic History of Europe, 1914–1920* (William Heinemann Ltd., London, 1957), pp.605–11.
12 Biskupski: *A History of Poland*, pp.70–2.
13 Norman Davies, *White Eagle, Red Star. The Polish-Soviet War, 1919–1920* (Macdonald, London, 1972), pp.188–225.
14 Garlicki: *Józef Piłsudski*, pp.103–4.
15 Peter D. Stachura, 'National identity and the ethnic minorities in early interwar Poland', in Peter E. Stachura (ed.), *Poland between the Wars, 1918–1939* (Macmillan Press, Ltd., Basingstoke, 1998), p.62.
16 Joseph Marcus, *Social and Political History of the Jews in Poland, 1919–1939* (Mouton Publishers, Berlin, 1983), pp.261–2.
17 Ibid., p.394.
18 Ibid., pp.296–9.
19 Narkiewicz: *The Green Flag. Polish Populist Politics 1867–1970*, p.170.
20 Holzer: *PPS, Szkic Dziejów*, pp.96–7.
21 Ibid., pp.108–10.
22 Ibid., p.143.

23  Krystyana Trembicka, *Miedzy Utopią a Rzeczywistością. Myśl polityczna Komunistycznej Partii Polski (1918–1938)* (Wydawnictwo IMCS, Lublin, 2007), pp.101–2.
24  M.K. Dziewanowski, *The Communist Party of Poland. An Outline of History* (Harvard University Press, Cambridge, MA, 1959), pp.90–5.
25  Trembicka: *Miedzy Utopią a Rzeczywistością*, pp.126–7.
26  Ibid., pp.144–5.
27  Ibid., pp.270–2.
28  Narkiewicz: *The Green Flag*, pp.160–4.
29  Ibid., pp.169–81.
30  Ibid., p.154.
31  Stanisław Lato, *Ruch Ludow wobec sanacji* (Krajowa Agencja Wydawnicza, Rzeszów, 1985), pp.34–6.
32  Wapiński: *Roman Dmowski*, pp.290–1.
33  Lato: *Ruch Ludow wobec sanacji*, pp.7–8.
34  Antony Polonsky, *Politics in Independent Poland 1921–1939. The Crisis of Constitutional Government* (Clarendon Press, Oxford, 1972), pp.22–7.
35  Garlicki, *Józef Piłsudski*, pp.133–4.
36  Eva Plach, *The Clash of Moral Nations, Cultural Politics in Piłsudski's Poland, 1926–1935* (Ohio University Press, Athens, OH, 2006), pp.24–31.
37  Ibid., pp.85–91.
38  Bogdan Głowacki, *Polityka Polskiej Partii Socjalistycznej 1929–1935* (Książka i Wiedza, Warszawa, 1979), pp.49–50.
39  Garlicki: *Józef Piłsudski*, p.147.
40  Lato: *Ruch Ludow wobec sanacji*, pp.132–9.
41  Zakrzewski: *Wincenty Witos*, pp.270–5.
42  Garlicki: *Józef Piłsudski*, pp.178–9.
43  Tadeusz Kowalik, *Historia Ekonomii w Polsce 1864–1950* (Ossolineum, Wrocław, 1992), pp.273–6.
44  Narkiewicz: *The Green Flag*, pp.228–9.
45  Holzer: *PPS, Szkic Dziejów*, pp.135–8.
46  Ibid., pp.156–9.

## CHAPTER 4

1  Piotr S. Wandycz, *France and Her Eastern Allies, 1919–1925: French-Czechoslovak-Polish Relations from the Paris Peace Conference to Locarno* (University of Minnesota Press, Minneapolis, 1962), pp.46–8.
2  Ibid., pp.216–18.
3  J. Kozeński, *Czechosłowacja w Polskiej polityce zagranicznej w latach 1932–1938* (Instytut Zachodni, Poznań, 1964), pp.127–8.
4  Anita Prażmowska: *Eastern Europe and the Origins of the Second World War*, pp.144–7.
5  Anita Prażmowska, 'The role of Danzig in Polish-German relations on the eve of the Second World War', in John Hiden and Thomas Lane (eds.), *The Baltic and the Outbreak of the Second World War* (Cambridge University Press, Cambridge, 1992), pp.88–9.
6  Anita Prażmowska, *Britain, Poland and the Eastern Front, 1939* (Cambridge University Press, Cambridge, 1986), pp.40–1.
7  Ibid., pp.53–6.
8  Małgorzata Gmurczyk-Wrońska, *Polska – niepotrzebny aliant Francji?* (NERITON, Warszawa, 2003), pp.100–2.
9  Prażmowska: *Britain, Poland and the Eastern Front, 1939*, pp.166–7.

10 A. Reid and D. Fisher, *The Deadly Embrace: Hitler, Stalin and the Nazi-Soviet Pact, 1939–1941* (W.W. Norton, New York, 1988), pp.250–6.
11 Prażmowska: *Britain, Poland and the Eastern Front, 1939*, pp.186–7.
12 Anita Prażmowska, *Britain and Poland, 1939–1943. The Betrayed Ally* (Cambridge University Press, Cambridge, 1995), pp.4–9.
13 Ibid., pp.10–12.
14 John Coutouvidis and Jaime Reynolds, *Poland 1939–1947* (Leicester University Press, Leicester, 1986), pp.25–9.
15 Tomasz Strzembosz, *Rzeczpospolita Podziemna* (Wydawnictwo Krupski i S-ka, Warszawa, 2000), pp.84–5.
16 Anita Prażmowska, 'Polish military plans for the defeat of Germany and the Soviet Union, 1939–41', *European History Quarterly* 31/4 (October 2001), pp.602–4.
17 Prażmowska: *Britain and Poland, 1939–1943*, pp.94–7.
18 Ibid., pp.179–80.
19 Jan Gross, *Revolution from Abroad. The Soviet Conquest of Poland's Western Ukraine and Western Belorussia* (Princeton University Press, Princeton, NJ, 1988), pp.28–35.
20 Ibid., pp.187–92.
21 Stanisław Jaczyński, *Zygmunt Berling. Między Sławą a Potępieniem* (Książka i Wiedza, Warszawa, 1993), pp.144–5.
22 Jan T. Gross, *Polish Society under German Occupation. The Generalgouvnement, 1939–1944* (Princeton University Press, Princeton, NJ, 1979), pp.45–50.
23 Ibid., pp.160–83.
24 Stefan Korboński, *The Jews and the Poles during World War II* (Hippocrene Books, New York, 1989), pp.41–4.
25 Józef Gierowski, 'Ethical problems of the Holocaust in Poland', in A. Polonsky (ed.), *'My Brother's Keeper'. Recent Debates on the Holocaust* (Routledge, London, 1990), pp.184–232.
26 Anita Prażmowska, *Civil War in Poland, 1942–1948* (Palgrave/Macillan, Basingstoke, 2004), pp.33–40.
27 Jan Ciechanowski, *The Warsaw Uprising of 1944* (Cambridge University Press, Cambridge, 1974), p.67.
28 Stanisław Dąbrowski, *Koncepcje Przebudowy Polski w progamach i publicystyce ruch ludowego, 1939–1945* (Ludowa Spółdzielnia Wydawnicza, Warszawa, 1981), pp.82–94.
29 Prażmowska, *Civil War in Poland, 1942–1948*, pp.36–8.
30 Ibid., p.57.
31 Ibid., pp.40–42.
32 Ibid., pp.41–3.
33 Krystyna Kersten, *The Establishment of Communist Rule in Poland, 1943–1948* (University of California Press, Berkley, 1984), pp.11–14.
34 Antony Polonsky and Boleslaw Drukier, *The Beginnings of Communist Rule in Poland. December 1943–June 1945* (Routledge & Kegan Paul, London, 1980), p.11.
35 Jan T. Gross, *Fear. Anti-Semitism in Poland after Auschwitz. An Essay in Historical Interpretation* (Princeton University Press, New York, 2006), pp.10–12.
36 Prażmowska: *Civil War in Poland, 1942–1948*, pp.116–17.
37 Antony Polonsky (ed.), *The Great Powers and the Polish Question 1941–1945* (London School of Economics and Political Science, London, 1976), pp.220–26.
38 Kersten: *The Establishment of Communist Rule in Poland*, pp.118–60.

## CHAPTER 5

1  Andrzej Paczkowski, *The Spring Will Be Ours* (The Pennsylvania State University Press, PA, 2003), p.146.
2  Prażmowska: *Civil War in Poland, 1942–1948*, pp.160–66.
3  Bernadetta Nitschke, *Wysiedlenia ludności niemieckiej z Polski w latach 1945–50* (Wyższa Szkoła Pedagogiczna in Tadeusza Kotarbińskiego, Zielona Góra, 1999), pp.101–11.
4  Eugeniusz Mironowicz, *Polityka narodowościowa PRL* (Wydanie Białostockiego Towarzystwa Historycznego, Białystok, 2000), pp.51–3.
5  Paczkowski: *The Spring Will Be Ours*, pp.161–4.
6  Krystyna Kersten, *Narodziny Systemu Władzy 1943–1948* (SAWW, Warszawa, 1984), pp.279–85.
7  Anita Prażmowska, 'The Polish Socialist Party, 1945–1948', *East European Quarterly* XXXIV/3 (Fall 2000), pp.345–7.
8  Prażmowska: *Civil War in Poland, 1942–1948*, pp.118–42.
9  Kersten: *Narodziny Systemu Władzy, 1943–1948*, pp.357–9.
10  Tadeusz Kowalik, *Spory o Ustrój Społeczno-Gospodarczy w Polsce, lata 1944–1948* (Wydawnictwo Key Text, Warszawa, 2006), pp.21–4.
11  Ibid., pp.39–40.
12  Ibid., pp.24–9.
13  Kersten: *Narodziny Systemu Władzy, 1943–1948*, pp.176–7.
14  Kowalik: *Spory o Ustrój Społeczno-Gospodarczy w Polsce*, pp.39–46.
15  Padraic Kenney, *Rebuilding Poland. Workers and Communists 1945–1950* (Cornell University Press, Ithaca, NY, 1997), pp.29–30.
16  Kowalik: *Spory o Ustrój Społeczno-Gospodarczy w Polsce*, pp.93–101.
17  Krystyna Kersten, 'The terror, 1949–1945', in A. Kemp-Welch (ed.), *Stalinism in Poland, 1944–1956* (Macmillan Press Ltd., Houndmills, 1999), pp.78–84.
18  Ryszard Wilczewski, 'Rozwój przemysłu w Polsce w latach 1947–1955', in Janusz Kaliński i Zbigniew Landau (eds.), *Gospodarka Polski Ludowej 1944–1955* (Książka i Wiedza, Warszawa, 1978), pp.250–55.
19  Janusz Kaliński, *Polityka Gospodarcza Polski w latach 1948–1956* (Książka i Wiedza, Warszawa, 1987), pp.122–4.
20  Antoni Dudek and Ryszard Gryz, *Komuniści i Kościół w Polsce, 1945–1989* (Znak, Kraków, 2006), pp.44–7.
21  Ibid., pp.63–8.
22  Paweł Machcewicz, 'Social protest and political crisis in 1956', in A. Kemp-Welch (ed.), *Stalinism in Poland, 1944–1956*, pp.99–102.
23  Paczkowski: *The Spring Will Be Ours*, pp.267–8.
24  Paweł Machcewicz, 'Social protest and political crisis in 1956', in A. Kemp-Welch (ed.), *Stalinism in Poland, 1944–1956*, pp.102–3.
25  Paczkowski: *The Spring Will Be Ours*, pp.269–72.
26  Ibid., pp.72–3.
27  Ibid., pp.273–4.
28  Ibid., pp.274–8.
29  Dudek and Gryz: *Komuniści i Kościół w Polsce, 1945–1989*, pp.147–50.
30  Ibid., pp.217–32.
31  Andrzej Skrzypek, *Mechanizmy autonomii. Stosunki polsko-radzieckie 1956–1956* (ASPRA-JR, Warszawa, 2005), pp.148–52.
32  Paczkowski: *The Spring Will Be Ours*, pp.297–9.
33  Ibid., pp.299–303.
34  A. Kemp-Welch, *Poland under Communism, A Cold War History* (Cambridge University Press, Cambridge, 2008), pp.148–63.

## CHAPTER 6

1 Osęka: *Marzec '68* (Znak, Kraków, 2008), pp.55–73.
2 Kemp-Welch: *Poland under Communism*, pp.180–4.
3 Paczkowski: *The Spring Will Be Ours*, pp.347–53.
4 Janusz Rolicki, *Edward Gierek. Życie i Narodziny Legendy* (Iskry, Warszawa, 2002), pp.31–40.
5 Ibid., pp.72–5.
6 Kemp-Welch: *Poland under Communism*, pp.178–9.
7 George Sanford, *Polish Communism in Crisis* (Croom Helm, Ltd., Beckenham, 1983), pp.17–19.
8 Ibid., pp.28–30.
9 Ibid., pp.31–5.
10 Jan Zielonka, *Political Ideas in Contemporary Poland* (Avebury, Aldershot, 1989), pp.15–29.
11 Dudek and Ryszard Gryz, *Komuniści i Kościół*, pp.281–95.
12 Ibid., pp.295–310.
13 Ibid., pp.340–49.
14 Jacek Tittenbrun, *The Collapse of 'Real Socialism' in Poland* (Janus Publishing Company, London, 1993), p.65.
15 Kemp-Welch: *Poland under Communism*, pp.212–23.
16 Ibid., pp.243–63.
17 Janusz Rolicki, *Edward Gierek*, pp.312–4.
18 Ibid., pp.314–9.
19 Kemp-Welch, *Poland under Communism*, pp.272–6.
20 Sanford, *Polish Communism in Crisis*, pp.113–7.
21 Martin Myant, *Poland: A Crisis for Socialism* (Lawrence and Wishart, London, 1982), pp.176–9.
22 Jan B. De Weydenthal, Bruce D. Porter, and Kevin Devlin, *The Polish Drama: 1980–1982* (Lexington Books, Lexington, MA, 1983), pp.78–81.
23 Dudek and Gryz: *Komuniści i Kościół*, pp.361–9.
24 Ibid., pp. 370–2.
25 Warner G. Hahn, *Democracy in a Communist Party. Poland's Experience since 1980* (Columbia University Press, New York, 1987), pp.195–202.
26 Kemp-Welch: *Poland under Communism*, pp.330–1.
27 Ibid., pp.325–7.
28 Andrzej Garlicki, *Rycerze Okrągłego Stołu* (Czytelnik, Warszawa, 2004), pp.5–19.

## CHAPTER 7

1 Kemp-Welch: *Poland under Communism*, pp.362–71.
2 Ibid., pp.394–9.
3 Garlicki: *Rycerze Okrągłego Stołu*, pp.45–7.
4 Paczkowski: *The Spring Will Be Ours*, pp.500–4.
5 Kemp-Welch: *Poland under Communism*, pp.406–12.

# BIBLIOGRAPHY

Ascherson, Neil. (1981). *The Polish August: The Self-Limiting Revolution*, London: Allen Lane.

Ascherson, Neil. (1987). *The Struggle for Poland*, London: Joseph.

Askenazy, Szymon. (1994). *Napoleon a Polska*, Warszawa: Wydawnictwo Bellona.

Berend, Ivan T. (2003). *History Derailed. Central and East Europe in the Long 19th Century*, Berkley: California Press.

Biskupski, Marian et al. (eds.). (2005). *The History of Polish Diplomacy X–XXC*, Warszawa: Sejm Publishing House.

Biskupski, Mieczysław B. (2000). *The History of Poland*, Westport, CT: Greenwood Press.

Blit, Lucjan. (1971). *The Origins of Polish Socialism. The History and Ideas of the First Polish Socialist Party 1878–1886*, Cambridge: Cambridge University Press.

Blobaum, Robert. (1984). *Feliks Dzierżyński and the SDKPiL: A Study of the Origins of Polish Communism*, East European Monographs, Boulder, CO.

Blobaum, Robert. (1995). *Rewolucja. Russian Poland, 1904–1907*, Ithaca, NY: Cornell University Press.

Chwalba, Andrzej. (2005). *Historia Polski, 1795–1918*, Kraków: Wydawnictwo Literackie.

Ciechanowski, Jan. (1974). *The Warsaw Uprising of 1944*, Cambridge: Cambridge University Press.

Cienciala, Ann M. & Komarnicki, Titus. (1984). *From Versailles to Locarno, Keys to Polish Foreign Policy, 1919–25* (University Press of Kansas, KS, 1984), pp.46–50.

Ciołkoszowie, Lidia i Adam. (1966). *Zarys Dziejów Socjalizmu Polskiego*, Vol. I, London: Gryf Publications Ltd.

Coutouvidis, John and Reynolds, Jaime. (1986). *Poland 1939–1947*, Leicester: Leicester University Press.

Dąbrowski, Stanisław. (1981). *Koncepcje Przebudowy Polski w progamach i publicystyce ruchu ludowego, 1939–1945*, Warszawa: Ludowa Spółdzielnia Wydawnicza.

Dmowski, Roman. (1953). *Myśl Nowoczesnego Polaka*, 7th edition, London: Koło Młodych Stronnictwa Narodowego.

Drozdowski, Marian M. (1981). *Ignacy Jan Paderewski. A Political Biography*, Kraków: Interpress.

Dudek, Antoni and Gryz, Ryszard. (2006). *Komuniści i Kościół w Polsce, 1945–1989*, Kraków: Znak.

Dziewanowski, M.K. (1959). *The Communist Party of Poland. An Outline of History*, Cambridge, MA: Harvard University Press.

Fountain, Alvin Marcus II. (1980). *Roman Dmowski: Party, Tactics, Ideology 1895–1907*, East European Monographs, Boulder, CO.

Garlicki, Andrzej. (1995). *Józef Piłsudski, 1867–1935*, Aldershot: Scolar Press.

Garlicki, Andrzej. (2004). *Rycerze Okrągłego Stołu*, Warszawa: Czytelnik.

Gerson, Louise L. (1972). *Woodraw Wilson and the Rebirth of Poland 1914–1920*, CT: Archon Books.

Gierowski, Józef. (1990). 'Ethical problems of the Holocaust in Poland', in A. Polonsky (ed.), *'My Brother's Keeper'. Recent Debates on the Holocaust*, London: Routledge.

Gmitruk, Janusz. (2003). *Ruch Ludowy w Polsce. Zarys dziejów*, Warszawa: Muzeum Historii Polskiego Ruchu Ludowego.

Gmurczyk-Wrońska, Małgorzata. (2003). *Polska – niepotrzebny aliant Francji?* Warszawa: NERITON.

Gross, Jan. (1988). *Revolution from Abroad. The Soviet Conquest of Poland's Western Ukraine and Western Belorussia*, Princeton, NJ: Princeton University Press.

Gross, Jan. (1979). *Polish Society under German Occupation. The Generalgouvnement, 1939–1944*, Princeton, NJ: Princeton University Press.

Gross, Jan. (2006). *Fear. Anti-Semitism in Poland after Auschwitz. An essay in Historical Interpretation*, New York: Princeton University Press.

Hahn, H.H. (1991). 'Prymus modernizacyjny i uścisk integracyjny – rola państwa w kształtowaniu mentalności politycznej Polaków w drugiej połowie XIX wieku', in Jerzy Topolski et al. (eds.), *Ideologie, Poglądy, Mity w dziejach Polski XIX I XX wieku*, UAM, Poznań.

Hahn, Warner G. (1987). *Democracy in a Communist Party. Poland's Experience since 1980*, New York: Columbia University Press.

Hauser, Przemysław. (2004). 'Polska Odrodzona w Europie', in Wojciech Wrzesiński (ed.), *Polska a Europa (X-XX wiek)*, Wrocław: Wydawnictwo Uniwersytetu Wrocławskiego.

Holzer, Jerzy. (1977). *PPS. Szkic Dziejów*, Warszawa: Wiedza Powszechna.

Jaczyński, Stanisław. (1993). *Zygmunt Berling. Między Sławąa Potępieniem*, Warszawa: Księżka i Wiedza.

Kancewicz, Jan. (1984). *Polska Partia Socjalistyczna w latach 1892–1896*, Warszawa: Państwowe Wydawnictwo Naukowe.

Kemp-Welch, A. (2008). *Poland under Communism: A Cold War History*, Cambridge: Cambridge University Press.

Kenney, Padraic. (1997). *Rebuilding Poland. Workers and Communists 1945–1950*, Ithaca, NY: Cornell University Press.

Kersten, Krystyna. (1984). *Narodziny Systemu Władzy 1943–1948*, Warszawa: SAWW.

Kersten, Krystyna. (1999). 'The terror, 1945–1949', in A. Kemp-Welch (ed.), *Stalinism in Poland, 1944–1956*, Houndmills: Macmillan Press Ltd.

Kersten, Krystyna. (1984). *The Establishment of Communist Rule in Poland, 1943–1948*, Berkley: University of California Press.

Komarnicki, Titus. (1957). *Rebirth of the Polish Republic: A Study in the Diplomatic History of Europe, 1914–1920*, London: William Heinemann Ltd.

Korboński, Stefan. (1989). *The Jews and the Poles during World War II*, New York: Hippocrene Books.

Kowalec, Krzysztof. (1996). *Roman Dmowski*, Warszawa: Editions Spotkania.

Kowalik, Tadeusz. (2006). *Spory o Ustrój Społeczno-Gospodarczy w Polsce, lata 1944–1948*, Warszawa: Wydawnictwo Key Text.

Kozeński, J. (1964). *Czechosłowacja w Polskiej polityce zagranicznej w latach 1932–1938*, Poznań: Instytut Zachodni.

Latawski Paul (ed.). (1992). *The Reconstruction of Poland, 1914–23*, London: Macmillan in association with the School of Slavonic and East European Studies, University of London.

Leslie, R.F et al. (1980). *The History of Poland since 1863*, Cambridge: Cambridge University Press.

Lukowski, Jerzy. (1991). *Liberty's Folly: The Polish–Lithuanian Commonwealth in the Eighteenth Century, 1697–1795*, London: Routledge.

Lukowski, Jerzy. (1999). *The Partition of Poland 1772, 1773, 1795*, London: Longman.

Lundgreen-Nielson, Kay. (1992). 'Aspects of American policy towards Poland at the Paris Peace Conference and the role of Isaiah Bowman', in Paul Latawski (ed.), *The Reconstruction of Poland, 1914–23*, London: Macmillan.

Ładyka, Teodor. (1972). *Polska Partia Socjalistyczna (frakcja Revolucyjna) w latach 1906–1914*, Warszawa: Książka i Wiedza.

Macmillan, Margaret. (2001). *Peacemakers. The Paris Conference of 1919 and Its Attempt to End War*, London: John Murray.

Machcewicz, Paweł. (1999). 'Social protest and political crisis in 1956', in A. Kemp-Welch (ed.), *Stalinism in Poland, 1944–1956*, Houndmills: Macmillan Press Ltd.

Micewski, Andrzej. (1971). *Roman Dmowski*, Warszawa: Wydawnicto 'Verum'.

Mironowicz, Eugeniusz. (2000). *Polityka narodowościowa PRL*, Białystok: Wydanie Białostockiego Towarzystwa Historycznego.

Myant, Martin. (1982). *Poland: A Crisis for Socialism*, London: Lawrence and Wishart.

Müller, Michael G. (1990). 'Czy rozbiory uniemożliwiły wejście Polski na drogęnowoczesności?', in Andrarzej Ajnenkiel et al. (eds.), *Sens Polskiej Historii*, Warszawa: Uniwersytet Warszawski.

Naimark, Norman M. (1979). 'The history of the "Proletariat". The emergence of Marxism in the Kingdom of Poland, 1870–1887', *East European Quarterly (Boulder)*.

Narkiewicz, Olga A. (1976). *The Green Flag. Polish Populist Politics 1867–1970*, London: Croom Helm.

Nitschke, Bernadetta. (1999). *Wysiedlenia ludności niemieckiej z Polski w latach 1945–50*, Zielona Góra: Wyższa Szkoła Pedagogiczna in Tadeusza Kotarbińskiego.

Osęka, Piotr. (2008). *Marzec '68*, Kraków: Znak.

Paczkowski, Andrzej. (2003). *The Spring Will Be Ours*, PA: The Pennsylvania State University Press.

Polonski, Antony. (1976). *The Great Powers and the Polish Question*, London: London School of Economics.

Polonsky, Antony. (1972). *Politics in Independent Poland 1921–1939: The Crisis of Constitutional Government*, Oxford: Clarendon Press.

Polonsky, Antony (ed.). (1976). *The Great Powers and the Polish Question 1941–1945*, London: London School of Economics and Political Science.

Polonsky, Antony and Drukier, Boleslaw. (1980). *The Beginnings of Communist Rule in Poland: December 1943–June 1945*, London: Routledge & Kegan Paul.

Prażmowska, Anita. (1986). *Britain, Poland and the Eastern Front, 1939*, Cambridge: Cambridge University Press.

Prażmowska, Anita J. (1995). *Britain and Poland, 1939–1943. The Betrayed Ally*, Cambridge: Cambridge University Press.

Prażmowska, Anita J. (2000). *Eastern Europe and the Origins of the Second World War*, Houndmills: Macmillan Press Ltd.

Prażmowska, Anita. (2004). *Civil War in Poland, 1942–1948*, Houndmills: Palgrave Macmillan.

Prażmowska, Anita. (Fall 2000). 'The Polish Socialist Party, 1945–1948', *East European Quarterly XXXIV/3*.

Prażmowska, Anita. (October 2001). 'Polish military plans for the defeat of Germany and the Soviet Union, 1939–41, *European History Quarterly 31/4*.

Prażmowska, Anita. (1992). 'The role of Danzig in Polish-German relations on the eve of the Second World War', in John Hiden and Thomas Lane (eds.), *The Baltic and the Outbreak of the Second World War*, Cambridge: Cambridge University Press.

Rolicki, Janusz. (2002). *Edward Gierek: Życie i Narodziny Legendy*, Warszawa: Iskry.

Sanford, George. (1983). *Polish Communism in Crisis*, Beckenham: Croom Helm Ltd.

Skrzypek, Andrzej. (2005). *Mechanizmy autonomii. Stosunki polsko-radzieckie 1956–1956*, Warszawa: ASPRA-JR.

Snyder, Timothy. (2003). *The Reconstruction of Nations: Poland, Ukraine, Lithuania, Belarus, 1569–1999*, New Haven, CT: Yale University Press.

Stachura, Peter D. (1998). 'National identity and the ethnic minorities in early inter-war Poland', in Peter E. Stachura (ed.), *Poland between the Wars, 1918–1939*, Basingstoke: Macmillan Press Ltd.

Strzembosz, Tomasz. (2000). *Rzeczpospolita Podziemna*, Warszawa: Wydawnictwo Krupski i S-ka.

Sukiennicki, Wiktor. (1984). *East Central Europe during World War I: From Foreign Domination to National Independence*, Vol. I, East European Monographs, Boulder, CO.

Szporluk, Roman. (1990). 'Polska: Powstanie teorii i praktyki nowoczesnego narodu (1770–1870)', in Andrzej Ajnenkiel et al. (eds.), *Sens Polskiej Historii*, Warszawa: Uniwersytet Warszawski.

Tittenbrun, Jacek. (1993). *The Collapse of 'Real Socialism' in Poland*, London: Janus Publishing Company.

Trzeciakowski, Lech. (1990). *The Kulturkampf in Prussian Poland*, New York: East European Monographs.

Wandycz, Piotr S. (1992). *The Price of Freedom. A History of East Central Europe from the Middle Ages to the Present*, London: Routledge.

Wandycz, Piotr S. (1974). *The Lands of Partitioned Poland, 1795–1918*, Seattle: University of Washington Press.

Wandycz, Piotr S. (1962). *France and Her Eastern Allies, 1919–1925: French-Czechoslovak-Polish Relations from the Paris Peace Conference to Locarno*, Minneapolis: University of Minnesota Press.

Wapiński, Roman. (1980). *Narodowa Demokracja 1893–1939*, Wrocław: Zakład Wydawniczy im. Ossolińskich.

Wasilewski, Stefan. (2002). *Pięćdziesiąt Lat Zwątpienia, Nadziei i Walki*, Warszawa: Książka Polska.

De Weydenthal, Jan B., Porter, Bruce D. and Devlin, Kevin. (1983). *The Polish Drama: 1980–1982*, Lexington: Lexington Books.

Wilczewski, Ryszard. (1978). 'Rozwój przemysłu w Polsce w latach 1947–1955', in Janusz Kaliński and Zbigniew Landau (eds.), *Gospodarka Polski Ludowej 1944–1955*, Warszawa: Książka i Wiedza.

Zakrzewski, Andrzej. (1977). *Wincenty Witos chłopski polityk i mąż stanu*, Warszawa: Ludowa Spółdzielnia Wydawnicza.

Zamoyski, Adam. 1987). *The Polish Way. A Thousand-Year History of the Poles and Their Culture*, London: John Murray.

Zamoyski, Adam. (1997). *The Last King of Poland*, London: Weidenfeld & Nicolson.

Zamoyski, Jan. (1991). *Powrót na mapę. Polski Komitet Narodowy w Paryżu 1914–1919*, Warszawa: Państwowe Wydawnictwo Naukowe.

Zielonka, Jan. (1989). *Political Ideas in Contemporary Poland*, Aldershot: Avebury.

Zienkowska, Krystyna. (1998). *Stanisław August Poniatowski*, Wrocław: Zakład Narodowy im. Ossolińskich.

# INDEX